Francis Suárez

On the Essence of Finite Being As Such, On the Existence of That Essence and Their Distinction

(DE ESSENTIA ENTIS FINITI UT TALE EST, ET DE ILLIUS ESSE, EORUMQUE DISTINCTIONE)

MEDIAEVAL PHILOSOPHICAL TEXTS IN TRANSLATION
No. 24

James H. Robb, L.S.M., Ph.D., Editor

Francis Suárez

On the Essence of Finite Being As Such, On the Existence of That Essence and Their Distinction

(DE ESSENTIA ENTIS FINITI UT TALE EST, ET DE ILLIUS ESSE, EORUMQUE DISTINCTIONE)

Translated from the Latin
With an Introduction

by

Norman J. Wells
Professor of Philosophy,
Boston College

MARQUETTE UNIVERSITY PRESS
MILWAUKEE, WISCONSIN
1983

Library of Congress Catalogue Card Number: 82-081397
©Copyright, 1983, The Marquette University Press
Milwaukee, Wisconsin
Printed in the United States of America
ISBN 087462-224-7

Acknowledgements

Let me acknowledge my thanks to the following benefactors. First, to the *American Council of Learned Societies* for a helpful grant-in-aid; to Dr. James H. Robb of Marquette University for taking valuable time out from a Fulbright research-year abroad to search out and acquire invaluable microfilms; to the *Pontifical Institute of Mediaeval Studies* and to the late Dr. Anton C. Pegis, the first for the use of the microfilms and the latter for suggesting the possibility of such a translation; to John P. Doyle of St. Louis University for generous help with an early version. Special thanks are in order to Rev. Richard Arnold, S.J. for his painstaking reading of Suárez's original text and of my humble renderings and for his generous suggestions on behalf of optional renditions. Finally, thanks are due to my wife, Lenore, who well knows why.

CONTENTS

Translator's Introduction

In the history of philosophy in the West, the translation of philosophical documents needs no justification.[1] However, this translation of a sixteenth-century metaphysical tract, dealing with a highly sophisticated philosophical issue, would seem to require something of an explanation. Accordingly, then, the reasons for this translation at this time are no less than those of an integral philosophical perspective itself: historical and anhistorical, temporal and atemporal, immanent in time and yet transcendent thereto. Anything less than this is unworthy of the muse of philosophy.

The historical reasons are both remote and proximate. It has been sometime now since Mgr. Grabmann indicated that the problem of essence and existence and their distinction in Francisco Suárez should be examined, not only in a directly doctrinal way, but also from an enlightened historical perspective.[2] The extensive historical annotations accompanying this translation are presented on behalf of that important task.

Furthermore, the problem of essence and existence in Francisco Suárez affords a unique contribution to the "purgative way" of contemporary Thomism[3] since it clearly indicates the wide divergence obtaining between the *Thomistae* and their master, Thomas Aquinas.[4] This historical conclusion is scarcely without its anhistorical consequences.

More proximate historical reasons for this translation are afforded by the essence-existence context of much of the discussion within contemporary Existentialism.[5] Indeed, a persistent comparison of present with past and past with present is an indispensable feature of a viable and vigorous philosophical enterprise.

Further, on this score, this work of Francisco Suárez offers a more than appropriate occasion to assess Martin Heidegger's charge of a *Vergessenheit des Sein* on the part of Western metaphysics from its onset down to the present day.[6]

However, lest history blind us to the anhistorical dimension of the philosophical quest, we must heed throughout the echo of an old refrain: "We should enter into association with a thinker of the past, not only to become acquainted with his views but in the last resort to learn something about reality." [7]

I. The Life of Francisco Suarez

Francisco Suárez was born in Spain at Granada, January 5, 1548, into a prominent legal family of the day. Directed early towards an ecclesiastical career, Suárez studied at the University of Granada and in 1561 matriculated to the University of Salamanca to pursue the study of canon law. On June 16, 1564, he entered the Society of Jesus but not before his first request had been once refused due to an apparent lack of talent and poor health. His ultimate entrance was clearly on a trial basis. Paradoxically, once within the Jesuit course of studies, it was the very study of philosophy which almost proved his undoing as a candidate. Indeed, he had to suffer the indignity of having to be tutored. Inexplicably, however, the tutored became, in turn, the tutor. From rather questionable beginnings, he finally achieved unquestioned eminence and prominence, not only in philosophy, but in theology, as well.

Assigned to teach philosophy at the Jesuit College at Segovia in 1571, where he was also ordained in 1572, Suárez successively taught theology from 1547 to 1580 at Valladolid, again at Segovia and then at Avila. In 1580 he was called to the Jesuit college at Rome, the famous *Gregorianum*, to continue his theological teaching. In failing health, he came to Alcala in 1585, replacing Gabriel Vasquez who had replaced Suárez in Rome. In 1593 he went to Salamanca where he began to publish his theological works and to prepare for publication his *Disputationes Metaphysicae*. At the behest of no less than Philip II of Spain, Suárez was appointed to the principal chair of theology at the University of Coimbre in Portugal. It was during this period from 1606-1617 that there was a marked increase in his writing and publication, coinciding with a decrease in his teaching burdens. He died at Lisbon, September 25, 1617. [8]

II. Works

The bulk of Suárez's written work, edited as well as unedited, reflect his various teaching positions as philosopher and as theologian. [9] However, a number are inspired directly by his state as a religious and a member of the Society of Jesus. [10] Still others have their origin in the legal and political disputes of the day. [11] The structure and contents of most of these works, their extent and quality, can be viewed with convenience in the twenty-six (or twenty-eight) volume edition of Vives.[12]

A. *Disputationes Metaphysicae*

It is against this over-all backdrop, especially the theological tracts, that Suárez's famous *Disputationes Metaphysicae* must be seen, if for no better reason than that this is the way Suárez viewed his metaphysical investigations themselves. For in both the *Ad Lectorem* as well as the *Prooemium* to this work, Suárez indicates the occasion and purpose of his metaphysical work with explicit consideration of its relation to his theological inquiries.

Sensitive to the pedagogical demands upon a discipline, Suárez confesses that in the course of his theological teaching, he has had to make rather spontaneous, frequent and extensive reference to metaphysical considerations. And this was required for the simple reason that "metaphysical principles and truths are so closely interwoven with theological conclusions and arguments, that if knowledge and full understanding of the former are lacking, knowledge of the latter must necessarily suffer." [13] Such asides, Suárez finds, are not only burdensome to the *legentes*, but personally embarrassing, since it demanded of his hearers a blind faith in his judgment.[14]

In addition to these immediate pedagogical problems, there are more substantive and overriding reasons presiding at the origins of the *Disputationes Metaphysicae*. Suárez sees clearly that, though sacred and supernatural theology is founded upon divine illumination and principles revealed by God, due to its human condition, such theology must utilize truths which are naturally known as well.[15] It is in this latter area that metaphysics proves so indispensable, for of all the sciences known to man, it comes closest to the science of divine things.[16] Moreover, without any proper knowlege of metaphysical problems, the Christian mysteries could scarcely be probed and discussed.[17] In short, Suárez is convinced that "our philosophy ought to be Christian and the servant of divine theology."[18]

In the matter of the internal organization of such a discipline as metaphysics, Suárez takes a stand that is significant both historically and methodologically. For he finds himself at odds with the then current practice in the history of Western metaphysics: the medieval technique of commenting on an authoritative text by way of the *quaestio* elaborated, somewhat erratically, within the context of the books of Aristotle's *Metaphysics*.[19] By way of a methodological corrective, Suárez insists that the *ordo doctrinae*, required and demanded by the very object of this discipline, must be heeded in the sequence and hierarchical arrangement of problems and discussions.[20] On this latter score, Suárez also finds himself quite disenchanted and critical of

Aristotle's own method, sequence and organization.[21] Consequently, observing the *ordo doctrinae* as Suárez sees it, the *Disputationes Metaphysicae* begin with an initial consideration of the object of the metaphysical enterprise, its dignity and utility. This is followed by an extensive consideration of the meaning and significance of that object, *ens*, its properties and its causes. This, in turn, is complemented by a consideration of the *inferiores rationes* of *ens*, i.e., the division of *ens* into *creatum-creator* and further divisions including all the special genera and grades of *ens*, [22] closing with a consideration of *ens rationis* in Disputation 54.[23]

B. Disputation Thirty-one

As part of this latter division, the thirty-first Disputation, comprised of fourteen separate sections of varying length, is explicitly concerned with laying bare the structure of finite being.[24]

The first section serves as a general introduction to the historical as well as the doctrinal dimensions of this problem.[25] Sections two to four constitute a more specialized introduction wherein Suárez's own basic and guiding principles are set down and established.[26] Sections five to seven are, for the most part, of a critical character, negatively as well as positively.[27] The remaining bulk of the discussion, comprising sections eight to fourteen, deal with the consequences and particular difficulties arising from the various historical traditions in this matter. Hence, they are meant to bolster and confirm, directly and indirectly, Suárez's own principles and conclusions as well as support his negative criticisms.[28]

III.   Suárez, Historian and Critic

A. Introduction

Consistent with his method and style throughout his *Disputationes Metaphysicae*, Francisco Suárez situates this particular discussion on the structure of finite being within the historical context of positions coming to him from the later Middle Ages. But there is also evidence that Suárez is acutely aware of a variety of positions taken by his predecessors and contemporaries at Salamanca. The interplay of the remote context with this more proximate context constitutes one of the more elusive historical considerations in this area of research and one on which much more work needs to be done.[29]

Yet, in order that Suárez's historical survey of these positions and his succeeding remarks be intelligible and not vitiated by the persistent specter of equivocation,[30] Suárez prefaces his historical record with a glossary or dictionary of the terms in this centuries-old controversy. Herein, he takes pains to make it clear that by *esse* or *existentia* he does not mean essential being (*esse essentiae*), nor subsistential being (*esse subsistentiae*), nor the being of a true proposition (*esse veritatis propositionis*). On the contrary, the existence of a creature means the actual existence by which the essence of a creature is actually constituted outside its causes. It is something real and intrinsic to the structure of created beings. It is this use of *esse* which Suárez signifies explicitly by the term *esse existentiae* or existential being.[31] Reflecting now on that widely varied yet persistent problem of essence and existence in the history of medieval metaphysics, Suárez sees that this history is, in fact, polarized around three basic metaphysical traditions or options.

The first is that of the *Thomistae*, the professed disciples of Thomas Aquinas, who propose a real distinction between the essence and the existence of a finite being, i.e., as between *duae res*.[32] Admittedly, this is not a formulation faithful to Aquinas' position. Indeed, it is reminiscent of Giles of Rome, even though Giles and the likes of Capreolus, Soncinas and Cajetan offer disclaimers that such a formula should not be taken in a proper sense, as *duo entia*.[33] Indeed, at Salamanca, there was considerable discussion among the *Thomistae* as to whether such a formulation did justice to the authentic teaching of Aquinas.[34] Moreover, some *Thomistae* at Salamanca were not above espousing the second tradition to be noted below because of problems arising from the *duae res* perspective and also because it was not inconsistent with the position of Thomas Aquinas.[35]

The second tradition is purportedly embraced by the *Scotistae*, the professed followers of John Duns Scotus, who, like the *Thomistae*, also stand for a real distinction, but of a more diminished sort, than that of the first tradition. Suárez prefers to label this a modal distinction. For, unlike the first tradition, existence is here not so much a *res* as a *modus rei*. Yet, in both these traditions there is a fundamental agreement on essence as a *res* in its own right.[36]

The third and last tradition, represented by philosophers and theologians of divergent perspectives, insists upon an actual identity between the essence and existence which constitute a finite being. In exercising this option, they consistently oppose the types of real distinction put forth by the two previous positions and argue on behalf of only a conceptual distinction of some sort.[37]

With this historical dossier set down, Suárez unhesitatingly throws in his lot with the third and last tradition.[38] Indeed, he notes that the succeeding sections of the thirty-first disputation will be concerned with setting down and exposing the basic principles underlying his metaphysical option.[39]

That Suárez's initial principle should have to do with the status of a creature's essence prior to its production by God, should not be too surprising. It is to be expected because of the teaching on essence contained in the first two traditions.[40] With its origins deep in Greek metaphysics as far back as Parmenides, this teaching came to be the common coinage of medieval metaphysics, Islamic as well as Christian, fashioned each in his own image by such men as Avicenna, Albert the Great, John Duns Scotus, Henry of Ghent, Giles of Rome and others. However cast, the prevailing feature is that of an essence which in and of itself enjoys a being or reality apart from any creative efficient causality of God. So much is this the case that essences continue to perdure, though the actual things which embody them have ceased to exist.[41]

In this light, the essences of finite beings, unlike their existence, are eternal, necessary and uncaused by an efficient cause. Since the existence of a creature is produced by an efficient cause, it is not eternal but temporal, not necessary but contingent and not uncreated but created. It remains only to make the point that one and the same thing cannot be and not be by an efficient cause in order to secure the real or modal distinction between the essence and existence of a creature.[42]

B. CRITIC OF THE REAL AND MODAL DISTINCTIONS

This tradition that essence is or has a reality in its own right is a constant among the *Thomistae* and others explicitly cited by Suárez in his initial catalogue of men and texts on behalf of the real and modal distinctions. It is dominant in Capreolus,[43] Cajetan,[44] Javellus,[45] Scotus,[46] Henry of Ghent,[47] and Giles of Rome[48] and it is found in those influenced by such men. This is especially the case at Salamanca where it was explicitly espoused by *Thomistae* such as Francisco de Vitoria,[49] Domingo de Soto,[50] Mancio del Cuerpo de Cristo,[51] Bartolomé de Medina[52] and Pedro de Ledesma.[53]

Not only is Suárez aware of this long-standing and prevalent tradition, he is also privy to a modification of that tradition by some *Thomistae*, e.g. Soncinas,[54] Sylvester of Ferrara[55] and, at Salamanca, continued by Bañez,[56] to the effect that the essences of creatures are genuinely created by an efficient cause. However, though there are no longer eternal essences, there are eternal, uncreated truths which, in the absence of eternal essences, serve as the foundation for an ongoing metaphysical enterprise. But as we shall see, Suárez is no less unsympathetic with this second facet of the tradition than he is with the first.[57]

Moreover, not only is Suárez in possession of an extensive knowledge of this tradition on essence endowed with an essential being of its own, he is also aware of and in sympathy with a long-standing and vigorous criticism of the *duae res* and *res/modus rei* traditions on the essence and existence of creatures. [58] For it has been noted that the *duae res* and *res/modus rei* characterizations of the distinction between essence and existence in creatures have left them vulnerable to a devastating criticism forthcoming from Ockham and the Nominalist tradition. To be sure, "if they were two things, then no contradiction would be involved if God preserved the essence of a thing in the world without its existence, or vice versa, its existence without its essence, both of which are impossible." [59]

Indeed, though this argument from separability is abroad in Giles of Rome, [60] it does not appear in any of the *antiqui Thomistae* whom Suárez explicitly lists on behalf of the real distinction. To be sure, Capreolus explicitly confronts this difficulty and denies its validity. [61] However, this argument is referred to by Soto whom Suárez has cited on behalf of the modal distinction. [62]

On the other hand, there is every indication that the *Thomistae* at Salamanca were considerably vexed over this issue of the separability of essence from existence and existence from essence. And Suárez himself devotes an extensive consideration to this very problem, referring to the various positions in the customary anonymous fashion. [63] But it is obvious he is privy to much of the controversy among the *Thomistae* at Salamanca on this issue. He is aware of those who would hold for an essence being preserved without existence [64] as well as of those who would maintain that existence can be preserved without essence. [65] In each case, Suárez proceeds to spell out the untenable consequences forthcoming from each of these positions, reinforcing his critique and rejection of the tradition of those proposing the real and modal distinctions between the essence and existence of creatures.

Fully aware, then, of the extent and significance of this tradition on essence as a genuine *res* in its own right in the history of medieval metaphysics, especially as it has been espoused by Capreolus and the *Thomistae* after him, Suárez sets it down straightway, and defends as a basic and fundamental principle of his option for the third tradition, that prior to the creative production of God, the essence of a finite being is absolutely *nihil*. Far from being a *res aliqua*, it enjoys no truly real existence in and of itself and apart from existential being. Straightway, one of the infamous *duae res* is literally annihilated, as far as Suárez is concerned. [66] Implicit in this is Suárez's rejection of any exemplary causality of essence prior to existence and his reduction of such exemplary causality to efficient causality. [67]

In taking such a stand, Suárez again makes it clear that he is working within a prevailing problem in medieval theology and metaphysics. However, in dealing with such a problem, Suárez has no desire to perpetuate a controversy which, in part at least, he considers to be but a *dissensio in modo loquendi.* [68] On the contrary, he would hope to put an end to it or, at least, to put it in its proper perspective. This is the significance of Suárez's defense of John Duns Scotus against some *Thomistae* who have taken the latter rather severely to task for his stand on the *esse objectivum* or *esse cognitum* enjoyed by the essences of creatures in the divine mind. [69] This is also the significance of Suárez's citation of a text of John Capreolus, *Princeps Thomistarum,* wherein a position not unlike that of Henry of Ghent on an eternal *esse essentiae* is maintained. [70] Finally, this is the significance of Suárez's insistence that it could never enter into the mind *alicuius doctoris catholici* to claim that the essence of a creature, of itself and apart from the free, efficient causality of God, is a *vera res,* possessed of a real being distinct from the being of God Himself. [71]

In addition to these points, Suárez is also bent on showing that not only Scotus, but Capreolus and others as well, agree with his first principle as stated: that the essences of created things, prior to coming from the hand of God, are absolutely nothing. [72] Indeed, with this in hand, what Suárez considers to be one of the spurious foundations for the real and modal distinctions is abolished. For, with the alleged eternal essences of his adversaries reduced from a *res* to a *nihil,* there is no longer any sound basis for a *duae res* or *res et modus rei* designation to bedarken future discussions of essence and existence. In principle, with this despatching of the creature's essence as an actual eternal *res,* the identity between an actual essence and its actual existence is secured.

However, as Suárez's adversaries are quick to indicate, this critique adds up to no less than a Pyrrhic victory. [73] For the upshot of the Suárezian annihilation of the eternal *esse essentiae* has surely been the identity of actual essence and actual existence. This, in turn, has led him to maintain that, when actual existence perishes, the essence vanishes accordingly. [74] Consequently, any scientific knowledge, metaphysics included, which is considered to focus upon real essences or *aeternae et necessariae veritates,* has been dealt a mortal blow. For with actual essence now identified with a contingent actual existence, essential propositions are now no longer necessary and endowed with eternal truth. All truths and the sciences thereof are condemned to the region of contingent truths because now, not only the existence, but also the essence of a creature is derived from an efficient cause. [75]

In the face of such a direct challenge, Suárez is not of a mind to embrace any sort of ambiguous compromise or accommodation. In fact, he pursues his critique with dispassionate consistency and renewed vigor against some *Thomistae* who espouse just such an ambiguous compromise. For, to save a metaphysics of the eternal truths, in spite of agreeing with Suárez that the essences of creatable things are not eternal, they contend that the bonds of the essential predicates with the creatable essences are eternal, uncreated and necessary. Hence, the essence of a creature derives from an efficient cause, along with its existence, but the *veritas essentiae* does not. In this fashion, *scientia*, as the knowledge of these necessary and eternal truths, remains intact.[76]

Suárez makes an outright and uncompromising rejection of this attempt to save scientific knowledge in general and metaphysics in particular. If the essence of a creature is created by an efficient cause, then the truth of essence equally derives from the self-same efficient cause since they are really identified.[77] It is the definitive Suarezian perspective that the essence of a creature can never be adequately appreciated apart from an efficient cause. For, any attempt to do so is to court the disaster of confusing such an essence with a mere *ens rationis*. His adversaries may well be guilty of such a confusion but Suárez is not about to yield to it in turn.[78]

For Suárez is quite confident that he has neutralized both strains of the *Thomistae* (and those of the *Scotistae* who partake of their perspective on essence as an uncreated, eternal *res*), those deriving from Capreolus who come very close to maintaining that the essence is an actual eternal *res*[79] and those following Soncinas and Sylvester of Ferrara who would insist that the essences of creatures are genuinely created but the necessary and eternal essential truths are not created and yet are endowed with actual truth.[80] Against Capreolus *et al.* Suárez makes it plain that any actual *esse essentiae* or actual essence, precisely as *actual*, must be dependent on God, as upon an actual efficient cause.[81] Lacking that actual efficient causality, such essences are in no way actual in themselves. To be sure, the only actual existence such essences enjoy is the actual existence of their cause. That is, they are in act in their cause, not in themselves.[82] In this instance, they exist in God in virtue of an *esse cognitum*,[83] a-being-of-being-known, or an *esse objectivum*,[84] a-being-of-being-an-object, wherein any eternity is that of the divine mind, or in virtue of an *esse potentiale objectivum*,[85] a-being-of-being-an-object-of-divine-omnipotence. In each case we are in the presence of an extrinsic denomination,[86] forthcoming in the first two instances from divine knowledge and in the latter instance from divine omnipotence.

As Suárez never ceases to repeat, there is nothing actual or positive which is intrinsic to creatures prior to their creation, neither in regard to essence nor to existence. Nor should his adversaries, rebuffed in the matter of an actual essence, take doctrinal comfort in some sort of possibility intrinsic to the essences themselves. We have only

God's omnipotence and *non-repugnantia*, or the negation of impossibility, on the part of the essences of creatures. [87] As Suárez will insist in his reverent interpretation of Capreolus, the essences of creatures, prior to their being produced by God, possess real essences in potency; not by an intrinsic potency on their part, but in virtue of the extrinsic power of the creator. In short, "they are said to have real essences, not in themselves, but in their cause." [88]

In keeping with his ongoing practice, Suárez is here bringing his adversaries up short for misreading the data of the problem and, at the same time, reaching some sort of accommodation with their perspective. The *Thomistae* have wrongly accredited an actual existence to essences existing within their cause because they have failed to recognize that the only actual existence involved is that of the cause itself. Consequently, the denial by Capreolus of a creative efficient cause of *esse essentiae* is grossly misplaced. For, since the actual existence of the creative cause is alone involved, there is obviously no creative efficient cause of God Himself. But if this be the thrust of Capreolus' position, it affords no aid and comfort on behalf of a denial that the essences of creatures are caused by a creative efficient cause.

Suárez, then, can tell the *Thomistae* that their vaunted real distinction between *esse essentiae* and *esse existentiae* makes sense only if it is accurately understood as a distinction between a *non-ens* and an *ens;* between an essence as possible and that essence as actual. [89]

Once again Suárez is in a position to insist that the *Thomistae* purportedly following Capreolus are guilty of another misreading of the problem. Their denial of any actual efficient cause of essence makes sense only if the essence is, not actual, but possible, enjoying an *esse potentiale objectivum* in its cause. In this instance, it is quite true, and Suárez is only too ready to agree, that such essences have no actual efficient cause. Moreover, Suárez is able to insist as well that there is no actual efficient cause of such a negative consideration as *non-repugnantia,* or the negation of impossibility. [90] It remains to be seen if such essences are equally dispossessed of a potential efficient cause. [91]

If Suárez's reverent rendering of Capreolus is tenable, then the *Thomistae* who would follow in that tradition have no basis for insisting on a real distinction, *ut duae res*, between an actual eternal essence, on the one hand, and an actual temporal existence, on the other.

Versus Soncinas and Sylvester of Ferrara *et al.*, Suárez uses much the same sort of tactic so successful against Capreolus, accusing his opponents of misreading the data and concluding beyond the evidence, and then achieving some sort of accommodation with their perspective. As noted, Suárez rejects outright the position that the *connexio* or *veritas essentiae* is not created even though the essence itself is created. For he wishes to know what something actually eternal is doing outside of God and lacking an efficient cause. [92] Further, Suárez insists that any connection, eternal or otherwise, is a union which is a *res* or a mode of something. [93] Consequently, if there is no actual eternal *res*, there can be no eternal union or connection. Indeed, the creative efficient cause which produces the essence also produces the essential connections. [94]

Unfortunately, Soncinas and Sylvester of Ferrara labor under an equivocation, failing, as their position does, to distinguish between the different meanings of *esse* and the different meanings of the copula *est* involved in those essential predications purportedly manifesting actual eternal truth. If *esse in actu* is meant, then the essence and its essential truths are dependent on an actual efficient cause. [95] But if *esse in potentia* is indicated, or a non-existential use of the copula *est* is employed, then Suárez is again quick to agree, as he was in the case of Capreolus, that no actual efficient cause of the essence, nor its eternal truth, is involved. [96] However, Suárez emphatically and explicitly insists that the presence of a potential efficient cause is still required. [97] Suárez wants nothing to do with a position which would allow for essential connections, propositions or actually eternal truths in regard to creatures which escape completely any and all relations to an efficient cause. Thus, when an actual essence ceases, there are no longer any essential propositions enjoying some sort of actual existential truth as Soncinas and Sylvester of Ferrara have claimed. For, if these *Thomistae*, in agreement with Suárez, insist on denying uncreated, eternal essences, as abroad in Capreolus, then there can be no case of essential propositions which have actual eternal truth. [98] In making a claim on behalf of such actual eternal truths, these *Thomistae* run afoul of their own objection initially made against Suárez. [99] Far from making a case for a Pyrrhic victory against Suárez, the objection strikes home against the *Thomistae* themselves, leaving Suárez's position intact, as we shall see. If their distinction between essence and existence be understood accurately, as a distinction between a *non-ens* and an *ens*, between an essence as possible and that essence as actual, then the possibility of any future metaphysics is not placed in jeopardy.

IV. Suárez, Critic and Proponent of a Distinction of Reason

Suárez's rejection of the real and modal distinctions between actual essence and actual existence by no means leads immediately to a blind and unqualified avowal of the perspective abroad in the third tradition noted above. Rather, his attitude is one of caution and circumspection. For, in that house there are many mansions and

Suárez is not about to take lodgings indiscriminately. For this reason he takes pains to eliminate various explanations of the conceptual distinction or distinction of reason in regard to essence and existence as inadequate, unclear or downright inaccurate.

For instance, some contend that the essence-existence couplet is reducible to essence as specific nature and the individual, i.e., essence in relation to existence is but the relation of species to individual; it is but the relation of *man* to *Socrates*. Hence, the distinction of reason or conceptual distinction obtaining here is but the conceptual distinction which obtains between the species and the individual. [100] Suárez does not deny a similarity here but sets himself against any such facile reductionism of one distinction to the other. For essence is not merely and exclusively specific. It can be, and is, singular and individual. Moreover, existence is not exclusively singular, for it can be conceived of in a general way. [101]

Furthermore, Suárez is not about to abide any attempt to see existence as indicating that the essence is related to an efficient cause and that actual existence is that relation. This is patently false, since, for Suárez, actual existence indicates something absolute and not relative. For he notes that it can hardly be a predicamental relation which presupposes that the creature is already created and existing. Nor is it a matter of a transcendental relation, a relation of dependence upon God. For this latter is not the existence of a creature but the causality thereof, wherein a real, rather than a conceptual, distinction obtains. [102] Moreover, Suárez can hardly allow that existence alone involves some consideration of the presence of an efficient cause. It is his constant position that this is the case with the essence of any creature as well. Consequently, any conceptual distinction which fails to appreciate this point in the context of essence and existence is hardly adequate.

In addition, Suárez finds a further attempt to appreciate the conceptual distinction between essence and existence as a matter of conceiving one and the self-same thing now abstractly, now concretely, as irrelevant. As far as Suárez is concerned, essence and existence, essential being and existential being, signify in exactly the same fashion and are subject to the same manner of conceiving. Indeed, as these terms designate true, real being, far from differing conceptually as abstract and concrete, at best they only differ verbally or nominally. [103]

However, while allowing some merit in the latter perspective, Suárez realizes that a greater difference must obtain between essence and existence than he has confronted thus far; the conceptual distinction must be one wherein actual existence can with truth be denied of the essence of a creature. [104] Otherwise, with an identity of essence and existence abroad in creatures as well as God, the difference and distinction between God and creature would be placed in deadly jeopardy. [105]

To support the denial of actual existence of a creature's essence, Suárez finds the fitting conceptual distinction in a still further version of a distinction of reason. However, in its unmodified form it is not without its difficulties. For, to the extent that this position contends that essence and existence differ conceptually inasmuch as *essentia* signifies a thing absolutely and not outside its causes, while *existentia* signifies the self-same thing but now with *esse* in itself and outside its causes, it is not unlike the position of Henry of Ghent already found wanting. Moreover, in Suárez's eyes, this position overlooks the critical point that *esse et non esse extra causas* is a consideration common to essence as well as existence, since each is equally subject to the creative efficient causality of God. *Essentia*, as well as *existentia*, is outside its causes when the thing is created and *existentia*, as well as *essentia*, is only in the potency of its causes before the thing comes to be. Consequently, because existence in potency is absolutely identified with essence in potency just as existence in act is identified with essence in act, no support is offered for the denial of the existence in regard to the essence. [106]

However, Suárez notes that it is one thing to speak of *essentia* and *existentia* by extending such terms to the same or similar signification, e.g., essence in potency, existence in potency; essence in act, existence in act. It is still another thing to take them properly and strictly. It is in this latter context, a modified version of the last attempt on behalf of a distinction of reason, that Suárez finds the true teaching in this matter and the proper fashion in which to maintain a conceptual distinction adequate to support a denial of existence on the part of the created essence. [107]

For *existentia*, strictly taken, does not properly signify existence *in actu signato* or existence as conceived in an intellect and/or in the potency of its causes. Rather, this term signifies existence *in actu exercito* or existence in act and outside its causes. Consequently, by the very fact that a thing or essence is abstracted from existence *in actu exercito*, then this state or this actual exercise of existing is not contained in the concept of a creature's essence. In light of this, it is correct to say that existence adds to essence, namely, the *actus essendi extra causas suas*. Moreover, as a further consequence, it is now possible, as well as correct, to deny existence of the created essence. For Suárez can now affirm that *existentia* is not *de essentia creaturae* since the concept of a creature's essence, abstracting as it does from the creature's existence, does not include this actual exercise of existing signified by the term *existentia*. [108]

In stating as much, Suárez is explicitly aware that such a position amounts, on the one hand, to conceiving of the creature's essence as possible, creatable or as essence in the potency of its causes, with no intrinsic reality or actuality proper to itself, and, on the other hand, to considering that self-same essence in act, as existent and existing with actuality outside its causes so intrinsic and proper to itself that such an essence is identified with it. It is this latter state which is signified and indicated by the Suarezian use of the term *existentia*. For *existentia*, strictly taken, means the essence of a creature conceived of as *in actu extra causas*. [109] Suárez's solution here amounts to a diversity in concept greater than that between the abstract and concrete, since it entails a concept of the essence as possible and a concept of the essence as actual rather than two different conceptions (abstract and concrete) of what is actual as actual. This is the distinction which Suárez noted at the outset of the thirty-first Disputation and which is variously disignated as either a conceptual distinction or a real negative or real privative distinction; a distinction which obtains between *essentia* as *ens in potentia* and *existentia* as *ens in actu* or between *non ens* and *ens*. [110]

Nevertheless, however much Suárez is satisfied with the implications of this latter distinction, expecially when it enables him to indicate that the so-called real distinction of the first two traditions are actually reducible to this and nothing more, he also realizes that it falls short of his explicitly stated intention; to maintain, in regard to a creature, a conceptual distinction between *existentia actualis seu esse in actu exercito* and *essentia actualis*, sufficient to support the denial of the former in regard to the latter. [111]

What makes this latter problem doubly difficult to solve is the fact that Suárez himself constantly insists on the real and actual identity of *existentia* (strictly taken) and *essentia actualis*, and that further, he also insists that *existentia* cannot be prescinded from an actual entity. [112] Consequently, *essentia actualis* and *existentia* (strictly taken) would seem to be synonymous terms indicating, not two different conceptions, but one and the self-same concept, thereby frustrating, in principle, the possibility of any sort of viable conceptual distinction with a foundation in created things. [113] Despite these difficulties, one might even say, inspired by them, Suárez, true to his initial intention, proceeds to claim, justify and defend a conceptual distinction between *essentia actualis* and *actualis existentia*.

Herein, for Suárez, we are confronted with an existent creature in which actual essence and existence are really identical. However, we can and do conceive that existent thing under different aspects. On the one hand, we conceive of it under the aspect of *essence* when we consider an existent thing according to the grade, type, order or level of being it embodies. On the other hand, we conceive of that self-same existent thing under the aspect of *existence* when we consider it as *in rerum natura* and outside its causes. [114] Though these two aspects are really identified in the existent creature itself, still that creature is the occasion for two conceptual considerations which differ one from the other. [115] The diversity is thus explicitly on the conceptual level and not on the level of some composite structure intrinsic to the creature itself. [116] This is the conceptual distinction or the distinction of reason which Suárez considers as adequate and sufficient to his needs.

However, Suárez is also bent on indicating and clarifying the real basis or foundation for such a conceptual distinction lest it appear to be the work of the intellect alone in some sort of arbitrary or unfounded fashion. Suárez locates this in the imperfection which pervades all creatures because they do not have existence of themselves, must receive it from another, and can cease to exist. It is this basic imperfection which affords the occasion for our two-fold consideration. [117] Accordingly, we can consider the creature as indifferent to being or not being in act by way of an abstractive precision. [118] In doing so, we conceive of the creature as an essence which has the role of potency to existence, here considered as its act. [119]

V.   Comments

For all the vaunted and genuine success of his critical sallies against the *Thomistae* and *Scotistae* of the *duae res* and *res et modus rei* types of real distinction, and on behalf of his own claim for a real identity between actual essence and existence, the success of Suárez's position on their conceptual distinction is subject to serious misgivings.

The villain of the piece would seem to be the fluctuating notions of essence, potency and possibility on the level of creatures prior to their creation and thereafter. For essence is taken as actual, as possible and then just in itself. [120]

Essence is actual in at least three fashions, *extra causam, in causa* and *in intellectu*, the latter two tending to fuse in the instance of an intellectual cause. In the first instance, the essence of the creature enjoys an intrinsic actual existence in itself. [121] Such is not the case in the latter two instances. Rather in the second case, the actual existence in question is the actual existence of the cause itself and does not belong intrinsically and properly to the essence of the creature itself. [122] In short, though the essence is actual, it is not a genuine actual essence. Something similar is involved in the third instance. For the essence of a creature existing in an intellect possesses no actual existence proper and intrinsic to itself. Rather, it possesses the-being-of-being-conceived, an *esse cognitum* or *cognosci* and/or the-being-of-being-an-object, an *esse objectivum*. [123] Again, though the essence is actual, it is not an intrinsically actual essence.

Suárez's position on essence as possible is considerably more complex. This is certainly so terminologically wherein the reader is somewhat overwhelmed by the likes of *ens possibile, esse essentiae, esse possibile, essentia creabilis, ens in potentia, potentia objectiva, potentia logica, entitas in potentia, ens in potentia objectiva, res possibilis, esse potentiale objectivum, potentia extrinseca* etc. [124] These are all similar in that, in no case, is the essence *extra causam*. Consequently, we are again dealing with creatures *in causa* as well as *in intellectu*. [125] However, this consideration does not focus on their *esse cognitum* or *esse objectivum*. Rather, it regards the aptitude or non-repugnance on the part of the still unproduced essence of the creature to be posited *ad extra* by God. [126] Accordingly, the designation *possible*, in addition to involving an extrinsic denomination from the omnipotence of God, [127] indicates something on the part of the creature even though it is *in causa*, still unproduced and *omnino nihil*. [128] This is *non repugnantia*. Indeed, in virtue of this latter, the unproduced essences of creatures are distinguished from fictitious and impossible notions like chimerae. [129]

It is at this point that we are at a critical juncture of the Suarezian perspective, the significance of which is scarcely acknowledged, much less spelled-out, by Suárez himself. On the one hand, we have the likes of *esse potentiale objectivum, potentia objectiva* and *ens in potentia objectiva* and their variations, all signifying that the as yet uncreated essence of a creature is an object of creative power. To be sure, there is an explicit reference to divine omnipotence which parallels that involving divine knowledge and *esse cognitum* or *esse objectivum* wherein an instance of extrinsic denomination is involved. For, in this instance of the-being-of-being-an-object-of-divine-omnipotence, we are again in the presence of an extrinsic denomination. This time it is forthcoming from divine omnipotence and not from divine knowledge. [130]

As we have seen, Suárez has used such data against the *Thomistae* and *Scotistae,* and with devastating success, to show that there is no such thing as an eternal essence possessed of genuine existence in its own right. They have misread these instances of extrinsic denomination as if they were genuine intrinsic denominations. [131] For what Suárez's adversaries have failed to realize, and what Suárez never refrains from stating, is that *esse potentiale objectivum* explicitly includes a negation, indicating that the essence of the creature has not yet been actually produced by God. [132] Accordingly, of itself an essence enjoying such existence involves an exclusion of actual efficient causality and, consequently, an exclusion of actual existence, the term of that causality. Indeed, as such it cannot even receive actual existence. [133] Thus the *Thomistae* and *Scotistae* are once more vulnerable to a charge of misreading the data on still another count. This time they have confused a genuine *potentia objectiva* which cannot receive actual existence with a *potentia subjectiva* which genuinely does receive it. But there is no justification at all for them to claim, as they do, such a *potentia subjectiva* on the part of an eternal essence when the latter is *nihil*. For how can anything be impressed upon that which is nothing. [134]

If this were the extent of the Suarezian critique, his victory over his adversaries in the first two traditions on essence and existence would be secured beyond reproach. But such is not the case. And this is because the designation *possible,* as noted above, involves *non-repugnantia*. From among his varied vocabulary on this matter, the term, *potentia logica,* infrequently used by Suárez, seems reserved exclusively for designating this *non repugnantia* without any explicit reference to divine omnipotence. That is, such a designation is not an extrinsic denomination forthcoming from that divine omnipotence. [135] In the presence of a possible essence, Suárez's position is that we are confronting what involves at least two negations, a negation of actual existence *extra causam* (and, accordingly, a negation of an actual efficient cause) and a negation of repugnance. As such, it can scarcely involve anything positive on its own part and, as far as Suárez is concerned, justly merits being characterized as *omnino nihil* and *non ens.* [136]

But the point which has to be made at this juncture, despite all of Suárez's efforts to deny any and every intrinsic actual or possible being on the part of the essences of creatures *in causa,* is that *non repugnantia,* as expressing a two-fold negation, reinstates the positive dimension which Suárez is convinced he has exorcised and dispatched from this conflict. [137] Moreover, if the negation of actual existence *extra causam,* indicated in the instance of *esse potentiale objectivum,* involves an exclusion by way of a privative or negative abstraction, and not merely by means of a precisive abstraction, then Suárez's stated difference between *ens in potentia* and *ens rationis* would be severely jeopardized. [138] For the latter, as involving some repugnance or implication of contradiction, clearly excludes actual existence and the possibility thereof. Consequently, lest Suárez's metaphysics succumb to lapsing into logic, his position on *non repugnantia* and *potentia logica* cannot be affected by the negative exclusion abroad in the instance of *esse potentiale objectivum.* [139]

In addition to essence as actual and essence as possible, the status of essence just in itself is also abroad in Suárez, for it involves something other than the two states cited previously which surely antecede every intellectual consideration. It implies a precision and abstraction on the part of the intellectual consideration involved. [140] Indeed, an abstractive precision is at work whereby the essence is considered apart from *creatura creata et creabilis*, that is, apart from any actual existence within or without a cause and apart from any possible existence. [141] Moreover, it is important to note that no explicit exclusion or separation (*abstractio vel praecisio negativa*) of either state is involved. [142] Accordingly, the content focused upon by this abstractive precision can only be the *non repugnantia* noted above, which is in turn labeled, though improperly so, *essentia realis* or *ens reale*. [143] The justification for this last point derives from the fact that, in an *essentia realis*, there is no repugnance (or there is an indifference) to being actually produced *ad extra* as a proper *ens reale* or *essentia realis in actu*. [144] However, there is, in fact, no such *essentia realis* genuinely existing in itself apart from an *esse possibile* in the sense of *esse potentiale objectivum*, or *esse cognitum/esse objectivum*, which are all *in causa*, or apart from an *esse actuale* which is *extra causam*. [145] It now remains to see how these considerations function within Suárez's two conceptual distinctions between essence and existence.

As noted above, the first conceptual or real negative distinction obtains between the actual essence *extra causam* and the possible essence *in causa*. Herein, as noted, the distinction is between an *ens* and a *non ens* or *nihil*. [146]

The other conceptual distinction purports to be between the actual essence and its actual existence *extra causam* which Suárez has established to be really identical. [147] But when all is said and done, the essence in question is scarcely the actual essence as initially promised. It is the *essentia realis* noted above, abstracting precisively from actual (as well as possible) existence. [148] Granted it does not exclude actual existence, it surely stands as indifferent thereto. [149] One can genuinely question whether this distinction differs from the former one wherein essence is conceptually distinguished from actual existence as a *non ens* from an *ens*. For if there is no difference, then Suárez may be able to sustain the negation of existence in regard to the essence but only at the price of foregoing a conceptual distinction between a really identical actual essence and actual existence. [150] Indeed, Suárez can sustain the negation of actual existence with respect to *essentia realis* (but not with respect to *essentia actualis*), for a real essence is indifferent to actual existence which is certainly not indifferent to itself. A real essence, then, is not identified with actual existence. Or one might even say, given the identity of actual essence and actual existence, a real essence is not identified with an actual essence. [151]

But if Suárez can sustain this negation of actual existence (or *essentia actualis*) with respect to *essentia realis*, he would seem to do so at an even higher price for the Suarezian perspective. For, at this point, Suárez runs the very great risk of restoring a vestige of the eternal essences of his adversaries. To be sure, not only does the burden of Suárez's double-negative formulation in his use of *non repugnantia* express a positive structure possessed of its own intrinsic ontological density, but his persistent consideration and use of *essentia realis* risks interpreting the *potentia logica* involved therein as a genuinely actual *potentia subjectiva*. [152] One can only say that this would appear to be too high a price to pay when the consistency of the Suarezian perspective is at issue.

VI.   Suárez, Metaphysics and the Eternal Truths

It remains to appreciate the impact of these positions on the structure and perspective of the metaphysical enterprise according to Suárez. For Suárez himself, in the early stages of the thirty-first Disputation, has made explicit retrospective reference to his earlier treatment thereof. [153] Moreover, we have yet to assess the positive dimension of Suárez's posture in regard to the previously mentioned charge that his position on the identity of actual essence and actual existence, and their separability, saps the very possibility of all scientific knowledge, metaphysics included. [154]

Without doubt, Suárez is concerned to show that his position on essence and existence, especially his position on their separability, does not frustrate the possibility of any future metaphysics. In addition, he is particularly preoccupied to make it clear that his extensive negative criticisms of the actual essences abroad in the followers of Capreolus and the actual eternal truths abroad in Soncinas and Sylvester of Ferrara, in no way contribute to the total destruction of the metaphysical enterprise. For Suárez well knows that a genuine metaphysics is at stake here, understood, of course, as one dealing with *aeternae veritates* and the necessities of essential predication, even though Suárez wants nothing to do with the actual eternal essences embraced by the followers of Capreolus nor with the actual eternal truths, divested of any actual eternal essence, in Soncinas and Sylvester of Ferrara.

It is this context which gives a distinctive cast to Suárez's discussion with the latter two *Thomistae*, for the prior discussion, with Capreolus and the *Thomistae* partaking of that persuasion, was carried on in the context of the divine intellect and divine knowledge, involving *esse cognitum* and *esse objectivum*. It was also carried on in the context of divine omnipotence, involving *esse potentiale objectivum*, and the attendant discussion of extrinsic denominations.

Moreover, forthcoming from such considerations is Suárez's claim that the essences of creatures prior to their creation are *omnino nihil*. So if his critical contentions here are correct, as they are, then a metaphysics of eternal essences would be reduced to the study of *omnino nihil*. But there can be no such metaphysics of *omnino nihil*, for the science of nothing is itself nothing. [155]

Suárez sees only too clearly, as purportedly did Soncinas and Sylvester of Ferrara, that a metaphysics of eternal truths cannot be saved in such a context as this, where possibility is understood in the context of *esse potentiale objectivum*, containing a negation of actual existence. [156] Also Suárez is aware that his position on the essences of creatures prior to creation as *omnino nihil* tends to compound the problem of distinguishing such essences from chimerae, for the latter are equally *omnino nihil*. [157] Still further, Suárez is aware, as are his adversaries, that while it is all very well to have said, versus the *Thomistae* following Capreolus, that the *non repugnantia* on the part of finite essences prior to creation and designated by *esse potentiale objectivum* is to be appreciated in the context of an *esse objectivum* or a-being-of-being-an-object in the divine intellect, this again compounds the problem of distinguishing such essences from chimerae. A chimera equally possesses such credentials as an *esse objectivum*, [158] for God knows them as well, just as we do. So the basis for the obvious distinction between essences and chimerae must be sought elsewhere than in their mutual mental existence within the context of divine knowledge. [159]

Consequently, this whole issue is brought to bear upon an intrinsic *potentia logica*, purportedly independent of divine omnipotence, and not upon the extrinsic consideration involved in the *esse potentiale objectivum* in reference to God's omnipotence. [160] But in moving beyond the divine intellect and the *esse objectivum* enjoyed by both chimerae and essences, as well as moving beyond the exemplary causality here of which Suárez is so wary, [161] it will remain to be seen whether Suárez also moves beyond God as potential efficient cause as the likes of Soncinas and Cajetan have done. [162]

In any case, because the very possibility of metaphysics is at stake, the role of *potentia logica* or *possibile logicum*, and the *essentia realis* which embodies it, tends to figure more prominently in this later discussion than in the initial one. In doing so, Suárez's consideration rejoins his initial perspective at the very outset of the *Disputationes Metaphysicae* where *essentia realis* bulked large. [163]

On behalf of his own metaphysics of the eternal truths, Suárez wants it clearly understood that such eternal truths are based on some sort of *esse*. [164] To be sure, it is not any *esse reale in actu*, neither of essence nor of existence nor of any eternal truths purportedly abroad in Capreolus, Soncinas and Sylvester of Ferrara.[165] Rather, when we say: *homo ex aeternitate est animal*, the *est* is not to be taken in a proper existential sense, nor in the sense of an actual *esse essentiae*, but it indicates only the intrinsic connection or identity of subject and predicate.[166] Accordingly, this connection is based on *esse potentiale*[167] and the necessity in question is decidedly not the absolute necessity of his adversaries. For Suárez comes down emphatically on behalf of a conditional necessity[168] in the instance of the eternal essential truths. That is to say, if man were to be created, he would be a rational animal.[169] Against Capreolus *et al.*, where the context of divine knowledge was so prominent, especially God's *scientia simplicis intelligentiae*,[170] Suárez could very well make the point that, in knowing *homo est animal rationale* and the identity therein, God does not know an eternal, positive reality. Nor does he know any actual intrinsic reality and truth *ab aeterno*, properly taken, on the part of the essences in question. For this is the teaching of his adversaries, not his teaching.[171] On his own behalf, Suárez is insisting that God is knowing the existence such an essence would have, if it were created. For God knows that if these essences were to enjoy actual existence, they would necessarily be such and such. In knowing this, God knows something "real", hypothetically real and hypothetically true, if you will.[172] However, any *eternal* actuality in regard to the vaunted eternal essential truths belongs to God alone and not to the *aeternae veritates* in themselves. They are eternally actual because God knows them, actually and eternally. The *esse* in question, then, is the *esse veritatis propositionis*.[173] This perspective on possibility, from the vantage point of God's *scientia simplicis intelligentiae*, would seem to have an obvious post-existential cast. That is, God knows that, if such a connection were to exist, nothing contradictory would result, i.e., if man were to be existentially linked to animal, nothing repugnant would ensue.[174] Indeed, the post-existential cast to possibility here would be quite in order, given this context of *potentia objectiva, esse objectivum* etc., wherein Suárez is bent on indicating to the *Thomistae* that there is no eternal essence endowed with an actual being of its own, nor with any intrinsic sort of possibility.[175]

But Suárez's criticisms of Soncinas and Sylvester of Ferrara for detaching the eternal truths from any essential structures tend to restore those very essential structures on the level of *esse potentiale*,[176] and to give greater emphasis to *essentia realis* (but not to any *essentia actualis*) and *potentia logica* than surfaced in the confrontation with Capreolus. Furthermore, this later consideration would seem to have a definite pre-existential cast which would be quite in keeping with Suárez's insistence upon a potential efficient cause,[177] which, in turn, befits the non-existential and non-temporal meaning of the copula *est*. [178] For the necessary connections abstractively prescind from actual existence and indicate that in whatever temporal instant man will be, he ought to be such and so. [179] Even though Suárez again insists on the conditional necessity of such truths, the more Suárez moves within the context of *essentia realis* and *potentia logica,* the more his perspective tends to move in a context where possibility and the truths based thereupon are completely underived, and the reference even to a potential efficient cause is a decidedly extrinsic and extraneous consideration. [180] For the context of *essentia realis* is the context wherein God and creature are together conceived under the common concept of *ens* as a noun. [181] And within this context of the most abstract and confused concept of being, the creature does not entail a relationship to God. For herein a creature "is not conceived as finite and limited but only confusedly as existing *extra nihil.*" [182]

It is to this extent that Suárez fails to overcome the problems associated with a genuinely underived, intrinsic, pre-existential possibility in the case of creatures. To be sure, it is not the pre-existential possibility of his adversaries among the followers of Capreolus, involving an actual *esse essentiae,* nor is it any positive intrinsic possibility either. Rather, Suárez is saddled with an underived, intrinsic pre-existential possibility of a negative sort which is embodied in his doctrine of *non repugnantia* and *essentia realis.* [183]

But as the Suarezian metaphysical procedure moves, within the context of *ens ut nomen,* from an inadequate and confused, quasi-univocal consideration of God and creatures as not-nothing, to a more contracted consideration of creatures, properly taken, [184] the *non repugnantia* and *essentia realis* take on a manifest causal reference. It is this causal reference which had to be absent in the initial uncontracted moment, given the presence of the deity within this concept of being. For there is no cause, potential or otherwise, of divine being, [185] But in the instance of the *essentia realis* of creatures, we are dealing with a *non repugnantia* to exist outside one's causes and in dependence upon those causes which properly befits the status of a creature. [186] And to say as much as this is to acknowledge that we are in the presence of a genuine *potentia objectiva,* [187] and not a *potentia logica* possessed in common with the deity. [188]

It is to this extent that Suárez is convinced that he has solved the problems associated with an underived, intrinsic pre-existential possibility. But it must be said that his solution does not succeed in overcoming the specter of equivocation and ambiguity to which he was so sensitive. [189] For the notion of *essentia realis* and *non repugnantia,* from the origins of the Suarezian metaphysical enterprise to its termination, is fundamentally equivocal.

Suárez's whole discussion is flawed by his failure to acknowledge the tensions which obtain between *potentia logica,* on the one hand, and *potentia objectiva,* on the other, when dealing with the essences of creatures prior to their creation. Indeed, the very reason why he can initially agree with Aquinas against Capreolus *et al.* that the eternal truths are only eternal by enjoying existence in the eternal mind of the deity, and then turn around and later on disagree with this position of Aquinas, is because he has switched from the context of *potentia objectiva* to the area of *potentia logica.* [190]

So it is that Suárez's metaphysics of finite being oscillates obliviously from one to the other. When the status of a finite essence prior to its creation is at issue, forewarned by the alleged positions of Henry of Ghent and Capreolus, Suárez calls upon the resources of his doctrine on *potentia objectiva* to banish any specter of a genuinely actual essence or one possessed of positive, intrinsic possibility on the part of creatures prior to their creation, and not without some success. But when the status of a genuine metaphysics is at issue, recognizing that it has to do with *aeternae veritates* or the necessities of essential predication, Suárez's responses call upon the resources of his teaching on *potentia logica.* Despite all of Suárez's efforts to avoid any positive consideration for such *potentia logica,* his position tends to resurrect, at the very least, the specter of intrinsic possibility, in the very face of his negative formulation of *non-repugnantia.* And for all of his efforts to emphasize the purportedly post-existential, conditional necessities of such essential predication in the instance of the *aeternae veritates* dealing with finite beings, as well as the presence herein of a potential efficient cause, the possibility on the part of creatures prior to their creation remains genuinely pre-existential and independent of God's creative act when the consequences of the doctrine of *potentia logica* are brought to the fore.

In all of this, Suárez's position is not unlike that of Duns Scotus whom he has taken great care to defend explicitly against the criticisms of the *Thomistae* in the matter of *potentia objectiva,* and whose doctrine here Suárez has made his own. [191] But, somewhat unwittingly, Suárez is less than forthcoming in acknowledging Scotus' doctrine of *potentia logica* and in recognizing its presence in and negative impact upon his own position. [192] For it is clear that the initial ambiguities of Scotus on the *esse intelligibile* of creatures prior to their creation, extensively catalogued by William of Alnwick, [193] continue to plague, many centuries later, Suárez's discussion of the same issues. And if such a doctrine was an "apple of discord" for the Scotist tradition, [194] it has surely been an "apple of discord" for the commentators of Francisco Suárez.

The impact of this Suarezian perspective, dominated by *essentia realis, potentia logica* and *aeternae veritates,* upon succeeding metaphysicians in the history of Western thought must not be overlooked. This is especially so in the case of Descartes whose metaphysics moves within the same context of *essentia realis, potentia logica* and *aeternae veritates.* To be sure, Descartes does not speak in terms of *potentia logica,* to the best of my knowledge, but there is no doubt that *essentia realis* and the *aeternae veritates* continue to bulk large in his metaphysical teachings. [195] Moreover, Descartes affects the negative mode of speaking when dealing with such "real essences", going so far as to designate them as *non nihil,* [196]and thus in need of an actual efficient cause.

Indeed, the same preoccupation as in Suárez to distinguish a genuine possible from a mere chimera is abroad in Descartes. [197] For, as Suárez before him, Descartes is concerned to point out that the-being-of-being-possible, the-being-of-being-not-contradictory, or the-being-of-being-intelligible is something positive and intrinsic to the genuine essences found within the mind, however negatively formulated, and even though it be the case that these essences, as well as chimerae, are both extrinsically characterized as possessed of the-being-of-being-known or the-being-of-being-objects. [198] It is clear in Suárez that the phrase, *esse objective praesens,* is most often taken in the sense of *actu videri,* actually being seen or perceived, i.e. to be possessed of the-being-of-being-objectively-present, [199] and it indicates accordingly an explicit extrinsic denomination and an explicit activity of conscious awareness conferring upon the *essentia realis* in question this being-of-being-seen. [200] To be sure, Caterus has labored at length to explain to Descartes this very meaning of objective reality or objective presence with respect to ideas, with but little success. [201] But this is as it should be, for Descartes' concern, in speaking of *idea* taken objectively, is not with an extrinsic denomination such as the-being-of-being-known or the-being-of-being-an-object. Rather, Descartes is dealing with the-being-of-being-intelligible or the-being-of-being-conceivable, all of which is the clear burden of Descartes' phrases, *omne excogitabile artificium* [202] and *omnis perfectio cogitabilis.* [203]

In espousing such a position, Descartes, wittingly or not, is taking over, and adapting to his doctrine of innate ideas, the Suarezian position on another and an aptitudinal rendering of *esse objective praesens.* [204] Herein, for a real essence to be objectively present in an aptitudinal sense is for that real essence to be able to be known. [205] Thus, to be existing objectively, in this aptitudinal sense, is not necessarily to be existing objectively in the explicit sense of possessing the-being-of-being-known. [206] Descartes thus proceeds to take this aptitudinal objective presence as a positive and genuine intrinsic denomination. And well might he do so! For there can be no question that the *essentia realis,* even though negatively designated as *non nihil,* must be something positive and intrinsic, befitting its double-negative designation.[207] Metaphysics forthwith makes its entrance into the modern period under the auspices of a genuine *essentia realis,* wherein what is really real is what is non-contradictory, and given expression in the form of *aeternae veritates.*

VII. The Translation

As is obvious from the annotations, this translation has been rendered from the Vives text but with copious corrections offered from the 1597 Salamanca and 1605 Mainz editions. This has been done because the Vives text, though imperfect, is far more available than any other, certainly more available than the Salamanca and Mainz editions.

Moreover, in rendering Suárez's highly articulated vocabulary of *being,* an effort has been made to indicate every instance wherein *ens* and/or *essendi* and their variants have been used. In every other instance, where neither *ens* nor *essendi* and their variants are at issue, the reader should be aware that *esse* is being used in the original text.

Notes

[1] See J.T. Muckle, C.S.B., "Greek Works Translated Directly in Latin before 1350," *Mediaeval Studies* 4(1942), 33-42; 5(1943), 102-114.

[2] M. Grabmann, "Die *Disputationes Metaphysicae* des Franz Suárez in ihrer methodischen Eigenart und Firtwirkung," *Mittelalterliches Geistesleben* (München: Max Hueber, 1926), 552. See also J. Iturrioz, S.J., "Fuentes de la metafísica de Suárez," *Pensamiento* 4(1948), 34-36; 87-89 and in *Estudios sobre la metafísica de Francisco Suárez* (Madrid, 1949), 159-161.

[3] See J. Owens, C.Ss.R., *St. Thomas and the Future of Metaphysics* (Milwaukee: Marquette University Press, 1957), 51-52; "Scholasticism-Then and Now," *Proceedings of the American Catholic Philosophical Association* XL (1966), 1-12.

[4] See my article, "Capreolus on Essence and Existence," *The Modern Schoolman* XXXVIII (1960), 1-24; L.H. Kendzierski and F.C. Wade, S.J., *Cajetan Commentary on Being and Essence* (Milwaukee: Marquette University Press, 1964), [3]-[19]; A. Maurer, C.S.B., "Cajetan's Notion of Being in his Commentary on the 'Sentences'," *Mediaeval Studies* 23(1966), 268-278; my article, "On Last Looking into Cajetan's Metaphysics: A Rejoinder," *The New Scholasticism* XLII (1968), 112-117; L.A. Kennedy, C.S.B., "La doctrina de la existencia en la Universidad de Salamanca durante el siglo XVI," *Archivo Teológico Granadino* 35(1972), 5-71; "Thomism at the University of Salamanca in the Sixteenth Century: The Doctrine of Existence," *Tommaso D'Aquino nella Storia del Pensiero,* Atti del Congresso Internazionale, 1974 (Napoli, 1976), II, 254-258; C. Fabro, "L'obscurcissement de l'*esse* dans l'école thomiste," *Revue Thomiste* LVIII (1958), 443-472.

[5] See J.B. Lotz, S.J., "Sein und Existenz in der Existenzphilosophie und in der Scholastik," *Gregorianum* XL (1959), 401-466; "Being and Existence in Scholasticism and Existence-Philosophy," *Philosophy Today* 8(1964), 3-45.

⁶ M. Heidegger, *Briefe über den "Humanismus"* (Berne: A. Franke, 1947), 72ff. See also J. Doyle, "Heidegger and Scholastic Metaphysics," *The Modern Schoolman* XLIX (1972), 201-220; J.D. Caputo, "The Problem of Being in Heidegger and the Scholastics," *The Thomist* 41(1977), 62-91; C. Fabro, *God In Exile Modern Atheism* transl. and edit., A. Gibson (Westminster, Md.: Newman, 1968), 958-961. However, Caputo's remark (67): "In particular Suárez first made the distinction between *metaphysica generalis (ontologia)* and *metaphysica specialis....*" is both unsupported and unwarranted.

⁷ K. Rahner, *Theological Investigations* transl. C. Ernst, O.P., (Baltimore: Helicon Press, 1961), I, 10. See also Thomas Aquinas, *In I De coelo,* lect. 22; ed. Marietti, n. 228, 109: "Studium philosophiae non est ad hoc sciatur quid homines senserint sed qualiter se habeat veritas rerum."

⁸ R. de Scorraille, S.J., *François Suárez de la compagnie de Jésus d'apres ses lettres, ses autres ecrites inédits et un grand nombre de documents nouveaux,* 2 vols. (Paris: Lethielleux, 1913).

⁹ See the convenient listing in J. Iturrioz, S.J., "Bibliografiá Suareciana," *Pensamiento* 4(1948), 606-608; *Estudios...,* 59-65.

¹⁰ See R. de Scorraille, S.J., *François Suárez...* T. II, 129-142.

¹¹ *Ibid.,* 119-128; 165-221.

¹² See *Opera Omnia,* 26 vols. (Paris: Vives, 1856-1877). Since this is scarcely a critical edition by modern standards, I have made corrections throughout following the first edition, 1597 Salamanca, and the 1605 Mainz edition, as noted in the Introduction.

¹³ *Disputationes Metaphysicae,* Prooemium, XXV, 1ab. (Hereafter all references to this work will be cited as *DM*) Consequently, as de Scorraille notes, *op. cit.,* I, 330, n.1, the *Disputationes Metaphysicae* should be the initial volumes in any *Opera Omnia* of Suárez. On Suárez's *Prooemia,* see E. Elorduy, S.J., " Dedicatorias y Proemios de las Obras de Suárez," *Miscelanea Comillas* 9(1948), 323-345.

¹⁴ *Ibid.,* 1a. On the other hand, Suárez is not above indulging in a long theological digression in the midst of his metaphysics. See *DM* 31, 12, 14-23; XXVI, 287-293, where in paragraph 33 he notes: "Atque haec satis sint de hac digressione, quae hic necessaria visa est, ut constet, ea principia metaphysica a nobis tradi, quae verae Theologiae deserviant; hoc enim praecipue intendimus et optamus."

¹⁵ *Ibid.*

¹⁶ *Ibid.*

¹⁷ *Ibid.*

¹⁸ *DM Ad Lectorem;* XXV. See J. Iturrioz, *Pensamiento* 4(1948), 31-34; J. Owens, "The Analytics and Thomistic Metaphysical Procedure," *Mediaeval Studies* XXVI (1964), 103-106. Suárez is not above using the following expressions: "Addo vero ulterius, saepe hoc probationis genus excedere vim naturalis luminis intellectus humani, et pertinere potius ad metaphysicam divinam (ut sic dicam) vel supernaturalem quam naturalem.", *DM* 1, 4, 24; XXV, 33.

¹⁹ *Ibid.* However, Suárez does make a concession to this practice in producing an *Index Locupletissimus,* as noted in his *Ad Lectorem:* "Quia tamen erunt permulti, qui doctrinam hanc universam Aristotelis libris applicatam habere cupient, tum ut melius percipiant quibus tanti philosophi principiis nitatur, tum ut eius usus ad ipsum Aristotelem intelligendum facilior sit ac utilior, hac etiam in re lectori inservire studui, indice a nobis elaborato, quo, si attente legatur, facillime (ni fallor) potuerunt omnia quae Aristoteles in libris Metaphysicae pertractavit, et comprehendi et memoria retineri; rursusque prae manibus haberi quaestiones omnes quae inter alios libros exponendos excitari." See J. Iturrioz, *Pensamiento* 4(1948), 46-47; *Estudios...,* 74. In light of this, Suárez's perspective qualifies as a representative of a "reanimated Aristotelianism" noted by J. Owens, "Scholasticism and Metaphysics," *The Future of Metaphysics,* edit. R.E. Wood (Chicago: Quadrangle, 1970), 21.

[20] *Ibid.* See A. Maurer, C.S.B., *Medieval Philosophy* (N.Y.: Random House, 1962), 357: "...Suárez's *Disputationes Metaphysicae* is the first complete and systemic treatise in scholastic metaphysics."

[21] See *DM Index Locupletissimus*; XXV, 1vb; 1xb; Disp. 2, *Prooem.*; XXV, 64ab. See also J. Iturrioz, *Pensamiento* 4(1948), 43-49; *Estudios...*, 73-76; C.H. Lohr, S.J., "Jesuit Aristotelianism and Sixteenth-Century Metaphysics," *Paradosis* Studies in Memory of Edwin A. Quain, S.J. (N.Y.: Fordham University Press, 1976), 203-220, esp. 215-220.

[22] *DM Ad Lectorem*; XXV.

[23] *DM* 54; XXVI, 1014-1041.

[24] *DM* 31, *Prooem.*; XXVI, 224b. See J. Iturrioz, *Estudios...*, 34-35.

[25] *DM* 31, 1; XXVI, 224-228.

[26] *DM* 31, 1, 13; XXVI, 228; 2, 1 and 11; XXVI, 229 and 232b; 3, 1-2; XXVI, 233; 4, 1 and 7; XXVI, 235 and 237.

[27] *DM* 31, 5, 1; XXVI, 237; 6, 1; XXVI, 241-242; 7, 1; XXVI, 250b.

[28] *DM* 31, 8, 1; XXVI, 253; 9, 9, 1 and 25; XXVI, 258a and 261b; 10, 1-2, XXVI; 266-267; 11, 1; XXVI, 272; 12, 1; XXVI, 283a; 13, 1; XXVI, 298b; 14, 1; XXVI, 308. See the lament of Gabriel Vasquez purportedly directed at such an extensive discussion on this matter in Suárez: "Multa sane praeter haec disputant Recentiores de esse et essentia, variasque circa rem hanc quaestiones multiplicant, parvi sani, aut nullius momenti, quae ex dictis facile dilui possunt." *Commentariorum ac Disputationum in Tertiam Partem Sancti Thomae* (Lugduni, 1620), III, q.17, a.1, disp. 72, cap. 2; T.I, 484b.

[29] On Suárez's role as an historian of philosophy, see my "Suárez, Historian and Critic of the Modal Distinction Between Essential Being and Existential Being," *The New Scholasticism* XXXVI (1962), 419-444, esp. 419 n.1 and 443. See also J. Iturrioz, *Estudios...*, 159: "Podrá achacarse al Eximio que no siempre se bas en lecturas directas de los autores citados; que es impreciso a veces en la referencias por fiarse de su memoria; que se vale de referencias de segundo mano." For recent work on this proximate historical context at Salamanca, see the research of L.A. Kennedy, C.S.B., cited in n.4 above. For a wider ranging discussion, see P. Di Vona, *Studi sulla scolastica della Controriforma* L'esistenza e la sua distinzione metafisica dall'essenza (Firenze, 1968).

[30] Suárez's fear of equivocation is constant throughout the 31st Disputation. See *DM* 31, 1, 2; XXVI, 224b; 13; 228b; 2, 11; 232b; 4, 7,; 237b; 6, 13; 246a; 6, 24; 250b; 12, 42-44; 296-297. For Suárez's more global lament, see *DM Index Locupletissimus*, XXV, xliiib: "Q.3. Unde rursus pullulat alia quaestio, an in formis separatis quod quid est non sit aliud ab eo cujus est, in sensibilibus autem rebus haec distinguantur. Utrumque enim videtur Aristoteles docere in citatis verbis. Existimo autem esse magnam aequivocationem in his verbis et quaestionibus prout nunc tractantur in scholis, et prout Aristoteles eas ponit, ut in superioribus tactum est, et ex hoc loco fiet manifestum." In view of the fact that this fear is not at all limited to this Disputation (cf. his reference to a *dissensio in modo loquendi* in text cited in n.68 below), it appears that Suárez as historian also looks upon scholastic philosophy as a single "system" with most differences reducible to some aspect of inadvertent equivocation. See J. Owens, *Proceedings of American Catholic Philosophical Assoc.* XL (1966), 1-12, esp. n.22 In light of this, Suárez's reader must be constantly aware of his persistent bent at reconciliation, eg., "...ubi etiam assignavimus modum conciliandi varias opiniones et dicta Doctorum de hujusmodi entibus rationis...", *DM* 54, 2, 15; XXVI, 1022. For this matter of conciliation, see C.H. Lohr, *Paradosis...*, 208-211.

[31] *DM* 31, 1, 2; XXVI, 224-225. For the rendering of *esse essentiae, esse existentiae,* as "essential being" and " existential being", see J. Owens, "The Number of Terms in the Suarezian Discussion on Essence and Being," *The Modern Schoolman* XXXIV

(1957), 151-152. Throughout the translation I have attempted to remain constant in rendering *esse* as "being". To avoid the constant confusion with *ens*, the latter appears in parentheses, as do the instances of *essendi*.

32 DM 31, 1, 11; XXVI, 227-228,

33 For Giles of Rome, see *Theoremata de Esse et Essentia*, edit, E. Hocedez (Louvain, 1930), theorema XIX; 134. On whether Giles wishes to take this formula in the strict sense, see E. Hocedez, in his Introduction, (55)-(56). Capreolus' disclaimer about this formula occurs in a response to an objection of Peter Auriol, *Defensiones Theologiae Divi Thomae Aquinatis*, edit. Paban-Pègues (Turin: Alfred Cattier, 1900), *In I Sent.*, d.8, q.1, a.1; I, 327-328. Soncinas' disclaimer appears in his *Epitoma quaestionum in quatuor libros Sententiarum Joanne Capreolo Tolosano disputatarum* (Pavia, 1522), *In I Sent.*, d.8, q.1; fol. 45rb. Cajetan explicitly uses the *duae res* formula, *In De Ente et Essentia*, edit. M.-H. Laurent (Turin: Marietti, 1934), c.5, no. 102; 161. However, in response to an objection of Trombeta (154), Cajetan replies: "Ad tertium negatur major ad intellectum arguentis; non enim requiritur ad distinctionem realem quod utrumque eorum habeat propriam existentiam." The influence, forthcoming from the Nominalist tradition on what it means to be really distinct, must be considered here. See L.A. Kennedy, C.S.B., *Tommaso D'Aquino...*, 256. Also, in order to appreciate the sources and influences of the *duae res* formula in the essence-existence controversy, one must consider the role of the (now known to be spurious) work of Aquinas, the *Summa Totius Logicae*, where one finds: "Ubi nota quod in creaturis esse essentiae et esse actualis existentiae differunt realiter ut duae diversae res; quod sic patet...." See the citation of this text as a purportedly authentic deliverance of Aquinas by John of St. Thomas, *Naturalis Philosophia*, edit. B. Reiser (Turin, 1933), I, q.VII, a.IV; II, 132.

34 See L.A. Kennedy, *Tommaso D'Aquino...*, 255-256 who notes that "Francisco de Vitoria and Mancio del Cuerpo de Cristo said explicitly that Aquinas did not teach that essence and existence are two things." See also his article in *Archivo Teológico Granadino* 35(1972), 7-17; 40-47. Also, Kennedy notes that "Domingo Bañez and Pedro de Ledesma were aware that Aquinas did not teach this doctrine explicitly, but were sure that it was what he meant." *Tommaso D'Aquino...*, 256. See his "Peter of Ledesma and the Distinction Between Essence and Existence," *The Modern Schoolman* XLVI (1968), 25-38, esp. 30-32.

35 See F. Zumel, *In Primam D. Thomae Partem Commentaria* (Venetiis, 1597-1601), I, q.3, a.4; 92a: "Haec sententia (Scoti) est probabilis, et plurimi crediderunt esse sententiam D. Tho. Ita docuit Magister Vitoria, Soto et Cano." Peter de Ledesma makes the same claim, L.A. Kennedy, *The Modern Schoolman* XLVI (1968), 30. L.A. Kennedy also notes that "Mancio del Cuerpo de Cristo wrote: 'Scotus's opinion...is accepted by the Thomists of our time. Nor does it seem contrary to St. Thomas'." *Tommaso D'Aquino...*, 258 and *Archivo Teológico Granadino*. 35(1972), 43.

36 *DM* 31, 1, 11; XXVI, 227-228. See my article cited in n.29 above. For a significant Scotistic response to this linking of the Thomist and Scotist traditions on essence and existence, see B. Mastrius, *Disputationes in XII Arist. Stag. Libros Metaphysicorum* (Venice, 1646), Disp. VIII, q.II, 77; II, 94: "Toto insuper, ut aiunt, aberrant Coelo, qui cum hac nostra sententia coincidere dicunt opinionem quorundam Thomistarum ponentium inter essentiam et existentiam distinctionem modalem, non autem realem, ut loquitur Soto 2 Physic. q.2, Molin. loc. cit. Fonsec. 4 Met. c.2 q.4 Albertin. tom. 2 princ. 1 Philosoph. disp. 2 q.1 et alii nonnulli, quia isti non loquuntur de distinctione modali, ut solet accipi in Schola Scotistarum, qualis assignari solet ab eis inter rem ac modum eius intrinsecum,....Sed loquuntur de distinctione illa modali quam Moderni assignare consueverunt inter rem et modum eius extrinsecum...."

37 *DM* 31, 1, 12; XXVI, 228.

[38] *DM* 31, 1, 13; XXVI, 228b. If B. Mastrius is correct, we should look upon Suárez as representing a tradition known as the *Neutrales.* See *Disputationes...,* Disp. VIII, q.II; II, 93a: "Opposita ex diametro sententia affirmat nullo prorsus modo a parte rei distingui, sed solum per intellectum, ita ut existentia a parte rei sit eadem omnino entitas actualis essentiae et est communissima, et passim recepta apud Nominales et Neutrales quam docuit Alensis 4 Met. tex. 4 et lib. 7 tex. 22, Aureol. 1, d.8, q.1, Durand., ibid., q.2, Greg. 2, d.6, q.1, Gabriel 3, d.6, q.3, art. 1 et sequuntur neoterici passim Pererius, lib. 6, suae Philosoph., cap. 4, Suárez, disp. 31, Met...."

[39] *Ibid.*

[40] *DM* 31, 2, 1; XXVI, 229a. See J. Gómez Caffarena, "Sentido de la composición de ser y esencia en Suárez, *Pensamiento* 15(1959), 141: "Quiere sin duda evitar la impression, que podria dar, de conceder a la esencia una actualidad propia anterior a la existencia; éste es su empeño primordial en la Disputa, como vamos a ver ahora con mas detención."

[41] See E. Gilson, *Being and Some Philosophers,* 2nd edit. (Toronto, 1951); T.J. Cronin, S.J., *Objective Being in Descartes and Suárez* (Roma: Gregorian University Press, 1966), Appendix II, 167-199; my article "Existence: History and Problematic," *The Monist* 50 (1966), 34-43.

[42] *DM* 31, 1, 4; XXVI, 225; 1, 11; XXVI, 227b. Cf. E. Gilson, *History of Christian Philosophy in the Middle Ages* (N.Y.: Random House, 1955), 211: "The metaphysical complex resulting from the combination of Avicenna's notion of efficient causality as the origin of existence with the Proclean universe described in the *Book on Causes,* will become very common about the end of the thirteenth century." See as well E. Gilson, *Jean Duns Scot* (Paris: J. Vrin, 1952), 487 n.1: "Il était assurément plus difficile, au début du XIVe siécle, de distinguer entre la position d'Avicenne et celle de saint Thomas sur la composition d'essence et d'acte d'être, que ce ne l'est aujourd'hui pour nous...."

[43] See my article cited in n.4 above; J. Hegyi, S.J., *Die Bedeutung des Seins bei den Klassichen Kommentatoren des heiligen Thomas von Aquin; Capreolus, Silvester von Ferrara, Cajetan* (Munich, 1959).

[44] See E. Gilson, "Cajetan et l'existence," *Tijdschrift voor Philosophie* 2(1953), 267-286 and other references in n.4 above.

[45] *Totius Philosophiae Compendium* (Lugduni, 1568), *Tractatus de Transcendentibus,* cap. 4; I, 466-467.

[46] T. J. Cronin, *Objective Being...,* Appendix II, 167-199.

[47] *Ibid.;* J. Paulus, *Henri de Gand. Essai sur les tendances de sa métaphysique* (Paris: J. Vrin, 1938); J. Gómez Caffarena, S. J., *Ser participado y ser subsistente en la metafisica de Enrique de Gante* (Rome, 1958).

[48] *Quodlibeta* (Louvain, 1646), V, 3; 273a where the essence has enough actuality to be known but it does not have enough to exist. This is as close as Giles comes to the doctrine of eternal essences abroad among the *Thomistae.*

[49] See L. A. Kennedy, *Tommaso D'Aquino...,* 257-258; *Archivo Teológico Granadino* 35(1972), 7-17.

[50] *Ibid.; Archivo Teológico Granadino,* 22-32.

[51] *Ibid.; op. cit.,* 40-47.

[52] *Ibid.; op. cit.,* 47-50.

[53] L.A. Kennedy; *The Modern Schoolman* XLVI (1968), 31-33.

[54] *Quaestiones Metaphysicales* (Venetiis, 1498), Bk. 4, q.12; B4v-b5v.

[55] *Commentaria in Summa Contra Gentiles,* ed. Leonina (Roma, 1920-1930), II, 52; T. 13, 389.

⁵⁶ *Scolastica Commentaria in Primam Partem Summae Theologicae S. Thomae Aquinatis,* edit. L. Urbano (Madrid, 1934), I, q.10, a.3; I, 227: "Essentiae rerum...non sunt ab aeterno quantum ad esse existentiae, neque quantum ad esse quidditativum et essentiale....Quod homo sit animal, est ab aeterno, si dictio, *est,* dicat esse essentiale et connexionem animalis cum homine....Si dictio, *est,* dicat veritatem propositionis, hominem esse animal, non est ab aeterno, nisi in intellectu divino." For an English rendering of this see *The Primacy of Existence in Thomas Aquinas,* transl. B. S. Llamzon (Chicago: Regnery, 1966), 117-119. In a more complete edition of Bañez (Salmanticae, 1584), we find a more explicit rendering of the position of Soncinas and Sylvester of Ferrara, *In I Sum. Theol.,* q.44, a.1; col. 646: "Ad tertium negatur antecedens, et ad probationem dico quod illa maxima, essentiae rerum sunt aeternae, est vera quoad connexionem, non quia illae essentiae existant ab aeterno...." Bañez alludes to a second proof and cites Soncinas and Sylvester of Ferrara.

⁵⁷ *DM* 31, 12, 41-45; XXVI, 295-297.

⁵⁸ *DM* 31, 12, 1-5, esp. 5; XXVI, 283-285.

⁵⁹ L. A. Kennedy, *Tommaso D'Aquino...,* 256.

⁶⁰ *Theoremata de Esse et Essentia,* theorema XII; 67-68. See Suárez's reference to Giles on this point and in this work, *DM,* 31, 12, 35; XXVI, 293.

⁶¹ *Def. Theol., Ad nonum Godofridi;* I, 327a. Capreolus notes that the major premise, ("Quandocumque sunt aliqua distincta realiter, unum potest per divinam potentiam ab alio separari.") *a multis multipliciter glossetur.*

⁶² *In Octo Libros Physicorum Quaestiones* (Salmanticae, 1582), II, q.2; 34rb. See L. A. Kennedy, *Archivo Teológico Granadino* 35(1972), 22-32. Suárez cites Soto in *DM,* 31, 1, 11; XXVI, 227b. See my article cited in n.29 above, esp. 429. For Gabriel Vasquez's attack upon Suárez for attributing a real modal distinction to Soto, see the same article, 430-431.

⁶³ *DM* 31, 12, 1-5; XXVI, 283-285.

⁶⁴ See F. Zumel, *In Sum. Theol.,* I, q.3, a.4; 95a. See Peter of Ledesma in L. A. Kennedy, *The Modern Schoolman* XLVI (1968), 35-36. Bañez espoused this position initially but later repudiated it according to L. A. Kennedy, *Tommaso D'Aquino...,* 256-257.

⁶⁵ See Peter of Ledesma, *op. cit.,* 35-36. F. A. Cunningham., S.J., "The 'Real Distinction' in Jean Quidort," *Journal of the History of Ideas* VIII (1970), 19 n.116 refers to sources which indicate that the original edition of Bañez's Commentary on the *Summa Theologiae* maintained that the *esse* of the bread, in Transubstantiation, continued in existence without its essence.

⁶⁶ *DM* 31, 2, 1; XXVI, 229: "Principio statuendum est, essentiam creaturae, seu creaturam de se, et priusquam a Deo fiat, nullum habere, in se verum esse reale, et in hoc sensu, praeciso esse existentiae, essentiam non esse rem aliquam, sed omnino nihil." (For what it is worth, the comma after *et in hoc sensu* is lacking in the 1597 Salamanca edition) *Omnino nihil* is even more forcefully stated in *DM* 31, 2, 4; XXVI, 230b: "...quia quod est simpliciter et omnino nihil, non potest vere et realiter esse aliquid in aliqua ratione veri entis." It is repeated in *DM* 31, 2, 5; XXVI, 230b. B. Mastrius, *Disputationes...,* Disp. VIII, q.I; II, 77a, links Suárez with "...quidam enim absolute negant posse dici ens reale, sed potius non ens et nihil debere dici, ita contendit Hurtad. disp. 8 Met. sec. 2, Faber theor. 32, cap. 3 ab initio ac etiam Suárez ita loqui videtur disp. 31, Met. sec. 2 ubi ait essentiam secluso esse existentiae non esse rem aliquam, sed omnino esse nihil, cui modo dicendi etiam Scotus favere videtur I d.36 M ubi ait hominem ab aeterno tam esse nihil, quam chimeram...et hunc dicendi modum sequuntur Autores cit. num. 32 qui possibilitatem rerum ab aeterno negant esse positivam, et dicunt importare meram negationem repugnantiae, et solam realitatem privativam, omnes, inquam, isti dicunt rerum essentias esse merum nihil, nec ullo pacto iis convenire rationem entis prout a

nihilo contradistinguitur...." Suárez also uses the phrase *non ens* in *DM* 31, 1, 13; XXVI, 228b; 31, 3, 1; XXVI, 233a; 31, 6, 22; XXVI, 249b. Though apparently unequivocal, the strength and proper significance of *omnino nihil* and *non ens* has been the cause of some concern. See J. Owens, *The Modern Schoolman* XXXIV (1957), 167-186; T. J. Cronin, *Objective Being...,* 41-56; Max Rast, S. J., "Die Possibilienlehre des Franz Suárez," *Scholastik* X (1935), 340-368; J. Doyle, "Suárez on the Reality of the Possibles," *The Modern Schoolman* XLV (1967), 30 et seq.; J. Hellín, S.J., "El ente real y los posibiles en Suárez," *Espíritu* 10(1961), 152 et seq.: W. Norris Clarke, S.J., "What is Really Real," *Progress in Philosophy* (Milwaukee, 1955), 61-90; H. Seigfried, *Wahrheit und Metaphysik bei Suárez* (Bonn: H. Bouvier, 1967), 66-67; A. Gnemmi, *Il Fondamento Metafisico* Analisi di struttura sulle *Disputationes Metaphysicae* di F. Suárez (Milano: Vita e Pensiero, 1969), 315-318. This is especially so because of statements such as that by J. I. Conway, S.J., *Proceedings of the Jesuit Philosophical Association* 21(1959), 123: "From a consideration of the above texts it should be abundantly clear that when Suárez observes that a possible essence is nothing, he does not intend to deny that such an essence is real but only that it is not anything actual." But it is all the more so in virtue of Suárez's own purported qualification in *DM* 31, 2, 10; XXVI, 232a wherein the still unproduced essence of a creature (*omnino nihil*) is in some way an *ens reale* or *essentia realis*. See J. Gómez Caffarena, *Pensamiento* 15(1959), 143: "Suárez, que habia comenzado la seccion negandoles todo ser real, admite ahora, con Cayetano, que lo sean, en otro sentido más amplio del término, el de aptitud para el existir real, prescindiendo de la realización." Indeed, Mastrius, in the place referred to above in this note (77b), makes the same point: "...posseque in hoc sensu rem possibilem ens reale dici apellari, et hoc etiam concedit Suárez loc. cit., num. 10". Purportedly, then, *omnino nihil* and/or *non ens* appear to indicate only a negation of actual *ens,* actual essence, actual existence. It would not necessarily imply a negation of possible *ens,* possible essence and possible existence. Indeed, see Suárez, *In Sum. Theol.,* I, 25, Bk. III, cap. 9, 16; I, 228: "Quia non ens, ut illa negatio dicit negationem possibilitatis, seu capacitatis ad esse....Non ens autem, ut dicit ens possibile cum negatione actualis existentiae..." Also see Suárez, *DM* 31, 3, 3; XXVI, 233: "...in essentia possibili priusquam fiat, nihil rei esse (proprie loquendo ie positiva et actuali)..." which would contribute to the above interpretations. Moreover, given the twofold signification of *ens* in Suárez, *ut participium* and *ut nomen,* as in *DM* 2, 4; XXV, 87-92, the use of *non ens* in this discussion would appear to indicate only a negation of *ens ut participium,* so that what is *non ens* in this latter sense is still *ens ut nomen.* However, in using *omnino nihil,* Suárez intends not only to negate *ens ut participium* but also to insist that *ens possibile,* with respect to creatures prior to their creation, and as involving an exclusion of actual existence, is not to be considered within the range of *ens reale* or *essentia realis* encompassed by *ens ut nomen.* See J. Gómez Caffarena, *Pensamiento* 15(1959), 136 n.2: "En D.M. 2, 4, 7-11 había Suárez reservado el término *in potentia* para el ente con abstraccion *negativa* de actualidad: pero en la D.M. 31 no observa siempre esa restricción y llama *potentia* o *potentialis* aun a la esencia realis con mera abstraccion *praecisiva* de actualidad."; J. Hellín, *Espíritu* 10(1961), 147: "Esto supuesto, los posibles no se incluyen en el ente real en cuanto a la privación de existencia que tienen antes de ser creados: en este sentido son totalmente nada y no se pueden contener en el ámbito del ente real, objeto de la metafísica." As we shall see below, for Suárez to say here that creatures have some sort of possible being prior to their creation is to insist on a *potentia objectiva* which is, in turn, an extrinsic denomination. This is altogether consistent with his claim about *omnino nihil.* We shall also see that his claims here about *ens reale, essentia realis* and *ens ut nomen* involve a switch to the area of *potentia logica.* Indeed, the specter of ambiguity and equivocation on this issue would seem to be the price Suárez must pay for trying to reconcile such texts as that of Aquinas on *potentia objectiva* in n.87 below with that of Scotus on *potentia objectiva* in n.86 below and with that of Scotus on *potentia logica* in n.135.

⁶⁷ *DM* 31, 6, 17; XXVI, 247; 25, 2, 7-18; XXV, 912-916. This is Suárez's way of countering the influence of Henry of Ghent's doctrine of non-creative, eternal, exemplary causality of the essences of creatures upon Capreolus and the *Thomistae* following him. See Capreolus, *Def. Theol., In II Sent.,* d.1, q.II, a.3, ad 4 Aureoli contra quartam conclusionem; III, 76. Suárez's attack on his adversaries' doctrine of exemplary causality is frequent and as often misunderstood. For, in denying a distinctive exemplary cause of created essences and thereby proceeding beyond the divine intellect and the *esse cognitum* of his opponents, Suárez does not intend to go beyond divine omnipotence and a potential efficient cause. See *DM* 8, 7, 27; XXV, 304b.

⁶⁸ *DM* 30, 15, 27; XXVI, 178. See also T. J. Cronin, *Objective Being...,* Appendix II, 167-199.

⁶⁹ *Ibid.* See also *DM* 31, 2, 1-2; XXVI, 229; 54, 2, 7; XXVI, 1020a.

⁷⁰ *DM* 31, 2, 2-4; XXVI, 229-230. See my article on Capreolus in n.4 above.

⁷¹ *DM* 31, 2, 3; XXVI, 230a.

⁷² *DM* 31, 2, 5; XXVI, 230b. See n.66 above.

⁷³ *DM* 31, 12, 38; XXVI, 294b.

⁷⁴ *DM* 31, 12, 1-37; XXVI, 283-294, esp. 34-37; 293-294.

⁷⁵ *DM* 31, 12, 38; XXVI, 294b.

⁷⁶ *DM* 31, 12, 41-45; XXVI, 295-297. See nn.54-56 for references to Soncinas, Sylvester of Ferrara and Bañez.

⁷⁷ *DM* 31, 12, 42-45; XXVI, 295-297.

⁷⁸ *DM* 12, 45; XXVI, 297. This is the significance of his: "Quanquam in hoc possimus discrimen assignare...." Suárez is able to do this but not his adversaries. In a very muted fashion, Suárez is availing himself of a passage in Peter Fonseca, *Commentariorum In Metaphysicorum Aristotelis Stagiritae Libros* (Cologne, 1615), Bk. V, cap. 5, q.1; II, col. 325-326, where Fonseca claims against the same adversaries confronted by Suárez: "...entia omnia infra Deum, possunt quidem imperfecte considerari ut entia realia, sine ordine ad Deum, ut causam primam efficientem....perfecte autem ac distincte nullo modo concipi possunt, nisi quantenus pendeat a Deo, ut a prima causa efficiente." This would be quite consistent with Suárez's metaphysical perspective where, within the context of *ens ut nomen,* one moves from an inadequate and confused, quasi-univocal consideration of God and creatures as not-nothing to a more contracted consideration of creatures properly taken. See J. Doyle, "Suárez on the Analogy of Being," *The Modern Schoolman* XLVI (1969), 219-249; 323-341.

⁷⁹ See n.4 above.

⁸⁰ See nn.54-56 above.

⁸¹ *DM* 31, 2, 3-5; XXVI, 230.

⁸² *DM* 31, 2, 4; XXVI, 230; 31, 2, 7; 231.

⁸³ *DM* 31, 2, 7-8 and 10-11; XXVI, 231-232.

⁸⁴ *Ibid.*

⁸⁵ *DM* 31, 2, 2; XXVI, 230a: "Atque eodem modo et ratione, esse, quod appellant essentiae ante effectionem, seu creationem divinam, solum est potentiale objectivum (ut multi loquuntur, de quo statim), seu per denominationem extrinsecam a potentia Dei, et non repugnantiam ex parte essentiae creabilis." This is addressed directly to the *Thomistae* who follow Capreolus following Henry of Ghent (ct. n.67 above) but is too often overlooked by many today in the context of the problem noted in n.66 above. F. Albertinus indicates the influences at work upon Suárez in this matter, *Corollaria seu Quaestiones Theologicae* (Lugduni, 1616), disp. I, q.3; II, 12a: "Omnes Doctores conveniunt, creaturam esse ab aeterno in potentia objectiva; sed controversia est inter eos, quaenam sit ista potentia objectiva in creatura. Prima

sententia est Ervei quodl. 11. quaest. 1. Soncin. quaest. M. quaest. 4. Suar. in met. disp. 31 et aliorum, quos supra in prima quaestione citavimus, qui quoniam tenent esse essentiae nihil esse ante creationem, sed simul fieri essentiam, et existentiam in tempore, consequenter tenent esse essentiae in potentia objectiva, nihil aliud esse quam denominatione extrinseca objecti a potentia productiva."

[86] *Ibid.* For an extensive dossier of texts on extrinsic denomination, see J. Doyle, *The Modern Schoolman* XLVI (1969), 330. This is the burden of Suárez's defense of Scotus on this point in *DM* 31, 3, 2: XXVI, 233.

[87] *Ibid.; DM* 31, 3, 2; XXVI, 233. See E. Elorduy, S.J., "El concepto objetivo en Suárez," *Pensamiento* número extraordinario (1948), 384: "Esta doctrina sobre la potencia objetiva la interpreta Suárez diciendo que Escoto llamó *ens in potentia objectiva* al mismo *ens possibile.* A continuacion explica Suárez lo que es la potencia objetiva en los posibles, demostrando con varios argumentos que no puede ser ninguna cosa verdadera y positiva la que como sujeto reciba la acción creadora de Dios. Como observó Santo Tomas, I. th. 1, 9, a.2, 'creaturae non dicuntur possibiles nisi per denominationem ab aliqua potentia':..." Just as Suárez lectured the *Thomistae* in section two of Disputation 31 by quoting Aquinas, *De Potentia,* q.3, a.5, ad 2, so in section three he continues to use the same tactic in quoting *I Sum. Theol.,* q.9, a.2, *DM,* 31, 3, 3; XXVI, 233. Suárez is also convinced that he has reconciled Aquinas and Scotus on this matter and can use that alliance against the *Thomistae* and the *Scotistae* who hold for an eternal actual essence. However, one should be wary of the consistency of Suárez's position here in light of the comment of J. Gómez Caffarena, *Pensamiento* 15(1959), 142, n.33: "Quiza va aquí Suárez más lejos de lo que él mismo querría, en la negación de realidad intrinseca al término del conocimiento en cuanto tal. Expresiones como la presente se encuentran en abundancia en sus obras, pero hay otras de otro sentido."

[88] *DM* 31, 2, 2; XXVI, 229b.

[89] *DM* 31, 3, 1; XXVI, 233a. Suárez takes pains to indicate that this understanding of the real distinction (as a real negative distinction) is maintained by Soncinas among the *antiqui Thomistae.* But he is also addressing himself to the *Thomistae* at Salamanca since this same distinction is embraced by D. Bañez, *In Sum. Theol.,* I, q.10, a.3; I, 228a. Most importantly, Suárez himself will agree with this rendering of the real distinction. See *DM* 31, 1, 13; XXVI, 228b.

[90] Suárez would seem to be influenced in this by Hervaeus Natalis, *Quodlibeta* (Venice, 1513), I, q.10; fol. 23va, which would be quite consistent with the comment of Albertinus in n.85 above.

[91] See n.186 below.

[92] *DM* 31, 12, 42; XXVI, 295b.

[93] *Ibid.*

[94] *Ibid.,* 296a.

[95] *Ibid.*

[96] *Ibid.*

[97] *Ibid.*

[98] *DM* 31, 12, 44; XXVI, 296-297.

[99] *DM* 31, 12, 38; XXVI, 294b; 31, 12, 44; 297a.

[100] *DM* 31, 6, 16; XXVI, 247a. See Michael de Palacios, *In Primum Librum Magistri Sententiarum Disputationes* (Salmanticae, 1574), *In I Sent.,* d.8, disp. 2; fol. 82vb-83rb.

[101] *Ibid.*

[102] *DM* 31, 6, 17-18; XXVI, 247-248. Suárez is here opposing the position of Henry of Ghent, *Quodlibeta* (Paris: Jacobus Badius Ascensius, 1518), I, q.9; fol. 6v-7r, with its exemplary causality of essence and efficient causality of existence. See n.67 above. See also F. Cunningham, S.J., "Some Presuppositions in Henry of Ghent," *Pensamiento* 25(1969), 103-143.

[103] *DM* 31, 6, 19-20; XXVI, 248-249.

[104] *DM* 31, 6, 20; XXVI, 249a.

[105] *DM* 31, 6, 13-15; XXVI, 246-247.

[106] *DM* 31, 6, 21; XXVI, 249.

[107] *DM* 31, 6, 21-24; XXVI, 249-250.

[108] *DM* 31, 6, 21; XXVI, 249b; 6, 13-15; XXVI, 246-247.

[109] *DM* 31, 6, 21-24; XXVI, 249-250; 4, 5; XXVI, 234a. See the bald statement by Suárez, *DM* 31, 10, 18; XXVI, 271b: "At vero, juxta nostram sententiam, existentia, ut in re ipsa invenitur, non est tam actus essentiae quam ipsa essentia in actu,...." See also *DM* 31, 13, 18; XXVI, 304a.

[110] *DM* 31, 6, 24; XXVI, 250b; 6, 22; XXVI, 249b. Also see n.89 above.

[111] *DM* 31, 1, 13; XXVI, 228b; 6, 13; XXVI, 246a; 6, 22; XXVI, 249b. See J. Owens, *The Modern Schoolmen* XXXIV (1957), 167-186.

[112] *DM* 31, 6, 15; XXVI, 248b; 3, 5; XXVI, 234a; 6, 8; XXVI, 244a: "...quia effectus formalis nec mente praescindi potest a causa formali." *DM* 31, 13, 11; XXVI, 301-302; 15, 11; XXV, 560b: "Similiter dicendum est de existentia: nam licet haec non sit absolute de essentia rei creatae seu creabilis, est tamen de essentia ejus, ut existentis, seu constitutae in ratione entitatis actualis...." See also Suárez, *In III Sum. Theol.*, disp. 36, I, 4; XVIII, 261.

[113] *DM* 31, 6, 22; XXVI, 249 and especially *DM* 31, 13, 11-13; XXVI, 301-302. On Suárez's position on the pertinent *distinctio rationis ratiocinatae*, see *DM* 7, 1, 4-8; XXV, 251-252; 2, 28; XXV, 271.

[114] *DM* 31, 6, 23; XXVI, 250a.

[115] *Ibid.* See *DM* 7, 1, 4; XXV, 251a: "Alio ergo sensu dici potest distinctio rationis ratiocinatae...ratiocinatae vero, quia non est omnino ex mero opere rationis sed ex occasione quam res ipsa praebet, circa quam mens ratiocinatur. See also *DM* 3, 1, 6; XXV, 104b: "...quia distinctio rationis, quae oritur ex praecisione intellectus non est per conceptionem alicujus fictae entitatis, quae non sit in re sed per modum solum inadaequatum concipiendi veram rem..."

[116] For Suárez's position on *compositio* herein, see *DM* 31, 13, 7-13; XXVI, 300-302; *DM* 6, 9, 21-23; XXV, 243.

[117] *DM* 31, 6, 23; XXVI, 250a.

[118] *Ibid.* On *abstractio praecisiva vel negativa*, see *DM* 2, 4, 9-11; XXV, 90-91 and J. Gómez Caffarena, *Pensamiento* 15(1959), 136 n.2.

[119] This consideration of essence as a receptive potency in relation to existence as its act is not without its problems. See J. Owens, *The Modern Schoolman* XXXIV (1957), 183-184. See nn.133, 134 below.

[120] See J. Owens, *The Modern Schoolman* XXXIV (1957), 155-157; J. Hellín, S.J., "Existencialismo escolástico Suareciano," *Pensamiento* 12(1956), 163: "...será necesario distinguir tres estados del ente, a saber: en ejercicio actual de la existencia, en estado de mera possibilidad, y en estado absoluto, en que se retiene la existencia, sin determiner si está ejercitada o no está ejercitada."

[121] *DM* 31, 1, 2; XXVI, 225a.

[122] *DM* 31, 2; XXVI, 229-232, esp. paragraph 7; 231a: "...sed sufficit esse potentiale quod ut sic solum est actu in causa." See also *DM* 6, 4, 9; XXV, 219-220 and nn.66, 78, 85, 87 above as well as nn.132, 133 below.

[123] *Ibid.*, esp. paragraph 8; 231b and paragraphs 10 and 11; 232. See nn.68, 69 above.

[124] Just how critical a problem is involved here is indicated by Suárez, *DM, Index Locupletissimus;* XXV, xlvia: "Celebris est divisio entis in ens actu, et ens in potentia, seu in potentiam et actum....Est autem pro totius libri intelligentia advertendum,

aliud vero dividere ens in ens, quod est potentia, vel quod est actus; nam prior non est divisio in entia essentialiter diversa, sed in diversos status ejusdem entis secundum rationem existendi; et in hoc sensu pauca dicit Philosophus in toto hoc libro; illam vero divisionem nos applicamus in disp. 31, sect. 3...."

[125] *DM* 31, 2-3; XXVI, 229-235.

[126] *DM* 31, 2, 2; XXVI, 229-230; 3, 3-4; XXVI, 233b-234; 6, 4, 9; XXV, 220a. See J. Doyle, *The Modern Schoolman* XLV (1967), 40-47; XLVI (1969), 333-340.

[127] *Ibid.; DM* 31, 6, 7; XXVI, 244a; 6, 4, 9; XXV, 219-220. See nn.85-87 above.

[128] *Ibid.; DM* 30, 17, 10; XXVI, 209. See also *DM* 31, 6, 13; XXVI, 246a: "...nullum ens praeter Deum habere ex se entitatem suam, prout vera entitas est. Quod addo, ut tollatur aequivocatio de entitate in potentia, quae re vera non est entitas sed nihil, et ex parte rei creabilis solum dicit non repugnantiam, vel potentiam logicam." See nn.66, 85-87 above and 136, 139 below.

[129] *DM* 31, 2, 2; XXVI, 229-230; 10-11; XXVI, 232; 3, 3; XXVI, 233b; 6, 13; XXVI, 246a; 12, 45; XXVI, 297; 54, 2, 10; XXVI, 1018; *DM* 2, 4, 5; XXV, 89a. See n.78 above and 157 below.

[130] *DM* 31, 3, 2-4; XXVI, 233-234. see nn.85-87 above. However, Suárez does not always insist on this. See *DM* 31, 6, 7; XXVI, 243-244: "...licet essentia creaturae priusquam fiat, dici posset esse in pura potentia objectiva ex parte sui....cum possit illa essentia intelligi in sola potentia objectiva ex parte ejus, et effectiva ex parte creatoris."

[131] *DM* 31, 4, 5; XXVI, 234a: "...diximus autem essentiam in potentia nihil habere entitatis; non ergo ei fit additio proprie loquendo, nisi fortasse secundum rationem, quatenus essentia in potentia objectiva apprehenditur per modum entis,...." This should be related to *DM* 31, 2, 10; XXVI, 232a and to J. Doyle, *The Modern Schoolman* XLV (1967), 40, n.56.

[132] *DM* 31, 3, 4; XXVI, 234; 5-8; 234-235; 6, 15; 246-247; 9, 25; 266a; *DM* 6, 4, 9; XXV, 219-220. Herein we would seem to be in the presence of a negation or an exclusion by a privative or negative abstraction and not merely by means of a precisive abstraction. Indeed, this is the case in *DM* 2, 4, 11-12; XXV, 91 as noted by J. Gómez Caffarena, in text cited in n.66 above. But the oft-noted *non repugnantia* cannot be affected by this negation and exclusion. For if actual existence were positively excluded, the stated difference between *ens in potentia* and *ens rationis* would be jeopardized. B. Mastrius, *Disputationes...*, Disp. VIII, q.1, a.3; II, 80b-81a, notes that Aversa insists that *essentia rerum secundum se* ought not to be designated as *ens potentiale* because such a designation is understood negatively; that it does not exist in act. But Aversa wishes to say that essence is truly essence, and is essentially *ens,* even when it does not actually exist. A negation of existence is not to be considered with respect to the essence itself. Mastrius' comment on this issue is interesting, to the effect that: "...essentia praecisa existentia secundum ipsum participat rationem entis nominaliter, at ens nominaliter sumptum dicitur illud, quod esto non existat, ei tamen existere non repugnat, ergo dixi [sic] potest ens potentiale. Quamvis ergo nequeat dici ens potentiale potentia objectiva, quia haec revera opponitur actui ac in sua ratione involvit negatione existentiae, bene tamen dici potest ens potentiale potentia logica..." Compare B. Mastrius, *Disputationes Theologicae in Primum Librum Sententiarum* (Venetiis, 1698), Disp. 3, q.2. #52; 118b: "...nam *de fide* est res ab aeterno habuisse esse possibile, seu in potentia logica, quale non habuerunt chimerae, et figmenta; item fuisse in in potentia objectiva, id est, in virtute omnipotentiae Dei, et secundum tale esse fuisse ab aeterno cognitas a Deo, qui ab aeterno cognovit esse reale actuale in tempore eis non repugnare...." See n.66 above.

[133] *Ibid.* esp. *DM* 31, 9, 25; XXVI, 266a:"...si per essentiam intelligant rem in sola potentia objectiva, nos de illa non agimus, quia illa ut sic nihil est, neque vere fit aut est terminus effectionis..." *DM* 31, 6, 15; XXVI, 246-247:"...negamus esse de

essentia, quia praescindi potest a praedicto conceptu, et de facto potest non convenire prout tali conceptui objicitur." See J. Owens, *The Modern Schoolman* XXXIV (1957), 179-183.

   ¹³⁴ *DM* 31, 3, 5; XXVI, 234b; 12, 35; 293b; 46; 298a:"...semper ergo restat difficultas tacta, quomodo, scilicet, si objectum in se nihil est,..." On *potentia subjectiva,* See *DM* 31, 3, 3; XXVI, 233. See n.131 above.

   ¹³⁵ *DM* 31, 6, 13; XXVI, 246; 28, 1, 14; XXVI, 6a; 42, 3, 9; XXVI, 613a; 43, 4, 2; XXVI, 645-646; 43; XXVI, 633; 43, 1, 2; XXVI, 634. See Duns Scotus, *Ordinatio,* edit. Vat. (Rome, 1963), *In I Sent.,* d.36, q.1; VI, 296:"Nec est fingendum quod homini non repugnat quia est ens in potentia, et chimerae repugnat quia non est in potentia, — immo magis e converso, quia homini non repugnat, ideo est possibile potentia logica, et chimerae quia repugnat, ideo est impossibile impossibilitate opposita; et illam possibilitatem consequitur possibilitas objectiva, et hoc supposita omnipotentia Dei quae respicit omne possibile (dummodo illud sit aliud a se), tamen illa possibilitas logica, absolute-ratione sui-posset stare, licet per impossibile nulla omnipotentia eam respiceret." See texts of Mastrius cited in n.132 above; A. Gnemmi, *Il Fondamento Metafisico...,* 73-74; J. Doyle, *The Modern Schoolman* XLV (1967), 41 nn.62, 63; H. Deku, "Possibile Logicum," *Philosophisches Jahrbuch* 64(1956), 1-21.

   ¹³⁶ See n.66, 85, 87 above. See Mastrius, *Disputationes...,* Disp. VIII, q.1, a.3, #32; II, 69:"Aliqui enim, ne videantur creaturis ab aeterno tribuere aliquod esse positivum, per eam non repugnantiam nolunt intelligi possibilitatem positivam ad existendum, sed meram negationem repugnantiae, et impossibilitatis, quam vocant realitatem privativam, ita loquitur Smisinch. trac. 2 de Deo uno, disp. 4, q.4, nu. 99 et seq. quo etiam modo locutus est Fonsec. 4 Met. c.5, q.1, sec 4 ubi connexionem extremorum, quam importat logica possibilitas, explicat per negationem diversitatis praedicati a subjecto." Suárez is linked with this perspective in the text of Mastrius cited in n.66 above.

   ¹³⁷ See B. Mastrius, *Disputationes...,* Disp. VIII, q.1, a.3, #32; II, 69:"Hic dicendi modus non placet, quia conceptus objectivi rerum in mente divina sunt positivi, et important esse essentiale rerum, quod est esse positivum; tum quia negatio negationis est quid positivum, ut negatio tenebrae est lux, negatio caecitatis est visus, sed negatio repugnantiae est negatio negationis, quia est negatio impossibilitatis, ergo quid positivum importare debet." John of St. Thomas makes the same point about the double negative, *Cursus Theologicus,* I, disp. 18, a.1, n.6; II, 373-374. This aspect of Suárez's position is most often overlooked and the tendency to espouse a doctrine of underived possibility, negative or positive, in the area of *potentia logica,* remains unassessed. See A. Gnemmi, *Il Fondamento Metafisico...,* passim; J. Hellín, "La metafisica de la posibilidad," *Las Ciencias* 3(1956), 455-477: "Existencialismo escolástico Suareciano," *Pensamiento* 12(1956), 157-178; 13(1957), 21-38; "El ente real y los posibles en Suárez," *Espiritu* 10(1961), 146-163; "Las verdades esenciales se fundan en Dios según Suárez," *Revista de Filosofía* 22(1963), 19-42.

   ¹³⁸ *DM* 31, 2, 10; XXVI, 232: "Ad quartum respondetur, essentiam possibilem creaturae objectivam (1597 Salamanca edit. reads *objectam*) divinae scientiae, non esse ens confictum ab intellectu, sed esse ens revera possibile et capax realis existentiae, ideoque non esse ens rationis, sed sub ente reali aliquo modo comprehendi. Jam enim supra declaravi essentiam creaturae, etiam non productum, esse aliquo modo essentiam realem. Et in superioribus, tractando de conceptu entis, ostendimus non solum sub illo comprehendi id quod actu est, sed etiam quod aptum est esse." See *DM* 2, 4, 7; XXV, 89. This tends to fly in the face of Suárez's gloss of Capreolus (nn.85-87 above) where *esse potentiale objectivum,* or an extrinsic denomination from divine omnipotence, is involved. For here we are not in the presence of any extrinsic denomination as the text of Scotus in n.135 above clearly indicates. We here confront a massive problem, alluded to in n.66 above, which dominates Suárez's metaphysics as it moves from its beginnings, where God and creature are

on a par within the context of the objective concept of being as a noun (see J. Doyle, *The Modern Schoolman* XLVI (1969), 229 n.56, 240 and 329-331: "Hence what is common to both God and creatures insofar as they are apt to exist is non-repugnance or non-contradiction. And it is this which is signified by the common concept of being as a noun.") or on a par with respect to logical potency or possibility, to the point where Suárez confronts properly finite being as in the instance of Disputation 31. It is at this point that he has to acknowledge the dependence of such beings upon God. To do so, he moves to the perspective involved in *esse potentiale objectivum* which clearly cannot apply to the deity. See *In I Sum. Theol.*, Bk. I, cap. II, 7; I, 7b: "Neque etiam concipi potest divina natura ut in potentia objectiva, quomodo proprie dicitur essentia creaturae esse in potentia ut abstrahit ab actuali existentia."; *DM* 2, 4, 11; XXV, 91a; 31, 6, 15; XXVI, 247a. J. Hellín, *Espiritu* 10(1961), 163 sees no incoherencia herein: "No hay incoherencia en Suárez, sino máxima *coherencia.* Cuando dice que los posibles *no tienen realidad* alguna intrínseca, lo entiende de los posibles antes de ser producidos, no de la realidad que tendrían si fuesen producidos; y cuando dice que los posibles se contienen bajo *el ente real* y son por tanto entes reales, se ha entender de la existencia que tendrían si fueran producidos, no de realidad alguna interna y propia que les atribuya antes de ser producidos: hay pues máxima coherencia." However, the oscillation involved herein from *potentia objectiva* to *potentia logica,* as will be noted below, indicates that we are dealing with an equivocal notion of possibility.

[139] See n.132 above.

[140] See n.118 above; *DM* 6, 4, 11; XXV, 220.

[141] *DM* 31, 6, 24; XXVI, 250b: "Cum autem negatur esse de essentia creaturae actu existere, sumenda est creatura ut abstrahit seu praescindit a creatura creata et creabili, cujus essentia objective concepta abstrahit ab actuali esse aut entitate, et hoc modo negatur esse de essentia ejus actu existere, quia non clauditur in conceptu ejus essentiali sic praeciso." See Suárez on *secundum se* in *DM* 6, 3, 6; XXV, 213-214. However, Suárez is not always consistent on this abstraction from possible existence (because of the ambiguity of *potentia logica* and *potentia objectiva*) but this is surely the burden of his position on *ens ut nomen* and *essentia realis* in *DM* 2, 4, 11-12; XXV, 91. See text of J. Gómez Caffarena cited in n.66 above as well as the text of J. Hellín in the same place.

[142] See n.132 above.

[143] *DM* 31, 2, 10; XXVI, 232a, cited in n.138 above. Note: "Essentia ergo creaturae secundum se est ens reale primo modo, scilicet, in potentia, non vero posteriori modo, et in actu, quod est *proprie* esse ens reale...."

[144] *DM* 31, 2, 2; XXVI, 229b-230a.

[145] *DM* 6, 4, 11; XXV, 220; 6, 3, 6; XXV, 213-214; 31, 2, 11; XXVI, 232b.

[146] See nn.89, 110 above.

[147] *DM* 31, 4-6; XXVI, 235-250.

[148] See nn.141, 143; *DM* 31, 13, 12; XXVI, 302.

[149] *DM* 31, 6, 23; XXVI, 250a.

[150] See n.111 above; J. Owens, *The Modern Schoolman* XXXIV (1957), 178-187.

[151] See nn.138, 141 above.

[152] See nn.131, 134 above; J. Owens, *The Modern Schoolman* XXXIV (1957), 183-185; J. Gómez Caffarena, *Pensamiento* 15(1959), 140, 148. The latter's insistence on behalf of a "modal" distinction between actual essence and actual existence raises many questions beyond the scope of our present concern. Such a distinction, as "modal", is not of the real modal variety. It purports to be closer to the type referred to by Mastrius in n.36 above. Indeed, the specter of equivocation on "modal" can't be overlooked. A similar difficulty arises in Descartes. See my "Descartes and the Modal Distinction," *The Modern Schoolman* XLIII (1965), 1-22. A more expanded treatment can be found in my "Descartes On Distinction," *Boston College Studies In*

Philosophy I (1966), 104-134. In any case, see *DM* 31, 13, 20; XXVI, 304-305; 7, 1, 19; XXV, 257a; 31, 1, 12; XXVI, 228b: "Videtur etiam Fonseca, lib. 4 Metaph., C.3, quaest. 4, nihil in re dissentire ab hac sententia, ut a nobis declarabitur, licet secundum sequi verbis profiteatur." Thus Fonseca maintains a "modal" distinction tantamount to a distinction of reason.

153 See n.138 above.

154 See n.75 above.

155 This is the trust of the text of J. Hellín cited in n.66 above and it is repeated by M. Schneider, "Der angebliche philosophische Essentialismus des Suárez," *Wissenschaft und Weisheit* 24 (1961), 57 as cited by J. Doyle, *The Modern Schoolman* XLV (1967), 37 n.40.

156 See n.85 above.

157 *Tractatus de Anima*, BK. 4, 2, 4; III, 714; *DM* 54, *Proem.*, 1; XXVI, 1015a. See more texts in J. Doyle, *The Modern Schoolman* XLVI (1969), 331 n.175. See also n.66 above for text of Suárez distinguishing two meanings of *non ens*. So it is surely not inconsistent to suspect that Suárez is ready to distinguish between two kinds of *nihil*. But such an appeal on Suárez's part only succeeds in making all the more puzzling his vigorous attack upon Capreolus *et al.* for the latter's distinction between two types of *nihil*. See *DM* 31, 2, 4; XXVI, 230: "Si vero tandem quis fateatur, illud, quod nihil habet existentiae, esse simpliciter et omnino nihil, relinquitur frivolam et vanam esse distinctionem de nihilo essentiae et existentiae, quia quod est simpliciter et omnino nihil, non potest vere et realiter esse aliquid in aliqua ratione veri entis."

158 *DM* 31, 2, 11; XXVI, 232b:"...quod esse in veritate propositionis (i.e. *esse objectivum*), non solum habet locum in essentiis realibus, sed etiam in entibus et fictitiis;...."; *DM* 54, 2, 23; XXVI, 1025b: "...quanquam Deus per se et immediate non intelligat formando entia rationis, nihilominus tamen perfectissime cognoscere ipsa entia rationis,...."

159 See n.138 above as well as n.78.

160 See nn.135, 138 above.

161 See nn.67, 102 above.

162 See my "Descartes and the Scholastics Briefly Revisited," *The New Scholasticism* 35 (1961), 172-190. In order to distinguish the position of Suárez from that of his adversaries, e.g., the likes of Soncinas and Cajetan *et al.*, one must heed the remarks of J. Hellín, "Las verdades esenciales se fundan en Dios, según Suárez," *Revista de Filosofía* 22 (1963), 41: "2. Suárez, sin deshacer en lo más mínimo esta, hace ciertas hipótesis en que prescinde o excluye del todo las causas se que en funden ciertas verdades.

a) *Excluye* toda causa ontologica en las proposiciones que versan sobre sujetos imposibles:...

b) *Prescinden* de toda causa aquellas proposiciones de sujeto tan amplio que abarquen a Dios y a las creaturas, como son las que tienen por sujeto al ente.

c) Tambien prescinden de toda causa aquellas verdades sobre sujetos finitos, en que solamente se atiende a la ilación de los extremos, sin tener en cuenta para nada si los sujetos son posibles o imposibles. Y más, en esta hipótesis, las proposiciones serían verdaderas aunque no existiese ninguna causa que pudiera producir el sujeto; pero en este caso las proposiciones serían verdades con verdad de *ilación* y no con verdad de realidad posible."

163 See nn.66, 138.

164 *DM* 31, 2, 6-8; XXVI, 230-231. See n.171 below.

165 See nn.43, 54-56.

166 *DM* 31, 2, 8; XXVI, 231: "Ut autem vera esset scientia qua Deus ab aeterno cognovit, hominem esse animal rationale, non oportuit essentiam hominis habere ex

aeternitate aliquod esse reale in actu, quia illud esse non significat actuale esse et reale, sed solam connexionem intrinsecam talium extremorum;..."

[167] *Ibid.*

[168] *Ibid.*

[169] *Ibid.*

[170] *DM* 31, 2, 7; XXVI, 231.

[171] See nn.43, 54-56. Also note J. Hellín, *Espiritu* 10 (1961), 156: "Dios conoce *ab aeterno* la propia realidad de los posibles, pero no conoce que tienen realidad intrínseca y verdadera *ab aeterno;* solo conoce que la existencia que tendrían si fuesen creadas, sería una cosa realísima....Suárez responde que estas proposiciones son reales eternamente, pero su realidad no es algo intrínseco a elles, sino en la mente divina que las conoce: Dios las conoce eternamente, pero no conoce que las esencias tienen una realidad eterna e intrínseca: lo que conoce es que *si la esencias tuvieran real existencia, o se creasen, serian necesariamente así o así* (31, 2, 8)." Though Hellín does not note the following texts, they would seem to afford corroboration for his point. See *DM* 31, 2, 9; XXVI, 231-232: "...habet tamen in rebus fundamentum, vel prout actu existunt, vel prout existere possunt, et objective terminare scientiam qua cognoscuntur, talis naturae atque essentiae esse debere, si fiant."; 30, 15, 23; XXVI, 177: "...Deum non tantum cognoscere aut scire has creabiles secundum esse quod habent in ipsomet Deo, sed etiam secundum proprium et formale esse quod in seipsis habere possunt...."; *In I Sum. Theol.,* Bk. III, c.3, 5; I, 203b: "Addere vero hic possumus cognoscere Deum de entibus aliquid per modum affirmationis, ut quod possibilia sint, et quam essentiam, vel proprietates postulent, ve habere debeant, si fiant:...."; *ibid.,* Bk. III, c.2, 21; I, 202a. Add to this the text from Suárez's *Opuscula, Opusc.* II, Bk I, c.8, 9; XI, 329: "...si hoc modo velimus praesentiam objectivam explicare, nihil aliud est quam ipsum esse, quod res est suo tempore habitura;...." For all of this emphasis on post-existential possibility (see n.174 below), it remains to be seen if Suárez's position and Fr. Hellin's rendering of it can avoid any and every vestige of a pre-existential possibility, utterly underived, in the context of *potentia logica.* See n.182 below.

[172] J. Hellín, *Espiritu* 10 (1961), 156-157: "Estas proposiciones tienen una verdad o realidad hipotética, y expresan cómo serían las esencias si realmente fueron puestas en la realidad por creación." See also J. Hellin, *Revista de Filosofía* 22 (1963), 26-27; 28-29; 35.

[173] *DM* 31, 2, 8; XXVI, 231; 11; 232b. See n.171 above.

[174] Suárez is well aware of a doctrine of post-existential possibility. See *DM Index Locupl.;* XXV, xlviiib: "Q. 2 Ex eodem capite, in fine, sumptum est illud vulgare axioma continens definitionem possibilis, scilicet: *Possibile illud est, quo posito in esse nihil sequitur impossibile.*" See Suárez's own citation of this maxim in *DM* 42, 3, 9; XXVI, 613. See also J. Hellín, *Espiritu* 10 (1961), 148, where a post-existential possibility in Suárez is defended. Indeed, J. Hellín would seem to fuse pre-existential and post-existential possibility in *Las Ciencias* 3 (1956), 456. However, Suárez's insistence (nn.67, 78) on the presence of a potential efficient cause vis á vis the essences of creatures would clearly indicate a pre-existential perspective. Indeed, Suárez's position on *potentia logica* is quite consistent with this latter pre-existential perspective. See nn.135, 138 above and 177 below.

[175] See nn.66, 85, 87.

[176] *DM* 31, 12, 42; XXVI, 295-296.

[177] *Ibid.*

[178] *DM* 31, 12, 44-45; XXVI, 296-297.

[179] This is the rendering of Suárez's position by B. Mastrius, *Disputationes...,* Disp. VIII, q.1, a.4, nu. 64-65; II, 86-87. See n.183 below.

[180] See the text of Hellín in n.162 above.

181 See n.138 above.

182 See J. Doyle, *The Modern Schoolman* XLVI (1969), 240, 323-325, 329-331. Suárez's equivocation on *nihil,* noted above in n.157, is pertinent here.

183 See nn.66, 135-138. Indeed, Suárez has every opportunity to insist that the eternal essential truths are to be taken in a *negatively eternal* sense (see A. Maurer, C.S.B., "St. Thomas and Eternal Truths," *Mediaeval Studies* XXXII (1970), 101-102, 104). For Suárez knows this position and avails himself of this jargon in *DM* 6, 7, 7; XXV, 231a.

184 See J. Doyle, *The Modern Schoolman* XLVI (1969), esp. 323 and following; XLIX (1972), 208-209.

185 See n.138 above.

186 This reference to a non-repugnance to exist outside one's causes is acknowledged explicitly in *DM* 31, 3, 3; XXVI, 233: "Ex parte igitur creaturarum solum supponitur *non repugnantia ut ita fiant,* (italics mine) quia nihil rei in eis requiri aut supponi potest."; *DM* 31, 2, 2; XXVI, 230: "...ex parte illius solum dicit *non repugnantiam, ut fiat;...*" (italics mine); *DM* 31, 2, 2; XXVI, 229: "...sed ex parte creaturae dicat quam aptitudinem seu potius *non repugnantiam, ut in tali esse a Deo producatur;...*" (italics mine). Since this *aptitudo* is *ad existendum cum dependentia ab alio,* an *essentia realis* here cannot be appreciated without an essential relation to God as efficient cause. This is the meaning of Suárez's persistent claim about the presence of a potential efficient cause. But this is to be in the presence of a *potentia objectiva,* or an *essentia realis* in the context of *potentia objectiva,* rather than the presence of an *essentia realis* in the context of *potentia logica.* See n.66 above.

187 See nn.66, 85-87 above.

188 See nn.138, 162.

189 See n.30 above.

190 *DM* 31, 2, 8; 26, 231; 31, 12, 40; 294-295.

191 See n.87 above. But see also above nn.66, 85, 132, 186.

192 See n.135 above. But see also above nn.132, 137, 138.

193 *Quaestiones disputatae de esse intelligibile,* edit. A. Ledoux, O.F.M. (Quaracchi, 1937), esp. 41, 137, 145, 161, 170. See E. Gilson, *Jean Duns Scot* (Paris: J. Vrin, 1952), 284-285.

194 E. Gilson, *Jean Duns Scot,* 291.

195 For the notion of *essentia realis,* see the convenient dossier of texts in E. Gilson, *Index scolastico-cartésien* (N.Y.: Burt Franklin Reprint) under *Essence,* 103-106; *Possible,* 235-237; *Etre,* 106-107. For the *aeternae veritates,* see *Essence,* as well, since Descartes identifies them: "...or cette essence n'est autre chose que ces vérités éternelles....", A Mersenne Amsterdam, 15 Avril 1630, in *Descartes, Correspondance,* edits. C. Adam and G. Milhaud, Paris: Alcan, 1936), I, 135. For other texts of Descartes on the *aeternae veritates,* see my "Descartes and the Scholastics Briefly Revisited," *The New Scholasticism* XXXV (1961), 172-190.

196 *Medit.* III; A-T, VII, 41, 26-29; VII, 64, 6-11; 65, 4-5; *Resp. I^{ae};* VII, 103, 1-4. See E. Chauvinus, *Lexicon Philosophicum,* Reprint of Leeuwarden, 1713 edition (Dusseldorf: Stern-Verlag Janssen, 1967), 501a: "Possibile....Quatenus vero opponitur impossibili, dicitur illud quod potest esse, quod est non repugnans, quod non involvit praedicata contradictoria, sive actu existat, sive non, ut homo, ignis, etc. Aliter dicitur possibile logice et remote....Res quaelibet antequam actu existat non est purum nihil: Ergo est non-nihil seu aliquid, et per consequens entitatem quandam includit. Antecedens sic probant. Purum nihil est prorsus impossibile, id est, nunquam potest produci, seu nunquam potest terminare actionem efficientis: sed res antequam actu existat non est ejusmodi; eo quod sit possibilis, producibilis et capax terminandi actionem efficientis pro aliquo tempore. Et revera, si res possibilis

esset in se purum nihil, sequeretur possibile non differre ab impossibili, quod est etiam purum nihil; cum inter duo pura nihil nulla sit differentia; sicque homo possibilis, et Chimera impossibilis non differrent, quod absurdum.

[197] *Resp. 5*^{ae}*;* VII, 383, 16-20: "Nec inficior quin existentia possibilis sit perfectio in idea trianguli, ut existentia necessaria est perfectio in idea Dei; efficit enim illam praestantiorem quam sint ideae illarum Chimaeraerarum quarum existentia nulla esse posse supponitur." Since this is the case, then, for Descartes, the ideas of chimerae do not have a genuine *realitas objectiva* since there is no genuine intrinsic possibility therein nor any *existentia possibilis.* See also *Medit.* III; VII, 43, 24-26 where Descartes wonders whether the ideas of secondary qualities are *rerum quarumdam ideae, an non rerum,* and the French translation (IX, 34) adds: "...ou bien si elles ne me representent, que ces estres chymeriques, qui ne peuvent exister." Also see the convenient dossier of texts under *Etre,* in E. Gilson, *Index scolastico-cartésien,* 106-107.

[198] See *Medit.* III; VII, 37, 3-6 where Descartes, in cataloguing what we know, i.e. objects known and purportedly possessing *esse objectivum,* the-being-of-being-known, lists chimerae along with man, heaven, angel and God. See E. Chauvinus, *Lexicon Philosophicum,* 445: "Objective dicitur de esse rei vicario, seu de re quae habet tantum esse cognitum, vel quae non aliter existit quam per modum objecti: tunc enim dicitur esse objective. Quod quidem esse cognitum reale creditur a multis; quia esse cognitum plus est, quam omnino non esse, esse nihilum." Descartes' position on the objective reality of ideas as *non nihil* (see n.196 above) bears out Chauvinus' allusion, as does the position of Arnauld, equally known to Descartes, *Obj. 4*^{ae}*;* VII, 207, 6-9: "...cum idea positiva non dicatur secundum esse quod habet tanquam modus cogitandi, eo enim modo omnes positivae essent, sed ab esse objectivo quod continet, et menti nostrae exhibet."

[199] See *Opusc.* II, Bk. I, c.8, 9; XI, 329: "Et hoc sensu nihil aliud est esse objective praesens, quam actu videri; et de praesentia hoc modo explicata verissime dicitur non antecedere etiam secundum rationem ipsam scientiam; et ideo non posse ex tali praesentia rationem scientiae reddi, cum per illam formaliter fiat."

[200] See nn.85, 86 above.

[201] *Obj. 1*^{ae}*;* VII, 92, 13-23.

[202] *Resp. 1*^{ae}*;* VII, 105, 7.

[203] *Ibid.;* VII, 1, 12. And this must be read as the meaning of his somewhat less explicit statements, provided the subjunctive mood is given its due: "...sed sane indiget causa ut concipiatur, et de hac sola quaestio est." (*ibid.;* VII, 103, 17-19) and: "...nihil enim aliud quaeritur quam quae sit causa quare concipiatur...." (*ibid.;* VII, 103, 23-25).

[204] *Opusc.* II, Bk. I, c.8, 9; XI, 329: "Secundo modo sumi potest aptitudine, ut in sensibilibus dicitur objectum, quamvis actu non videatur, esse objective praesens, quando ita est propinquum, illuminatum, et dispositum, ut quantum est ex se videri possit."

[205] *Ibid.*

[206] See E. Ashworth, "Descartes' Theory of Objective Reality," *The New Scholasticism* XLIX (1975), 332: "Finally, to have an idea is sometimes to be the possessor of a specific mental content of which we may be ignorant, or not at the moment conscious of, but which may be summoned up. This last possibility is dwelt on in some detail when Descartes considers the idea of God. People may deny they have it, or honestly fail to recognize it, but it is there all the same." This has to be related to what Descartes means by "innate". See R. McRae, "Innate Ideas," *Cartesian Studies,* edit. R. J. Butler, (Oxford: Blackwell, 1972), 32-53, esp. 33-42; *Descartes' Conversation with Burman,* transl. J. Cottingham, (Oxford: Clarendon Press, 1976), xxiii-xxxvi.

[207] See nn.137, 198 above.

DISCUSSION XXXI

The essence and the being of a finite being (ens), and their distinction.

After a discussion of a first and supreme being *(ens)*, which is not only the primary object of the whole of metaphysics, but also the first thing signified and the primary analogate of the whole meaning and scope[1] of being *(ens)*, there must follow a statement about the second member proposed in the first division, that is, of finite and created being *(ens)*[2]. But because the latter is not absolutely one, but only one by reason of abstraction or a common character, and because it comprises within itself a number of varied types of being *(ens)*, two things must be done for the explanation of this member. First, it must be made clear in what the common character of a created or finite being *(ens)* is posited. This is what is proposed in this discussion.[3] Second, its divisions and subdivisions must be taught, down to the ultimate types of beings *(ens)* comprised within the object of metaphysics posited above.[4]

SECTION I

Is the being and the essence of a created being (ens) distinguished in reality.

1. Since, as was seen in the above sections, a being *(ens)*, to the extent it is a being *(ens)*, is called such from being, and [since] it is through being or through a relationship to being that it has the character of a being *(ens)*,[5] so, to make clear the meaning of a created being *(ens)*, we start with a comparison of essence and being. In this regard, many points needing treatment come to mind, which are absolutely necessary for a grasp of the essence and the properties of a created being *(ens)* as such. However, the root of all these issues is the question we have proposed, namely, how are being and essence distinguished?

2.   To avoid an equivocation in terms[6] and to make it unnecessary later to make distinctions about an essential being,[7] an existential being or a subsistential being or a being of truth in a proposition, I suppose by being we understand the actual existence of things. For essential being, if it is truly distinguished from existence, adds nothing real to the essence itself, but only differs from it in the way it is conceived or signified.[8] Hence, just as the essence of a creature as such, in virtue of its concept, does not say that it would be something actually real with being outside its causes, so the essential being as such, by standing precisely in this, does not express an actual being by which an essence outside it causes would be constituted in act. For if to be actual in this latter way is not of the essence of the creature, neither will it be able to pertain to its essential being. Hence, the essential being of a creature as such will prescind[9] of itself from actual being outside its causes by which a created thing comes to be beyond nothing, by which[10] name we designate actual existential being. But subsistential being is also more contracted than existential being, for the latter is common to substance and accidents. The former is proper to substance. Besides, subsistential being (as I suppose from what is to be proved below)[11] is something distinct from the existential being of a substantial created nature and separable from it, because it does not constitute a nature in the order of actual entity, which pertains to existence. Now the being of truth in a proposition of itself is not a real and intrinsic being, but it is an objective being in the intellect as it is composing; hence it belongs also to privations. For we say, accordingly: *Blindness is* or *A man is blind,* as Aristotle discusses at greater length in 5 *Metaph.,* chapter seven.[12] Hence, the discussion is about created existence concerning which, furthermore, we suppose that it is something real and intrinsic to an existing thing; this seems self-evident. For through existence a thing is understood to be something in the nature of things. Therefore, it is necessary that existence be both something real and intrinsic, that is, within the existing thing itself. For a thing cannot be existing by some extrinsic denomination or some being *(ens)* of reason. Otherwise, how would existence constitute a real being *(ens)* in act and beyond nothing?

THE FIRST OPINION AFFIRMING THEY ARE REALLY DISTINGUISHED.

3.   Hence, there are different opinions about this existence of a creature. The first is that existence is a thing altogether really distinct from the essential entity of a creature. This is considered to be the opinion of St. Thomas[13] which, in this sense, almost all the old Thomists have followed. The principal texts in St. Thomas are, part

1, q.3, art.4,[14] *2 Against the Gentiles, c.52,*[15] *On Being and Essence, c.5,*[16] 4 *Metaph.*, lect.2.[17] These are interpreted accordingly by Capreolus, in 1, dist. 8, art.1, q.1;[18] Cajetan in the texts cited, part 1.,[19] *On Being and Essence,;*[20] Ferrara in the text cited, *Against the Gentiles,;*[21] Soncinas in, 4 *Metaph.*, quest. 12;[22] Javellus, *Treatise on Transcendentals.*[23] In addition, Giles in, 1, d.2, quest. 4, art. 1,[24] and throughout *On Being and Essence.*, q.9, and following,[25] and *Quodl.*, q.7.[26] Albert, *On Book of Causes,* propos. 8;[27] and Avicenna, in the fifth book of his *Metaph.*, the first chapter,[28] are also cited.

4.   There are many arguments by which this opinion is customarily advocated. First,[29] because the essential predicates belong to a creature without the intervention of an efficient cause. This is the reason why it has been true from eternity to say: man is a rational animal. But existence does not belong to a creature except through an efficient cause. And so, a creature cannot be said to be actual unless it has come to be. Consequently, the being of a creature is a thing distinct from its essence, because it is not possible for one and the same thing to be and not to be by an efficient cause.[30] But were you to say that when a creature comes to be, not only does its being come to be, but also the essence of the creature, the answer is not that essence is absolutely[31] produced, but that an essence subject to being comes to be, or that an existing essence comes to be. So it does not follow that a produced essence is distinguished from essence absolutely, except by reason of the existence which adds to it.

5.   My[32] second argument is that the being of a creature is a being received in something; in an essence, that is, for nothing else can be thought of in which it would be received. Hence, being is a thing distinct from essence, for the same thing cannot be received into itself. The first antecedent is proved, because unreceived being is self-subsistent being in virtue of its own actuality. For, such being is entirely abstracted from a subject or potency in which it would be received. Therefore, it is the most perfect and supreme being, and so pure act and something infinite in the order of being *(essendi)*. Hence, it is repugnant for the being of a creature to be entirely unreceived. Also, the first antecedent is confirmed, because such being does not have that whereby it would be limited. For it is not limited by a potency in which it would be received, if it has not potency. Nor is it even limited by an act or a difference which would be related by way of an act in regard to existence. For existence, since it is the ultimate actuality, is not constituted by an act by which it would be limited. So, for the being of a creature to be finite and limited, it must be the act of the essence in which it is received and by which it is limited.[33]

6.   The third argument would be, that every creature is composed by a true and real composition. But the first and general real compo-

sition can consist only of being and essence. Therefore, every creature is composed of being and essence, as of an act and a potency really distinct. The major is established, because, if there were granted a creature in which there would be no real composition, an absolutely simple creature would be granted, as an angelic substance actually existing, if it were not composed of being and essence, it would be substantially and absolutely simple, and so, in a certain way, it would equal divine perfection. [34] But were you to say that in it a composition of genus and difference, or, of nature and supposit and of subject and accident can remain, nothing of them is satisfactory because the first composition is not real but one of reason; hence it does not exclude perfect real simplicity. The second composition, in the first place, is not universal to all things because it does not belong to accidents. In the second place, it has the same problem as the composition of being and essence. Hence, if the former is granted in created substances, why not also the latter? Finally, the third composition is not for constituting a substance, but now we are concerned with substantial composition and simplicity. Besides, a universal argument is derived from the preceding. For it follows, at least in the realm of the possible, that it is not repugnant to a creature to have this lack of all real composition and so to be supremely simple, which is something unfitting because this seems proper to God. The consequence is clear, both because there is no reason why it will be more repugnant for the other compositions to be excluded, than for this composition of being and essence to be excluded and also because a simple substantial nature can be conserved without any accident. [35]

7.   Fourth, in a substance composed of matter and form, being is something distinct from matter and form and from the nature compounded of both. Therefore, it is a reality distinct from the whole essence of such a substance. Consequently, the case will be the same in the rest of created being *(ens)*. [36] This consequence is evident with respect to less perfect things. But in regard to more perfect things, as are spiritual substances, it can appear weak because those substances, since they are more perfect, so they can be more simple. But still, as to subject matter, it is the best inference. First, because if in some created thing a real distinction of being from essence is admitted, no reason can be offered why a distinction would be denied in other things. For, if a distinction is not repugnant in virtue of essence and being as such, it will not be repugnant in virtue of such an essence and such created being. Secondly, because if in any creature being and essence are found distinct, the reason is not that it is such, but because it is a creature and because in it essence is related to being as potency to act, which is outside its quiddity, and without

which it can be conceived: characteristics which are common to every creature. It remains to prove the first antecedent. This is proved in the first place, because the being of a composite substantial nature is either one simple entity or a composite entity. As I shall show,[37] it cannot be composite. But if it be simple, it cannot be matter, as seems self-evident, nor even form, for two reasons. First, because the argument is practically the same. Secondly, because it will also be concluded at once that the essence of matter exists by an existence really distinct from it, since form is really distinguished from matter. Then all the arguments put forth will proceed to require that the same thing be said of any created essence whatsoever. Moreover, the entity could not be identified with the entire essence, compounded of matter and form, for a simple entity cannot be one and the same thing[38] as a thing compounded of distinct things. Indeed, an obvious repugnance is involved. Hence, if such being is a simple entity, it is necessarily a thing absolutely distinct from such an essence.

8.   The first proof to be given is that that being would not be a composite entity but a simple one because otherwise it would be necessary to distinguish in that being the parts of which it is composed. The first consequence of this would be that one of those parts would be the same as matter and the other as form. And thus matter will not have its being from form but of itself. Hence, it will not be pure potency but of itself it will have some act, contrary to the position common to the philosophers. Secondly, it follows that a simple unit does not come from matter and form because from two beings in act a simple unit does not come to be. Thirdly, it follows that matter, to the extent that it is of itself, can be without form, and any form without matter, not only with regard to the absolute power but of its very nature. However, the consequent in regard to the first part is against philosophy, but in regard to the second part it is also against faith; otherwise the souls of brute animals would be immortal. Now the consequence as to the first part is proved, for, if matter has a partial existence, either that is sufficient for constituting matter ouside its causes, and then the point is made, namely, that although form is lacking it will conserve it, or it is insufficient[39], and thus it is truly no existence, for it is of the nature of existence to be sufficient for constituting a thing outside its causes. Comparable is the repugnance that there be whiteness and that it be of itself inadequate for making something white. Also, because if matter cannot exist except as dependent upon form and upon the whole composite whose existence can be terminated and actuated, it would have been redundant for matter to be given a partial existence of its own. Also, because, if matter has an existence of its own, by reason of that it will be under-

stood to exist naturally prior to its actuation by form. Consequently, even though the actuality of form be taken away, matter will remain in virtue of its own existence, for the prior does not depend upon what follows. And these arguments also prove the second part, namely, that every form could remain naturally in existence even though it be separated from matter, for then it has its own existence sufficient for constituting it ouside its causes; by this it exists with natural priority and, to that extent, adequately. Thus the theologians, most of all St. Thomas,[40] conclude from this especially that the rational soul is immortal. For it carries with itself its own being which belongs primarily to it and through it is communicated to the whole man.

9.   Finally, it follows that one of these two partial existences is related to the other as potency to act; the conclusion is false. Therefore, the consequence if clear. For, in addition to these partial existences, it is necessary to establish an integral and total existence of the whole nature. This cannot be simple and absolutely distinct from the partial existences, as is self-evident from all that has been said. And, because otherwise the partial existences would be superfluous, and[41] in man it is clear that such a total and simple existence, absolutely distinct from the existence of the soul, cannot be imagined; for it would be neither spiritual nor corporeal, since it would be posited as perfectly accompanying and actuating the substance consisting of body and spirit and dependent on it. Consequently, such an existence must be made of the partial ones; therefore it is also necessary that these partial existences be essentially united in order to constitute one total existence. Otherwise, that total existence would not be essentially one but an aggregate of a plurality. Therefore, one of these partial existences must be related to the other as potency to act; otherwise they would not be essentially united. However, this last conclusion is proved to be false, for being is the ultimate actuality of any and every thing; indeed, by reason of its own character, it is pure actuality with no admixture of potentiality in itself, but by reason only of the essence or nature which has the being. Therefore, existence is said to be more perfect than every substantial form, for it has more actuality than form itself, as is taken from St. Thomas, first part, quest. 4, art. 1, to 3.[42]

10.   Fifth,[43] to the metaphysical arguments we can add a theological argument,[44] for a created essence is separated from its existence in the thing itself. For this reason it is really distinguished from it. The consequence is proved from what was said above about the distinctions of things.[45] Most are wont to give as proof of the antecedent that when created things are corrupted or annihilated, they lose their existence but not their essence. So by the corruption of a thing existence is separated from an essence. However, that antecedent

finds a better proof in the twofold mystery of faith. One is the mystery of the Eucharist; here, as a result of consecration, quantity loses it natural existence by which it was existing in the bread; and it acquires another which [46] exists in itself and is able to sustain the rest of the accidents. The other is the mystery of the Incarnation; here the humanity of Christ lacks a natural existence of its own; it was assumed with the result that it exists by the uncreated existence of the Divine Word. [47]

THE SECOND OPINION POSITING A MODAL DISTINCTION.

11.   The second opinion is that created being is indeed distinguished in reality [48] or (as others say) formally, from the essence which has the being and it is not a proper entity altogether really distinct from its essential entity, but it is its mode. This position is attributed [49] to Scotus, in 3, dist. 6, quest. 1; [50] and to Henry, *Quodl.* 1, q. 9 and 10; [51] their opinion I shall discuss later. [52] Soto has held the same opinion, 2 *Phys.*, quest. 2, [53] and in 4 *Sent.*, dist. 10, quest. 2. [54] And some moderns follow it. Their basis is because some distinction in reality between being and the essence of a creature seems altogether necessary. But no greater distinction is required than this modal or formal distinction. Hence, no greater is to be affirmed, for distinctions are not to be multiplied without necessary. First, all those points brought up in favor of the first opinion seem to prove the major. Second, it seems to be proved effectively, because what is extrinsic to the essence of the thing must be distinguished in reality, at least formally, from the essence of the thing. But being is extrinsic to the essence of a creature, as [55] seems evident, since it is separable from it. Thus this proposition, *A creature is,* is not, by itself, necessary and essential but contingent: therefore. Third, because otherwise the creature would be its own being, and consequently pure act; this is to attribute to a creature what is proper to God. So Hilary, in book 7 *On Trinity,* attributed to God as proper to Him "that being does not happen to him" [56] but He is subsistent being itself. And Boethius, in the book, *On Hebdom.,* c.1, "in created things (he says) that which is, is different from being". [57] The minor is proved, because this distinction suffices for one to be outside the essence of another and for a true and real composition, for wherever a distinction occurs in things, a true composition is forthcoming from extremes so distinct. Further, that distinction is sufficient for one extreme to be separable from another by divine power, even though it would not suffice for a mutual or convertible separation, as was said in previous sections. [58] From this the confirmation of this opinion is possible. For, although a created essence is separable from its own being, still, contrariwise,

that very being is not separable from the essence of the creature. For thus far it has not happened, nor is it likely that it can happen, that the existence of whiteness be conserved without whiteness being conserved, and that man has the existence of a white thing and not be white, and the same with regard to others. Hence, it is a sign that there is no real distinction between essence and existence, but only a modal distinction. I omit the other arguments customarily made to support these positions, because they do not have a special difficulty not found in the ones mentioned.

THE THIRD OPINION POSITING A MERE DISTINCTION OF REASON.

12.   The third opinion asserts that the essence and existence of a creature, proportionately compared, are not distinguished really or in reality as two real extremes, but are distinguished in reason only. This is the express tenet of Alexander of Alexandria, and he has explained it very well in 7 *Metaph.*, at text 22.[59] Aureolus also held it according to Capreolus, in 1, dist. 8, quest. 1,[60] where Capreolus lists also Henry,[61] Godfrey[62] and Gerard of Carmel[63] for the same opinion. And there Durandus, in the first part, d.8, quest. 2, holds the same,[64] also Gabriel, in 3, dist. 6,[65] and the rest of the Nominalists in the same place. And Harvey held it, *Quodl.* 7, quest. 8,[66] as does Gregory, in 2, dist. 1, quest. 6, on the arguments of Aureolus.[67] Moreover, the Scotists follow this opinion as is clear from Antonius Andreas, 4 *Metaph.*, quest. 3,[68] Lychetus, 3, dist. 6.[69] Alexander Achillinus holds the same position, book 1 *On Elements,* problem 23,[70] Palacios, in 1, d.8, disput.2,[71] as does John Altensteig, in the Theological lexicon, under the word *Being.*[72] Niphus also holds this opinion in reality, book 4 *Metaph.*, disp. 5, although he differs in words,[73] and insists at the end of the discussion that the controversy concerns the manner of speaking.[74] On the other hand, in the same place,[75] following the position of Aristotle and the Peripatetics, he distinguishes between corruptible creatures and incorruptible creatures, resulting in a distinction of existence from essence in the former, but not in the latter. And John of Ghent holds this too, 4 *Metaph.*, q. 3.[76] But this is not to be considered in this place, because it hangs on that question of whether, in the judgment of Aristotle, these things are produced by God or not. This has already been discussed above.[77] It appears that Fonseca too, book 4 *Metaph.*, c. 2, quest. 4,[78] does not really disagree with this opinion, as it will be explained by us.[79] However, he avows that he follows the second position in words.[80] In addition, all the theologians who hold that the humanity would not have been able to be assumed by the Word without its own existence, can be cited in favor of this opinion.[81] For

that cannot be rightly established except in the identity of the essence and the existence of the created nature. On this matter, one can read what we have written in tome one of the third part. [82]

THE THIRD OPINION IS EXPLAINED AND ACCEPTED.

13.   This third opinion must be set forth in such a way that the comparison takes place between actual existence, which they call actually exercised being, and the existent actual essence. Thus this opinion asserts that existence and essence are not distinguished in the thing itself, even though the essence, conceived of abstractly and with precision, as it is in potency, be distinguished from actual existence, as a non-being *(ens)* from a being *(ens)*. Moreover, I think that this opinion as set forth is absolutely true. [83] Its basis is, in short, because some thing cannot be intrinsically and formally constituted in the character of a real and actual being *(ens)* by something[84] distinct from it. For, by the very fact that one is distinguished from another, as a being *(ens)* from another being *(ens)*, both have the status of a being *(ens)*, as equally distinct from the other, and consequently not [constituted] formally and intrinsically by that [other]. But because the force of this argument and the complete resolution of this problem, along with the answers to arguments, hang on many principles, so to take things step by step and without equivocation of terms, which I fear to be frequent in this matter, we must move gradually and individual [principles] are to be set forth in separate sections.

Notes

[1] I read the *latitudinis* of the 1597 Salamanca edition rather than the *habitudinis* of the Vives text.

[2] See *DM* 2, I-IV; XXV, 70-92 and *DM* 28; XXVI, 1-21, esp. Section I.

[3] See *DM* 2, IV, 7; XXV, 90a; *DM* 31, XII, 9; XXVI, 301b and the Introduction to *DM* 32; XXVI, 312a.

[4] These divisions are treated in Discussions 32-54. See *DM* 32, Introduction; XXVI, 312a.

[5] See *DM* 2, IV; XXV, 87-92 and *DM* 3, esp. I, 7; XXV, 105b, and II, 4; 108b.

[6] The possibility of equivocation is mentioned by Suárez throughout. See *DM* 31, II, 11; XXVI, 232b; V, 15; XXVI, 241a; VI, 13; XXVI, 246a; VI, 24; XXVI, 250b.

[7] I am here using the translation of J. Owens, C.Ss.R., "The Number of Terms in the Suarezian Discussion on Essence and Being," *The Modern Schoolman* XXXIV (1957), 151-154.

[8] See the comments of J. Owens, "The Number of Terms...," 152-153.

9 I read the *praescindet* of the 1597 Salamanca edition instead of the *praescindit* of the Vives text.

10 I read the *quo* of the 1597 Salamanca edition instead of the *quod* of the Vives text.

11 *DM* 34, II, 1-20; XXVI, 353-359.

12 Aristotle, *Metaphysics,* V, 7, 1017a32.

13 On the significance of Suárez' hesitancy here, see J. Owens, "The Number of Terms...," 161-162.

14 *Sum. Theol.,* I, 3, 4; T. 4, 42.

15 *Sum. Cont. Gent., II, 52; T.13, 390.*

16 *De Ente et Essentia,* ed. Roland-Gosselin, c. 4. Suárez's reference to c. 5 is not necessarily incorrect as the chapter divisions of the various editions differ.

17 *In IV Metaph.,* ed. Cathala, 1926, 1. 2, 558; 187.

18 Capreolus, *Defensiones Theologiae Divi Thomae Aquinatis,* ed. Paban-Pégues (7 vol. Turin: Alfred Cattier, 1900), *In I Sent.,* d. 8, q. 1, a. 1; I, 301-315. Article 2 of the same question (315-331) contains Capreolus' answers to the many objections to his stand in the first article. See my article, "Capreolus on Essence and Existence," *The Modern Schoolman* XXXVII (1960), 1-24 and J. Hegyi, S.J., *Die Bedeutung des Seins bei Klassichen Kommentoren des heiligen Thomas von* Aquin, *Capreolus-Silvester von Ferrara-Cajetan* (Pullach: Verlag Berchmanskolleg, 1959).

19 Cajetan, *Commentaria in Summam Theologicam,* ed. Leonina Operum S. Thomae IV-XII (Romae, 1888-1906), *In I Sum. Theol.,* q. 3, a. 4; T. 4, 42-43.

20 Cajetan, *De Ente et Essentia D. Thomae Aquinatis Commentaria,* ed., M. H. Laurent (Turin: Marietti, 1934), cap. V; #100, 156-157.

21 Sylvester of Ferrara, *Commentaria in Summam Contra Gentiles,* ed. Leonina Operum S. Thomae XIII-XV (Romae, 1920-1930), II, 52; T. 13, 389a V.

22 Soncinas, *Quaestiones Metaphysicales Acutissimae* (Venetiis, 1588), Bk. 4, a. 12, 20a-22b.

23 Javellus, *Totius Philosophiae Compendium* (Lugduni, 1568), *Tractatus de Transcendentibus,* cap. 4; I, 466b-467a.

24 This reference is incorrect and I have been unable to find the correct one. It may be *2 Sent.,* d. 3, 1 p., q. 1, a. 2, as noted by Vasquez, *Commentariorum ac Disputationum in Tertiam Partem Sancti Thomae* (Lugduni, 1620), Disput. LXXII, cap. 1; T. I, 482a. Giles there discusses the question "Utrum in angelo sit compositio ex essentia et esse."

25 Giles of Rome, *Quaestiones Disputatae De Esse et Essentia* (Venetiis, 1503), q. 9, fol 17va-22rb. This is not to be confused with Giles' *Theoremata de Esse et Essentia,* ed. E. Hocedez, S. J. (Louvain: Museum Lessianum, 1930).

26 Giles of Rome, *Quodlibeta* (Lovanii: De Coninck, 1646), I, q. 7; 15-16. Thus the Vives reference to question 2 is incorrect.

27 St. Albert, *De Causis et Processu Universitatis,* I, 1, 8, *Opera Omnia,* ed. A. Borgnet (Paris, 1890-1899); X, 377.

28 Avicenna, *Metaphysica* (Venetiis, 1508), fol. 86va-87rb. St. Albert and Avicenna are not being cited as *Antiqui Thomistae* but as men who have been cited by some *Antiqui Thomistae.*

29 Suárez's response to and refutation of this first Thomistic argument can be seen below in Section XII, 38 et seq.

30 This argument is found in Capreolus, *Def. Theol.,* I, 301-306; Soncinas, *In IV Metaph.,* q. 12; 22a; Cajetan, *In De Ente...,* cap. 5; 157; Sylvester of Ferrara, *In Sum. Cont. Gent.,* II, 52; T. 13, 389aV; Javellus, *Tract. de Transc.,* cap. 4; 466b; Bañez, *In Sum. Theol.,* I, q. 3, a. 4; 147a. It is commonly attributed to the *Thomistae* by the men cited by Suárez on behalf of the distinction of reason between essence and existence.

[31] I read the *absolute* of the 1597 Salamanca edition which is deleted by the Vives text.

[32] One should not be misled by Suárez's use of the first person. He is not arguing for a position of his own. In the words of one of his historians, "...et mismo Suárez urge los argumentos ajenos como si fueran propios...", A. Astrain, S.J., *Historia de la compania de Jesús en la Asistencia de Espana 1581-1615* (Madrid, 1913).

[33] This argument can be found in Giles of Rome, *Quaestiones Disputatae De Esse et Essentia*, q. IX, fol. 18ra; 18vb; 19ra and q. XI, fol. 25ra; Capreolus, *Def. Theol.*, I, 305b-306a; Soncinas, *In IV Metaph.*, 22a; Cajetan, *In De Ente...*, cap. 5; #100, 156; Sylvester of Ferrara, *In Sum. Cont. Gent.*, II, 52; T. 13, 388b; Javellus, *Tract. de Transc.*, 466b; Bañez, *In Sum Theol.*, I, q. 3, a. 4; 147ab. Suárez's response to and refutation of this Thomistic argument can be seen below in Section XIII, 14 et seq.

[34] This argument is strangely absent from the texts of the *Thomistae* previously cited by Suárez.

[35] Suárez takes up this whole argument again in Section XIII, 24-27 below.

[36] This argument does not appear in so many words in any of the *Thomistae* listed. Its likely source seems to be Thomas Aquinas, *Sum. Cont. Gent.*, II, 52 as quoted by Capreolus, *Def. Theol.*, I, 312b.

[37] This is done immediately following in paragraphs 8-9, this section, below.

[38] I read the *una et* of the 1597 Salamanca edition which is deleted by the Vives text.

[39] The Vives text carries *in sufficiens* instead of *insufficiens*.

[40] *Sum. Theol.*, I, q. 76, a. 1 ad 5; T. 5, 210. See comment relevent to this in *DM* 31, XI, 12; XXVI, 276a.

[41] I read the *et* of the 1597 Salamanca edition which is deleted by the Vives text.

[42] *Sum. Theol.*, I, q. 4, a. 1 ad 3; T. 5, 50.

[43] Suárez's response to and refutation of this Thomistic argument can be seen below in Section XII, 14 et seq.

[44] The insertion of a theological argument into this discussion is altogether in keeping with Suárez's purpose in writing the *Disputationes Metaphysicae*. See his *Ad Lectorem* and *Prooemium*, I, 1.

[45] *DM* 7, II; XXV, 261-271; *On the Various Kinds of Distinctions,* trans., C. Vollert, S.J. (Milwaukee: Marquette Univ. Press, 1947), (40)-(61).

[46] I read the *qua* of the 1597 Salamanca edition instead of the *quae* of the Vives text.

[47] Giles of Rome is the only one of the *Thomistae* cited by Suárez who uses the argument from separability. See *Theoremata de Esse et Essentia*, ed. E. Hocedez (Louvain: 1930), theorema 12, p. 67-68. Cf. also *ibid.*, Introd., p. 63. Suárez would seem to have this work in mind when he refers to Giles and separability of essence and being in *DM* 31, XII, 35; 26, 293ab. For a collection of texts on the problem of one *esse* in Christ, see E. Hocedez, *Quaestio de unico esse in Christo a doctoribus saeculi XIII disputata,* Textus et Documenta, Series Theologica #14 (Roma: 1933). For a discussion of the problems arising from this doctrine of separability within the Thomist school, see L.A. Kennedy, C.S.B., "Thomism at the University of Salamanca in the Sixteenth Century: The Doctrine of Existence," *Tommaso d'Aquino nella storia del pensiero, Atti del Congresso Internazionale,* 1974; II, 254-258; "Peter of Ledesma and the Distinction between Essence and Existence," *The Modern Schoolman* XLVI (1968), 25-38; "La doctrina de la existencia en la Universidad de Salamanca durante el siglo XVI," *Archivo Teológico Granadino* 35 (1972), 5-71.

[48] "In reality" here translates *ex natura rei* which is used throughout this discussion sometimes as a generic designation for a real distinction and sometimes to designate a modal distinction. See A. Maurer, C.S.B., *Medieval Philosophy* (N.Y.: Random House, 1962), p. 360.

[49] The use of "...is attributed *(tribuitur)* to Scotus..." seems to indicate a caution or hesitancy on Suárez's part. It parallels his use of "...is considered *(existimatur)* to be the opinion of St. Thomas..." above in Section I, 3.

[50] Scotus, *Opus Oxoniense,* III, d. 6, a. 1; ed. Vives, T. 14, 305-314. But there is no explicit mention of any modal distinction between essence and existence. See my article, "Suárez, Historian and Critic of the Modal Distinction between Essential Being and Existential Being," *The New Scholasticism* XXXVI (1962), 419-444; A.J. O'Brien, S.J., "Duns Scotus' Teaching on the Distinction Between Essence and Existence," *The New Scholasticism* XXXVIII (1964), 61-77; A. B. Wolter, O.F.M., "The Formal Distinction," *John Duns Scotus, 1265-1965,* edit. J.K. Ryan and B.M. Bonansea, *Studies in Philosophy and the History of Philosophy,* Vol. 3, (Wash., D.C.: Catholic Univ., Pr., 1965).

[51] Henry of Ghent, *Quodlibeta* (Paris: Jacobus Badius Ascensius, 1518), I, q. 9; fol. 6v-7rv; q. 10; fol. 8r-9v. But again there is no explicit mention of any modal distinction between essence and existence.

[52] See *DM* 31, VI, 13-18; XXVI, 247a-248a.

[53] D. Soto, *In Octo Libros Physicorum Quaestiones* (Salmanticae, 1582), II, q. 2; 34rb. Thus the reference to 1 *Phys.,* q. 2 in the Vives edition is incorrect. The Mainz edition of 1605 and the Salamanca edition of 1597 have the correct reference.

[54] D. Soto, *In Quartum Sententiarum Commentarii* (Lovanii, 1573), d. 10, q. 2, a. 2; 274a.

[55] I read the *ut* of the 1597 Salamanca edition instead of the *et* of the Vives text.

[56] St. Hilary of Poitier, *De Trinitate,* Bk. 7; *PL* 10, 208. The Vives reference to "Book nine" is incorrect.

[57] Boethius, *De Hebdomadibus; PL* 64, 1311.

[58] *DM* 7, II, 6; XXV, 263ab.

[59] *In XII Aristotelis Metaphysicae Libros Dilucidissima Expositio* (Venetiis, 1572), Bk. 7, Tex. 22; 207rb-207vb. This is not Alexander of Hales but Alexander of Alexandria. See L. Veuthey, *Alexandre d'Alexandrie, maître de l'université de Paris et ministre général des frères mineurs* (Paris: Société et Librairie Saint-François D'Assise, 1932); C. Fabro, "Una fonte antitomista della metafisica Suareziana," *Divus Thomas* (Piacenza) 50 (1947), 57-68; R. Ceñal, "Alejandro de Alejandria: su influjo en la metafisica de Suárez," *Pensamiento* IV (1948), 91-122.

[60] *Def. Theol.,* I, 317b-320b. For Aureolus directly see *Scriptum super Primum Sententiarum,* I, d. 8, a. 21, ed. E. M. Buytaert (St. Bonaventure, N.Y.: Franciscan Institute, 1956), Vol. II, 884.

[61] *Def. Theol.,* I, 315ab. See *supra* n. 51 for complete reference to Henry's direct discussion of the problem of the distinction between essence and being in *Quodlibet* I, q. 9.

[62] *Def. Theol.,* I, 317ab. Capreolus himself is using Aureolus' recapitulation of Godfrey's position. See ed. Buytaert, 889-890. For Godfrey's own statement of his position, see *Les quatre premiers quodlibets de Godefroid de Fontaines,* ed. De Wulf-Pelzer, Quodlibet 3, q. 1; T. II, 156-177, esp. 164. See also J. F. Wippel, "Godfrey of Fontaines and the Real Distinction between Essence and Existence," *Traditio* XX (1964), 385-410;"Godfrey of Fontaines' and Henry of Ghent's Theory of Intentional Distinction between Essence and Existence," *Studia Anselmiana* 63 (1974), 289-321.

[63] *Def. Theol.,* I, 315b-317a.

[64] *In Petri Lombardi Sententias Theologicas. Commentarium Libri Quatuor* (Venetiis, 1571), I, d. 8, a. 2; fol. 35ra-36rb. The numeral missing in the Vives citation "in prima parte d., quaest. 2..." is 8.

[65] Gabriel Biel, *Collectorium Circa Quatuor Sententiarum Libros,* ed. W. Steinbach (Tubingen, 1501), 3 *Sent.,* d. 6, q. 2, a. 1; fol. 253va-254rb.

[66] Harvey Nédellec or Hervaeus Natalis, *Quaestiones Quodlibetales* (Venetiis, 1513), Quodlebet 7, q. 8; fol. 139rb-140rb. The Vives citation of "quaest. 9" is incorrect.

[67] Gregory of Rimini, *Super Primum et Secundum Sententiarum,* II, d. 1, q. 6, a. 2; Reprint of 1522 edition (St. Bonaventure, N.Y.: Franciscan Institute, 1955), fol. 25vb. The Vives reference of "dist. 6, quaest. 1 ad arg. Aureoli" is incorrect.

[68] Suarez apparently does not have the *Quaestiones super duodecim libros Metaphysicae* of Antonius Andreas in mind. A similar difficulty in locating the references to A. Andreas arises in *Uber die Individualität und das Individuationprinzip,* Text und Ubersetzung, herausgegeben, übersetzt von R. Specht (Hamburg: Felix Meiner, 1976), I, 338 n.5. It may be that Suarez has the *Expositiones* of Antonius Andreas in mind. However, this has not been available to me.

[69] Franciscus Lychetus, *In Opus Oxoniense,* (J. Duns Scoti, *Opera,* ed. Vives, Parisiis, 1893), Bk. 3, d. 6, q. 1; T. XIV, 306-307.

[70] Alexander Achillinus, *Opera Omnia in Unum Collecta* (Venetiis, 1545), *De Elementis,* Bk. I, dub. 23; fol. 103vb-104. The Vives reference to "dub.3" is incorrect.

[71] Michael de Palacios, *In Primum Librum Magistri Sententiarum Disputationes* (Salmanticae, 1574), d. 8, disp. 2; fol. 79vb-84ra. The Vives reference to "disput, 1" is incorrect.

[72] Johannes Altensteig, *Lexicon Theologicum* (Antwerp, 1576) 99v-100v. The abbreviation *Joan. Alens.* in the Vives text is in error. It should be *Joan. Altens.,* as in 1597 Salamanca edition.

[73] Augustinus Niphus, *Metaphysicorum Disputationum in Aristotelis Decem et Quatuor Libros Metaphysicorum* (Venetiis, 1559), Bk. 4, disp. 5; 118a-121b.

[74] *Ibid.,* 121b.

[75] *Ibid.,* 119b-120a.

[76] John of Jandun, *Quaestiones in XII Libros Metaphysicorum* (Venetiis, 1554), Bk. 4, q. 3, fol. 47v-48v. The Vives reference cites "c.3".

[77] *DM* 20, I, 24-26; XXV, 751b-753a.

[78] Petrus Fonseca, *Commentarium in Libros Metaphysicorum Aristotelis* (Francofurti, 1599-1605), Bk. 4, cap. 2, q. 4; col 746-761. The Vives reference to "c.3" is incorrect.

[79] See *infra* Section VI.

[80] *Op. cit.,* col. 755: "Tertia conclusio. Existentia creaturarum distinguitur ab illarum essentia ex natura rei non tamen formaliter, sed tanquam ultimum eius modus intrinsecus."

[81] See *supra* E. Hocedez in n. 47.

[82] *Commentaria ac Disputationes in Tertiam Partem D. Thomae,* Disp. 36, I and II; *Opera Omnia,* ed. Vives; T. 18, 260-272.

[83] This is important in view of Fr. Owens' ("The Number of Terms...," *The Modern Schoolman,* XXXIV (1957), 187) remark that this is the *only* type of distinction between essence and being operative in Suárez' metaphysics.

[84] I read the *aliquid* of the 1597 Salamanca text rather than the *aliud* of the Vives text.

Section II

What the essence of a creature is before it is produced by God. Solution of the question.

1.   To begin with, we must establish that the essence of a creature, or the creature of itself, and before it is made by God, has in itself no true real being and in this precise sense[1] of existential being, the essence is not some reality, but it is absolutely nothing. This principle is not only true but it is also certain according to faith. So Thomas of Walden, book 1 of *The Teaching of the Ancient Faith,* chapt. 8[2] rightly lists among the errors of Wyclif his statement that creatures from eternity have some real being distinct from the being of God. The Thomists take Scotus severely to task for having asserted that creatures have a certain eternal being which is a diminished being of theirs; that is, an objective being or the being of an essence enjoying the being of being known. This may be seen in Cajetan and others more recent, first part, question 14,[3] article 5. They think that the being of being known in the position of Scotus is some real being distinct from God's being; this, of course, they rightly attack as absolutely false and contrary to the principles of faith. However, they undeservedly attribute this to Scotus, for Scotus himself expressly shows that this being of being known, just as it is forthcoming in creatures from the knowledge of God, is not in them some real being intrinsic to them. Nor is it sufficient to ground a real relation but one of reason only. This may be seen in Scotus himself in 1, distinction 35, § *To these*[4] and distinction 36, § *To the second I say,*[5] and in 2, distinction 1, question 1, article 2[6] and in *Quodl.,* q. 1[7] and 14, article 2.[8] Nor could Scotus think otherwise, for he maintains that this being of being known befits creatures necessarily as well as it befits God Himself to know creatures, which does not depend on God's will or freedom. However, one would be in error to say that God necessarily and without freedom communicates to creatures some real being participated in from Himself, however diminished, since it is a matter of faith that God does all His works according to the counsel of His own will. Consequently, in this part, Scotus agrees with us in the principle put forth, because the essences of creatures, although they are known by God from eternity, are nothing; and they have not true real being, before they receive it when God freely effects it.

2.   But what's more, the very same Scotus, in the quoted distinction 36, [9] attacks Henry, for he maintained in a number of passages that, of themselves, the essences of things possess a certain essential being. This he calls a real being, eternal and unproduced, belonging to creatures independently of God; and this is supposed in them, not only prior to God's effecting, but also prior to His knowledge, so that by reason of that being they can be the objects of that divine knowledge which the theologians call simple intelligence. So writes Henry in this manner in *Summa,* third article, questions 23 and 25 [10] and *Quodl.* 8, questions 1 [11] and 9 [12] and *Quodl.* 9, questions 1 [13] and 2 [14] and *Quodl.* 11, q. 3. [15] The Thomists also oppose the position of Henry, as is clear from Hervaeus, *Quodl.* 11, q. 1 [16] and from Soncinas, 9 *Metaphysics,* question 4, [17] as do the more recent commentators on St. Thomas, part 1, q. 10, third article; [18] q. 46, art. 1. [19] However, Capreolus, in 2, dist. 1, quest. 2, art. 3, on the fourth argument of Aureolus against the fourth conclusion, would not vary much from Henry's opinion and manner of speaking. There, in response to Aureolus' question whether, when a thing is created, that which was absolutely nothing comes to be, Capreolus says [20] that indeed which was a nothing as to existential being comes to be; and he adds: "But beyond the nothingness, which is the lack of actual existence, there was an essence enjoying essential being; this essence, absolutely considered as a nature or quiddity, is withdrawable from the nothingness of existence and from the somethingness [21] of existence. This essence in itself is always something in the order of essences, both in intelligible being and in the active power of the Creator, although not in real actual being, as Henry, Godfrey and Bernard Gannaco maintain." [22] Later, [23] Capreolus so explains this essential being that, on the part of the creature, before it be produced by God, he does not judge it to be some true thing distinct from God which would be absolutely beyond nothing, but that, on the part of the creature, he would say that there is a certain aptitude or, rather, non-repugnance to being produced by God in such a being. For in this lies the distinction of creatures' essences from imagined and impossible things such as a chimera. In this sense, creatures are said to have real essences even though they do not exist; however, they are said to possess real essences, not in act but in potency, not by an intrinsic potency but an extrinsic one of the creator; and thus they are said to have real essences, not in themselves but in their cause, whether material, as a generable thing is said to be in the potency of prime matter; or efficient [cause], in the way in which an entire creatable being *(ens)* is contained in the potency of God before it comes to be, of whose possible essence in general we are now treating. Also in this way is such an essence, before it comes to be, called

real, not by a true reality of its own which it has actually in itself, but because it can be made real, by receiving true entity from its own cause; this possibility (as I shall soon say at greater length) [24] on the part of that essence alone bespeaks a non-repugnance to being produced; but on the part of the extrinsic cause it bespeaks the power to effect that essence. Further, in the same way and for the same reason, the being which they call essential prior to divine effection or creation, is only an objective potential being (as many say, about this immediately), [25] or by way of an extrinsic denomination from the potency of God and a non-repugnance on the part of the creatable essence.

3.   Nor could it have occurred to any Catholic Doctor to think that the essence of a creature of itself, and apart from the free effecting of God, be some true thing with some true real being distinct from the being of God. Ultimately, Capreolus expressly acknowledges this in the place cited, [26] quoting the words of St. Thomas, q.3 *On Power of God,* art. 5, to 2, where he speaks as follows: "From the very fact that being is attributed to a quiddity, not only the being but also the very quiddity is said to be created, because before it has being, it is nothing except perhaps in the intellect of the creator where it is not a creature but the creative essence." [27] It is proved by reason from the principles of faith, because God alone is a necessary being *(ens)* of himself and without Him nothing is made and without His effecting it there is nothing nor does it have in itself any real being. Hence, the holy Fathers rightly say that whatever is not created by God, either is God, or is nothing: Justin, *On the Exposition of the Faith;* [28] Cyril, Bk. I *On John,* cap. 6; [29] Augustine, Bk. I *On the Trinity,* cap. 6. [30] However, it is certain in faith that God did not make created essences from eternity, neither from necessity (as we were arguing against the opinion attributed to Scotus); [31] since, it is a matter of faith that God does nothing out of absolute necessity; nor from free will. For it is likewise a matter of faith that He began to operate in time. Furthermore, it is evident that, if the essences of things had been made by God from eternity, they also would have been existing from that time on, because every effecting is terminated [32] at existence, as I shall point out below. [33] This is confirmed, for otherwise God could not return something into nothing since something of the thing would always remain, namely, the essence. Also God would not have created all things from nothing but would have transferred them from one being to another being.

4.   Nor does it help any for Capreolus to reply as above, according to the opinion of others, [34] that God created all things from an existential nothing but not from an essential nothing. For what has nothing of existence is either simply and utterly nothing or it is not. If it is

not, then God absolutely and simply did not create all things from nothing nor did He produce all beings *(entia)* nor all that which is truly something real and consequently He, properly speaking, created no being *(ens)*, but produced one thing from another, as from a real receptive and unproduced potency, namely, existence or the existing thing from a real essence which is said to be the potency receptive of that being, and unproduced. A further result of this is that the creature can, so to speak, pride itself in having of itself something which it does not have from God nor has been given a share in by Him. But all these points and ones like them are against faith and natural reason. However, if, finally, someone admits that what has an existential nothing is simply and absolutely nothing, it is concluded that a distinction about an essential nothing and an existential nothing is worthless and meaningless, because what is simply and utterly nothing cannot truly and really be something in any order of true being *(ens)*. A further reason is that, with the removal of existence and of the effecting by the first cause removed, utterly nothing remains in the effect, as was shown. [35] Hence, then, an essence cannot remain subject to any true real being distinct from the being of the creator.

5.   This is finally made clear in this fashion: for let us grant that a created and existing essence is an entity really distinct in reality from existence and separable from it; and let us conceive of that essential entity, which is subject to existence, by mentally separating one from the other as, for example, the humanity of Christ, if that is only an essential entity. Accordingly, no Catholic can decide that that essential reality of the humanity, according to that whole which is conceived of in it after existence has been prescinded, has that entity in act from eternity, and that there was only lacking to it a union to the Word and to every other existence, otherwise an eternal and un-created entity outside God would be granted. Hence, it must, of necessity, be acknowledged that, when the existential entity, which is imparted to a creature by some effecting is removed, the essential entity is utterly nothing.

Objections against the proposed solution.

6.   Still, some objections are made against this truth, but of little weight. However, to satisfy everyone, I shall cite them. First, because the essence of a creature before it exists terminates the knowledge of God. But in order to terminate, it requires some being. Second, because essential predicates are predicated or can be predicated truly of the essence from eternity; every truth, however, is based on some being. Third, because created things in terms of essential

being are arranged under a definite genus and species; thus a rose is of the same species whether it exists or does not exist; indeed, the humanity of the created Peter and of the creatable Peter is numerically the same essence. Hence, in both states it retains some essential entity. Fourth, because if the essence of a creature in itself and as it is an object of God's simple intelligence is nothing real, then it will be a being *(ens)* of reason. How then is it truly said to be something creatable, since a being *(ens)* of reason is neither something nor can it be created? Also how is there science of real being *(ens),* since, properly speaking, it is about essence and not about existence? Next, how can an essence have a true exemplar or exemplary cause in God, for that[36] has no place in beings *(ens)* of reason? Finally, a threefold being is generally distinguished in creatures, namely, one of essence, one of existence and one of truth in a proposition, as can be seen in St. Thomas, in 1, dist. 33., q. 1, art. 1 to 1.[37] Hence, with existence removed, the essence can still retain essential being, for this it does not have from existence but from itself. Therefore, with all extrinsic effecting removed, it has such being and as a consequence has it from eternity.

THE OBJECTIONS ARE ANSWERED.

7. First.[38] In regard to the first one, without including the opinions of the Theologians touched upon above[39] and treated more at length in part 1, q. 14,[40] I concede that the essence of a creature, as it is the secondary object of divine knowledge, so terminates it, for it is not a moving but a terminating object only. However, for this no real being which it would have in act is necessary to it, because *to terminate* is neither something in the essence, nor is it something derived from it, but it is only an extrinsic denomination from God's knowledge; and this denomination posits nothing in the thing denominated nor even supposes, strictly speaking, some real being except such as is known by knowledge. For this very being is necessary for the truth of knowledge. Hence, since by the knowledge of simple intelligence God knows no creatures as having some real being in act but in potency only, then He does not require in them some real being to terminate knowledge of this sort; but potential being suffices which, as such, is in act only in a cause, as St. Thomas rightly said in part 1, quest. 14, art. 9[41] and I *Against the Gentiles,* cap. 66.[42] But if the discussion be about the knowledge of vision by which God regards existing things, that indeed requires existence in an object, in the measure of eternity, as they say.[43] Nevertheless, it does not enjoy a temporal duration of its own except for the time in which it is known to exist. So, from the very nature of the termination of knowledge, some real being is

not required in the thing known, but only that which is adequate to knowledge for its truth. And this is evident[44] in the knowledge which an Angel has of a possible rose or of a future eclipse.[45]

8. *Second. What is the eternal truth of propositions.* To the second one I will speak more at length when I solve the first argument set forth in the preceding section in favor of the first opinion.[46] For now, a brief response is given following St. Thomas in part 1, quest. 10, art. 3 to 3[47] to the effect that there has been no truth from eternity in those propositions except insofar as they were objectively in the divine mind, for, subjectively or really they were not in themselves nor objectively in another intellect. But for the knowledge to be true by which God knows from eternity that man is a rational animal, it was not necessary for the essence of man to have some real being in act from eternity, because that being does not signify an actual and real being but only the intrinsic connection between such extremes. But this connection is not based on an actual being but on a potential one. You will say that by that knowledge it is not known that man can be a rational animal, but that of necessity he is a rational animal. Hence, potential being alone is not a sufficient basis for it. This is answered by an absolute denial of the consequence, for that necessity is not an absolute one of being *(essendi)* in terms of some real being in act, but in this regard there is possibility only. Nevertheless, it involves a conditional necessity, for, surely, if man is to be produced, he will, of necessity, be a rational animal. This necessity is nothing else than a certain objective identity of man and animal; this identity God knows most simply, we, however, by the composition which the word *is* signifies when we say that man, from eternity, is a rational animal. This being pertains to that third way in which being is sometimes said to signify the truth in a composition.

9. *Third.* To the third one, it is to be said that possible things not yet produced are arranged under a definite genus and species in that way in which essential predicates are said to belong to them or rather to be truly ascribed to them, that is, insofar as they are objectively in the divine intellect or in any other. For this classification or arrangement under certain genera and species is not formally in things but in the intellect. Nonetheless, it has a foundation in things either as they exist in act or can exist and terminate objectively the knowledge by which they are known to be bound to be of such a nature and essence, if they come to be. Thus, when a possible thing and a created thing are said to be the same numerically or specifically, if the discussion concerns real or positive identity, it is false, because this kind of identity exists only between positive and real extremes. However, they are said to be one thing or of one species negatively, because a producible thing and one produced are not two things but

one; nor do they have two species or two essences, but one. But this negative unity or identity is apprehended by us in the manner of a positive type, because we compare a positive thing objectively existing in the intellect to the thing existing in act as if they were two positive extremes when, indeed, they are in reality only one, as will be established more fully from the following section. [48]

10.   *Fourth.* To the fourth one, the answer is that the creature's possible essence as objected [49] to divine knowledge is not a being *(ens)* fashioned by the intellect, but it is a being *(ens)* truly possible and capable of real existence. Thus it is not a being *(ens)* of reason but is in some way comprehended under real being *(ens)*. For I have already explained above [50] that the essence of a creature still unproduced is in some way a real essence. In the preceding sections, treating of the concept of being *(ens)*, we showed [51] that not only that which is in act is comprehended under it but also what is apt to be. Consequently, Cajetan rightly says in *On Being and Essence,* chap. 4, quest. 5 [52] that real being *(ens)* is taken in a twofold manner: in one way as it is counter-distinguished from being *(ens)* constructed by the intellect (which is properly a being *(ens)* of reason); in another way as it is distinguished from something not existing in act. Thus the essence of a creature in itself is a real being *(ens)* in the prior way, [53] namely, in potency but not in the latter way and in act, which is to be a real being *(ens)* properly, as Cajetan has noted in the same place. [54] Therefore, if the essence of a creature, taken precisely and in itself and not yet made, were considered as a being *(ens)* in act, or if being in act were attributed to it, then either it must not be considered in itself but in its cause, nor has it a real being other than the being of its cause, or if it were considered as having being in itself, it is thus true, according to that consideration, that it is not a real being *(ens)* but one of reason. For in itself it is not, but is only objectively in the intellect. Nonetheless, that nature is called creatable or possible, inasmuch as in itself it is real and apt for existing. In the same way it can have a real exemplar in God. For this does not always represent actual being *(ens)* but also possible being *(ens)*. Finally, in the same way, the sciences which consider things by abstracting from existence are not concerned with beings *(ens)* of reason but with real beings *(ens)*, because they consider real essences, not in terms of the status they have objectively in an intellect, but in themselves or insofar as they are apt for existing with such natures or properties.

11.   *Fifth. What is the meaning and various senses of essential being.* As to the fifth argument, it must be noted that an equivocation is possible in the first member, namely, essential being. For it is attributed to created things in two ways. In one way, in themselves, even as they are still uncreated and not existing in act. In this way essential being

is not a true, real and actual being in the creature as was demonstrated,[55] but it is a possible being; and is reduced to that third member dealing with the being of the truth in a proposition or of knowledge. For, as we have shown,[56] the essences of creatures in this way only have being[57] either in a cause or objectively in an intellect. Only a difference can be established between these two members because the being in the truth of a proposition not only has a place in real essences but also in beings *(entia)* of reason and imaginary beings *(entia).* For thus is it true that blindness is a privation, and a chimera is an imagined monstrosity; and thus in a peculiar way essential being is ascribed to created things before they exist, so that there is an indication that that truth is founded on potential being, apt for existing. Essential being is taken in another way, as in act it belongs to a creature already existing; and this being is undoubtedly real and actual, whether in the thing or in reason only it be distinguished, we shall see later[58] because it is certain that in the existing thing the essence itself is a being *(ens)* in act and consequently its essential being is actual being. Yet it does not have this actuality except by creation or production by an agent and when the essence is really joined to existence. Therefore, even though we may grant that essential being, taken in this way, is an actual being and distinct from existential being, nevertheless, the principle laid down is true and certain: that the essence of a creature does not have this essential being in act except by an effecting; and consequently that in itself and of itself and as unproduced, it has no being in act, neither essential nor existential. This distinction must be kept in mind to remove equivocation and to understand the efficacy of the arguments which are usually raised in this matter.

Notes

[1] I read the *et in hoc sensu praeciso esse existentiae* of the 1597, Salamanca edition without the comma after *sensu* in the Vives text.

[2] Thomas of Walden, *Doctrinale Antiquitatum Catholicae Ecclesiae* (Venetiis, 1557), Bk. I, cap. 8; T. I, 32a et seq. Elsewhere, Suarez does not think Wycliff said any such thing nor that such a position ever entered anyone's head. See Suarez, *In I Sum. Theol.,* Bk. III, cap. 5, #5; I, 211a.

[3] Cajetan, *In Sum. Theol.,* I, q. 14, a. 5; T. 4, 174-175. The Vives reference to "quaest. 17" is incorrect. For some *recentiores,* see D. Bañez, *In Sum. Theol.,* I, q. 14, a. 6; 338; F. Zumel, *In Primam D. Thomae Partem Commentaria* (Venetiis, 1597-1601), I, q. 14, a. 5, concl. 5; 290a.

[4] Scotus, *Opus Oxon.,* I, d. 35, q. 1; T. 10, 553b-557a.

[5] Scotus, *Opus Oxon.,* I, d. 36, q. 1; T. 10, 577b-582a.

[6] Scotus, *Opus Oxon.,* II, d. 1, q. 1; a. 2; T. 11, 22b et seq.

[7] Scotus, *Quaestiones Quodlibetales,* q. 1, #12; T. 25, 20b.

[8] *Ibid.,* q. 14, #14; T. 26, 52.

[9] Scotus, *Opus Oxon.,* I, d. 36, q. 1; T. 10, 564b-587.

[10] "La referencia que Suárez hace de la Suma de Enrique (ar. 3, q. 23 et 25) es totalmente equivocada." José Gómez Caffarena, "Sentido de la composición de ser y esencia en Suárez," *Pensamiento* 15(1959), 142 n. 29. See also J. Benes, "Valor 'Possibilium' apud S. Thomam, Henricum Gandavensem, B. Jacobum de Viterbo," *Divus Thomas* (Piacenza) 30(1927), 112-113, "Animadversio. — Auctores, qui tribuunt falso Henrico a Gandavo sententiam, ac si doceret essentias ut tales habere aliquod esse actuale, provocant ad diversas quodlibeta....Provocant etiam ad Summ. a. III (aliqui indicant a. II) q. 23 et 25. Sed nec art. III nec art. II Summae habet quaestiones sive 23 sive 25. Hanc animadversionem facit iam Henricus A. Burgus, Ord. Servorum B.M.V., in suo libro 'Henrici Gandavensis Paradoxa' (a. 1627 Bononiae), p. 116 col. 1. Haec citatio videtur esse reducenda ad aliquem marginistam Scoti..."

[11] Henry of Ghent, *Aurea Quodlibeta* (Venetiis, 1613), Quodlib. 8, q. 1; fol. 1r-3v.

[12] *Ibid.,* Quodlib. 8, q. 9; fol. 20v-26v.

[13] *Ibid.,* Quodlib. 9, q. 1; fol. 58r-62v.

[14] *Ibid.,* Quodlib. 9, q. 2; fol. 65v-68v.

[15] *Ibid.,* Quodlib. 11, q. 3; fol. 184v-193r.

[16] Hervaeus Natalis, *Quaestiones Quodlibetales* (Venetiis, 1513), Quodlib. 11, q. 1; fol. 179rb-180ra. However, A. Pelzer has found that the eleventh and twelfth Quodlibets of Hervaeus in the 1513 Venice edition (fol. 179rb-186vb) are really Quodlibets III and IV, brief redaction, of Godfrey of Fontaines. See *Les quatre premiers quodlibets de Godefroid de Fontaines,* Les philosophes belges, textes et études (Louvain, 1904), T. 2, x. See J. Wippel, "Godfrey of Fontaines and the Real Distinction between Essence and Existence," *Traditio* XX (1964), 386-387.

[17] Soncinas, *In 9 Metaph.,* q. 4; 230b-232b. Soncinas here uses the anonymous *aliqui* but *In 5 Metaph.,* q. 10 ad 1; 65b he cites Henry by name and refers his reader to Bk. 9.

[18] D. Bañez, *In Sum. Theol.,* I, q. 10, a. 3; 227a notes:"aliqui inter quos est Scotus..." Also it must be noted that Bañez is using Soncinas: "Ita Sonc. 9 *Met.,* q. 4 refert." See also F. Zumel, *In Sum. Theol.,* I, q. 10, a. 3; 155-156.

[19] This too may refer to D. Bañez, but to date I have not been able to check his commentary at this place.

[20] Capreolus, *Def. Theol., In II Sent.,* d. 1, q. 2, a. 3 ad quartum argumentum Aureoli contra quartam conclusionem; III, 73a.

[21] I read the *aliquidditati* of Capreolus' own text, as well as that of the 1597 Salamanca edition, instead of the *quiddidati* of the Vives text.

[22] For Bernard de Gannaco, see A. Pattin, "La structure de l'etre fini selon Bernard d'Auvergne O.P. (apres 1307)," *Tijdschrift voor Filosofie* 24 (1962), 668-737.

[23] *Def. Theol.,* III, 74b and 76a.

[24] *DM* 31, II, 10-11; XXVI, 232.

[25] *DM* 31, III, 2-4; XXVI, 233-234.

[26] See nn. 20 and 21, above.

[27] *De Pot.,* q. 3, a. 5 ad 2; ed. Pession, II, 49b. The argument to which this text is an answer should be noted.

[28] Justin Martyr, *Expositio Rectae Fidei,* 2, *Corpus Apologetarum Christianorum Saeculi Secundi,* ed. J.C.Th. Otto (Jena: F. Mauke, 1849), IV, 4-5.

[29] Cyril, *In Evangelio Joannis,* Bk. I, ch. 6; *Opera* (Basiliae: J. Hervagii, 1566), col. 24-26.

[30] St. Augustine, *De Trinitate,* Bk. I, ch. 6; *PL* 42, 825. The reference to "Bk. I" appears in the 1597 Salamanca edition but is deleted in the Vives text.

[31] See paragraph 1, this section, above.

[32] I read the *terminatur* of the 1597 Salamanca edition and the Mainz edition of 1605 instead of the *confirmatur* of the Vives text.

[33] See Section IX below.

[34] See paragraph 2, this section, above.

[35] See paragraph 3, this section, above.

[36] I read the *id* of the 1597 Salamanca edition which is deleted in the Vives text.

[37] St. Thomas, *In I Sent.*, d. 33, q. 1 ad 1; ed. Mandonnet, I, 766. See also *In III Sent.*, d. 6, q. 2, a. 2; ed. M.F. Moos (Paris: Lethielleux, 1953), III, 238.

[38] I read the *Prima* of the 1597 Salamanca edition instead of the *Primae* of the Vives text which numbers all five replies in the genitive.

[39] *DM* 30, XV, 27; XXVI, 178.

[40] See Suárez, *In Sum. Theol.*, I, q. 14, Bk. III, cap. 2, 1-21; I, 196a-202a.

[41] *Sum. Theol.*, I, q. 14, a. 9; T. 4, 181.

[42] *Sum. Cont. Gent.*, I, 66; T. 13, 184-185.

[43] Suarez is referring to the phrase *aeternitate mensuretur* used by Aquinas, *Sum. Theol.*, I, q. 14, a. 9; T. 4, 181. See also *Sum. Theol.*, I, q. 14, a. 13; T. 4, 186-187.

[44] I read the *evidens* of the 1597 Salamanca edition instead of the *evidentius* of the Vives text.

[45] Capreolus makes use of this example in *Def. Theol.*, *In I Sent.*, d. 38, q. 1, a. 2; II, 465b.

[46] *DM* 31, XII, 38-47; XXVI, 294b-298b.

[47] *Sum. Theol.*, I, q. 10, a. 3 ad 3; T. 4, 98. Herein St. Thomas says nothing about the *objective* presence of these eternally true propositions in the Divine intellect. See *DM* 31, XII, 40-41; XXVI, 294b-295b where Suárez indicates that he is not altogether happy with this text of Aquinas.

[48] See Section III below.

[49] I read the *objectam* of the 1597 Salamanca edition instead of the *objectivam* of the Vives text.

[50] See paragraph 2, this section, above.

[51] *DM* 2, IV, 6-7; XXV, 89a-90a.

[52] Cajetan, *In De Ente et Essentia,* cap. 4, q. 6; ed. Laurent, 92, 59. The Vives citation of "quaest. 5" is in error.

[53] I read the *priori* of the 1597 Salamanca and 1605 Mainz editions instead of the *primo* of the Vives text.

[54] See n. 52, this section, above.

[55] See paragraphs 2-5, this section, above.

[56] See paragraph 2, this section, above.

[57] For what it is worth, I read the *habent esse vel* word-order of the 1597 Salamanca edition instead of the *habent vel esse* of the Vives text.

[58] See Section VI below.

Section III

How and in what being (ens) in potency and in act,
or essence in potency and act, differ in creatures.

1.   In this section another principle and foundation for what is to be said must, of course, be determined: to wit, that in created things, a being *(ens)* in potency and one in act are distinguished immediately and formally as a being *(ens)* and a non-being *(ens)*, absolutely speaking. This distinction is called by some[1] a real negative distinction because one extreme is a true thing and the other is not. But it is called by others[2] a distinction of reason because there are not two things but only one which is conceived of and compared by the intellect as if there were two things. And this principle is commonly accepted, even in the school of St. Thomas, as is clear from Soncinas, 9 *Metaph.,* quest. 3 and from others.[3]

THE NATURE OF OBJECTIVE POTENCY.

2.   To grasp this principle which is very necessary for what we shall say, it must be noted that certain writers have thought that a being *(ens)* in potency indicates some positive mode of being *(essendi)* on the part of the thing which is said to be in potency, which is a diminished being and imperfect compared to that state in which a thing is said to be in act. According to this opinion one would have to say that those two extremes are positive and real. This opinion is usually ascribed to Scotus in 2, dist. 16, q. 1, § *Those reasons.*[4] For he distinguishes the potency by which a being *(ens)* in potency is denominated from active and passive potency. For this reason it is customarily called objective, following Scotus again in 2, dist. 12, q. 1.[5] According to this, it is thought to be something real and positive on the part of the being *(ens)* said to be potency. But neither did Scotus utter this last statement nor does it have any likelihood in itself. For Scotus never

understood a purely objective potency to be a real, positive thing, distinct from a producing cause and presupposed on the part of a possible thing for the action of that cause. Further, if you read carefully, the aforementioned distinction 12 [6] denies that clearly. Hence, he only called possible being *(ens)* itself a being *(ens)* in objective potency because it is related as an object to a productive potency. Hence, only in name does he differ when he calls a being *(ens)* in objective potency what we call potential being *(ens);* and he thinks that Aristotle in 9 *Metaph.* [7] is speaking of that objective potency when he says that potency and act are in the same genus. But there was a discussion above [8] about the meaning of the axiom and at the moment it is of no concern.

3.   Therefore, the fact that that being in potency or that objective potency could not be something true and positive in the thing itself which is said to be in potency is first manifest from what has been said in the preceding section, [9] because either that potency would be [10] produced or altogether unproduced; if it is unproduced, it is nothing distinct from the creator; if it is produced, it is produced either from eternity and out of necessity (and this cannot be said without error) or freely and in time; and thus, before it might be produced, it was in objective potency. Consequently, the whole thing, without such a potency in the produced thing, was in objective potency. Therefore, this being in objective potency expresses no real and positive potency which would be in act. Secondly, it is evident that that objective potency is not something real and positive in the thing which is said to be in potency, for either a potency of this sort remains in the produced thing or does not remain. If it does not remain, it can be nothing real and positive. For how would that being *(ens),* whatever it is imagined to be, be destroyed by the production of a being *(ens)* in act, if it were something positive and real? But if that potency remains in the produced thing, then that potency is not only objective but it is also subjective. Nor would things be made from nothing but from a presupposed potency, as from a subject or matter from which a thing is made. Thirdly, it was shown above [11] that there is no reality (speaking properly of a positive and actual thing) in the possible essence before it is made. Hence, there cannot be a real positive potency in it. For every real, positive potency is some true thing or based on some reality and entity. Therefore, as St. Thomas has rightly noted in part 1, quest. 9, art. 3 [12] creatures are not called possible except by denomination from some active potency or passive potency. But when this denomination is taken from a passive potency or from the active potency of a second cause, it supposes such a potency already produced by another; for neither a second cause nor any real passive potency can be entirely unpro-

duced. Accordingly (St. Thomas says), "All creatures, before they might exist, were not possible to be by some created potency, since nothing created is eternal; but they were possible by divine potency alone to the extent that God can produce them in being." [13] Hence, on the part of creatures, the only supposition is non-repugnance to be made in such a way, because no reality in them can be supposed or required.

4.   Nor can that potency, in terms of which they are said to be in objective potency, be something in them, but it is in the cause by which they can be produced, because being in objective potency is nothing else than the possibility of being an object of some power, or rather of the action or causality of some potency. But a thing cannot be an object of itself, just as it cannot be produced by itself, but can be produced by another. Hence, it is said to be in objective potency in relation to the potency of another and, by denomination from the latter it is called a possible thing. Thus it is concluded that a being *(ens)* in potency as such, does not express a positive state or mode of being *(ens),* but rather, in addition to the denomination from the potency of an agent, it includes a negation, namely, that it has not yet come forth in act from such a potency. Hence, it is said to be in potency because it has not yet issued into act. Furthermore, for that reason, when a thing is created, it ceases to be in potency, not because it would cease to be subject to divine potency and contained in it, but because now it is not only in it but also from it and in itself. Hence, that being in potency excluded this latter state.

WHAT ESSENCE IN ACT ADDS TO ESSENCE IN POTENCY.

5.   In the second place, a principal observation must be made about the other extreme, namely, a being *(ens)* or an essence in act: authors [14] frequently say that an essence in act adds existence to the essence itself. This manner of speaking, according to the opinion of those who affirm that the existing essence is not distinguished in reality from its being, must of necessity be understood to concern an addition according to reason or an addition improperly so called. For, if the discussion concern an essence in act in relation to an essence in potency, less properly speaking does it seem to add existence to it, because a real addition does not take place properly except to a real being *(ens),* for it has some entity to which the addition is made. But we have said [15] that an essence in potency has no entity. Hence, properly speaking, no addition is made to it, except perhaps according to reason, insofar as an essence in objective potency is understood after the fashion of a being *(ens).* It would be said more properly that an essence, as a being *(ens)* in act, is distinguished by

actual existence from itself as it is in potency. Hence, if the discussion concern an essence in act, it is in no way possible to say, according to this opinion, that an existing essence adds existence to an essence in act, because an essence, which is a being *(ens)* in act, formally and intrinsically includes existence. Indeed, by it it is constituted a being *(ens)* in act and distinguished from a being *(ens)* in potency, according to this opinion, as was said. [16] Therefore, the authors who think being is distinguished in reality from the essence of a creature more often use this manner of speaking, as is clear from the above citations. [17] From among them Giles, *Quodlibet* I, q.7 says "being is impressed on an essence when it is created and becomes existent." [18] This dictum, if it be understood of an essence as it was in potency or rather, was thought of prior to God's production, is either utterly false or is most improper and metaphorical. For how can an act be impressed on that which is nothing? Indeed, an act is not impressed except on a receptive potency. But an essence subject to this consideration is not in receptive potency but only in objective potency. Hence, in order that that statement, and ones like it, could have some true meaning in the opinion mentioned above, it must be understood as referring to an essence in act. This essence, when compared to being, is its receptive potency, though it is not an actual essence except when it actually receives the act of being *(essendi)*.

6.   Still, it is a necessary consequence of this that although an actual essence differs from a potential essence only when it is, or also because it is subject to an act of being *(essendi)*, yet formally and precisely it does not differ immediately in the act of being *(essendi)* but in its essential entity or in actual essential being. This, (I say) must be said when making a distinction in reality of an actual essence from existence, as a real potency from an act. For a being *(ens)* in objective potency, as we have shown, [19] is simply nothing or is not a being *(ens)* in act; therefore, any actual entity formally, immediately and precisely differs from a being *(ens)* in potency by that through which it is an actual entity in its own genus and ceases to be potential. But an actual essence in essential being differs from an essence in potency, as is self-evident. It does not differ formally and precisely by existence, but by that actuality which it has in itself and which is distinct from existence, because an actual essence did not have that in act while it was in potency. Therefore. The same point is to be made for a further reason: in terms of that actual entity, an actual essence is in receptive potency to existence in which it was not when considered in mere objective potency. Besides, it is clearly manifested in the humanity of Christ, if it be supposed to exist by the uncreated existence of the Word, because no less is the humanity of Christ, precisely conceived, a created actual entity; and so, even as precisely

conceived, it differs from itself as it was from eternity in mere objective potency. So it is now conceived as proximately apt for this union to the Word which it did not have before creation. Hence, that humanity as an actual essential entity differs from itself in potency by its very own created essential entity, and not only by God's uncreated being.

7. A fuller expression and confirmation of this is as follows: for if essence and existence are different things, just as an essence can be in potency and act, so a created existence is in potency and in act. And just as an essence cannot be actual unless joined to an existence, so neither can an existence be actual unless joined to an essence. Yet, formally and intrinsically, actual existence does not differ from itself as potential by essence but by its own actual entity which it did not have in act while it was in potency. Accordingly, the same pertains to essence if it be compared to itself in potency in terms of the precise actuality of the essence. Similarly, not only can we conceive of essence precisely and of existence precisely, but also of the whole composite of being and essence, as in potency, and as [20] in act, which is self-evident. However, this being *(ens)* in act is not adequately [21] distinguished from itself in potency because it adds existence to essence. For, in both states, it includes existence proportionately. But it differs by its entire adequate entity, because, to be sure, while it is in act, it has an essential and an existential actuality; but while it is in potency, it has neither.

8. Hence, it is universally true, according to the principle set down above, [22] namely, that a being *(ens)* in act and a being *(ens)* in potency are distinguished formally and directly as a being *(ens)* and a non-being *(ens)*, and not as adding one being *(ens)* to another being *(ens)*. Consequently, it is also true that an essence as an actual being *(ens)* is distinguished directly from a potential essence by its own actual entity whether or not it requires another entity or another mode to have that. For the argument is the same in the case of an essence in act as in the case of any being *(ens)* in act. Hence, to speak formally and to abstract from every opinion, one must not say that an actual essence is distinguished from a potential essence, because it has existence. For, although that too can be verified, either formally and proximately, or fundamentally and remotely, according to the different opinions, still, most formally and directly in every opinion an actual essence is separated from a potential one by its own actual entity which it has in the order of real essence.

Notes

[1] See Soncinas, *In 9 Metaph.*, q. 3; 230a; D. Bañez, *In Sum. Theol.*, I, q. 10, a. 3; I, 228a.

[2] See Alexander of Alexandria, *In 7 Metaph.*, text 22; 207vaF.

[3] See n.1, this section, above.

[4] Scotus, *Opus Oxon.*, II, d. 16, q. 1; T. 13, 25-28.

[5] Scotus, *Opus Oxon.*, II, d. 12, a. 1; T. 12, 556.

[6] *Ibid.*

[7] Aristotle, *Metaphysics*, IX, 8, 1049b17-27. See Fonseca, *In Metaph.*, IX, 1, q. 3; col. 517-521.

[8] *DM* 14, II, 13; XXV, 469ab.

[9] See Section II, 2-3 above.

[10] I read the *esset* of the 1597 Salamanca and 1605 Mainz editions instead of the *est* of the Vives text.

[11] See Section II, 2-3.

[12] *Sum. Theol.*, I, q.9, a. 2; T. 4, 91-92.

[13] *Ibid.*

[14] See nn.17, 18, this section, below.

[15] See Section II above.

[16] See Section I, 13, above.

[17] See Soncinas, *In 9 Metaph.*, q. 3; 230; *In 4 Metaph.*, q. 12; 21b. See also Capreolus, *Def. Theol.*, I, 310b and Javellus, *Tractatus de Transcendentibus,* cap. IV, 466b.

[18] Giles of Rome, *Quodlibet* I, q. 7; 16a where this exact text in so many words does not appear.

[19] See Section II above.

[20] I read the *ut* of the 1597 Salamanca and 1605 Mainz editions. It is deleted in the Vives text.

[21] The 1597 Salamanca edition reads *non distinguitur* & *adequate.* J. Hellin, S.J., "Existencialismo escolastico suareciano," *Pensamiento* 12 (1956), p. 165 n. 5 [bis] recommends reading *non distinguitur inadequate.* The Vives text does not carry the "&".

[22] See paragraph 1, this section, above.

Section IV

Whether the essence of a creature is constituted in its actuality by some real being indistinct from it with the name and character of existence.

1. We have spoken of the essence of a creature as possible and as in act, and of the sort of distinction between them. It remains to speak of the being by which an actual essence is most formally constituted.
2. Consequently, I state first: a real essence, which in itself is something in act, distinct from its cause, is constituted intrinsically by some real and actual being. This follows clearly from what has been said.[1] For every real entity is constituted by some real being since the term being *(ens)* is derived from being and a real being *(ens)* is named from real being. Hence, when a real entity ceases to be potential and becomes actual, it must be constituted by some real actual being. On the other hand, a real actual essence is a true and a real actual being *(ens)* in its own order, differing then from a being *(ens)* in potency. Hence, it must be formally constituted in such actuality by some real actual being conferred[2] on it by some efficient causation.
3. I state secondly: this constitution does not come about by a composition of such being with such an entity, but by an identity real in every way. It is proved in the first place from what has been said.[3] For an actual essence at once differs from its potential self immediately by its own entity. Accordingly, by that very entity it has that actual being by which it is constituted, etc.

Secondly, it is stated in this way. For, either an actual essence is distinguished in reality from existence or is not. If not, it is obvious that it has no distinct being by which it would be constituted in such an actuality. But if it is distinguished, then the actual essential being is also distinguished in reality from the actual existential being. Hence, the actual essential being is not distinguished in reality from the actual essence; otherwise there would be an infinite progression. Therefore, in every opinion, that being by which an actual essence is constituted as such cannot be distinct in reality from it.

PROPER[4] RESOLUTION OF THE QUESTION.

4. I say thirdly: that being by which the essence of a creature is formally constituted in essential actuality is the true existential being.
The two preceding statements,[5] as we set them forth, are common to
every opinion whether we hold that existence is distinguished in reality from essence or not. But this third statement is indeed granted,
and is even asserted of necessity by the ones who do not distinguish
existence from an actual essence. But it is more often denied by
those who maintain the opposite. Further, if they were to speak consistently, I do not see how they could admit it. Now this statement is
proved in a variety of ways. First, because this being, understood
precisely, is sufficient for the truth of this statement with a second
adjacent: *essence is.* Hence, that being is true existence. The consequence is clear, for according to the common meaning and human
conception, the *is* of a second adjacent, is not divorced from time.
But it signifies being in act in the realm of things, which all of us
understand by the name *existence* or by *existential being.* You will say
that the *is* is always said truly of an actual essence, yet not formally
because of the actuality of an essence, nor on account of that being
by which it is formally constituted in such actuality, but because it
never has this being without existence, although distinct from such
an essential being or actuality. But against this retort the antecedent
of the argument given is proved. For, by this actual essential being,
taken formally and precisely, such an essence is a being *(ens)* in act
and distinguished from a being *(ens)* in potency. Hence, by virtue of
that being, such an essence is, for the inference is correct: it is a being *(ens)* in act; therefore it is. For to be a being *(ens)* in act does not
reduce the character of being *(ens)* which includes the verb *is.* So,
even if we grant that this actual essential being depends on a further
limit or act, as on a necessary condition or something of this sort,
still that very being will formally constitute a being *(ens)* in act and
will distinguish the latter from a being *(ens)* in potency. Thus, by virtue of that being a thing is truly and absolutely said to be, just as an
accident by virtue of its being is said to be a being *(ens)* in act and to
be absolutely, even though that being requires an inherence in a
subject so that, without it, it could not exist naturally.

5. Secondly, I argue both directly and *ad hominem.* For all those
characteristics which are usually ascribed to existence agree with this
actual essential being, and further, all those features because of
which the authors of the first and second opinions[6] judge that existence is distinguished in reality from essence. Hence, it is true existential being. The antecedent is proved, for, in the first place, this
actual essential being is not eternal but temporal. For, as was shown

above, [7] creatures have had no real being from eternity, but essential being, as distinguished from existential being, is said to be eternal, and this cannot be true except of that potential being. Hence, actual being, just as it is temporal so also is it true existence. Furthermore, this being belongs contingently or not necessarily to a creature since also before it came to be, it did not have it, and, after it has it, it can be deprived of it. But these are the conditions of existence for which it is especially thought to be distinguished from essence. For essence is not said to belong to a thing contingently but necessarily and inseparably. Hence, this actual essential being has all the conditions of existence. You will say: if this argument is effective, it not only concludes that this being would be existence but also that it would be distinct from essence. The answer is that in the opinion of others it is so concluded. However, according to our way of thinking, the conclusion is rather that it is not rightly proved by those arguments that existence is distinguished in reality from essence; about this more below. [8] Hence, in addition, it belongs to actual essential being to be granted to the creature by the effecting of the creator, but existential being is proximately conferred by an effecting. Consequently, in this also, this being agrees with existence. Finally, no condition necessary for existential being can be thought of which does not belong to this being. Unless perhaps someone says, while begging the question, that one of the conditions required for existence is to be distinguished in reality from an actual essence; and this would be to utter a patent absurdity. For we are now looking into the conditions by which we can come to know what existence is and why it is to be distinguished from essence. Hence, it would be a wilful begging of the question to place a distinction of this sort among the necessary conditions for existential being, above all, because a distinction, since it is a certain negation or relation, is not a condition essentially required for the being of a thing. Rather, it is something resulting from the particular being of a thing. Hence, a distinction must not be posited as one of the necessary conditions for the being of a thing, whether essential being or existential being. But among the rest, a condition which would constitute real being in existential being and which would not be found in actual essential being cannot be imagined. Therefore, this is true existential being.

6.   Thirdly, this very point is made clear from the proper character of existence. For existential being is nothing else than that being by which some entity is formally and immediately constituted outside its causes and ceases to be nothing and begins to be something. But this being is the type by which a thing is formally and immediately constituted in essential actuality; therefore it is true existential being. The major is seen to be self-evident from the meaning of the

term itself and from the common conception of all. Also, it is made clear from the immediate and formal opposition noted above[9] between being *(ens)* in act and a being *(ens)* in potency. For a being *(ens)* in act is the same as an existing being, otherwise something between a possible being *(ens)* and an existing being *(ens)* could be granted; but this is unintelligible. Therefore, that being by which a being *(ens)* in act is constituted formally in itself and outside its causes, is also the being by which it is constituted as existing. Hence, that being is true existential being. Also, the major is clear because if, possibly or impossibly, this sort of being be understood to remain without any other distinct being, it is sufficient for distinguishing an actual entity from a possible entity, and, as a result, for constituting it in a new and temporal state which it does not have for eternity, and for terminating the action of an agent, or, for grounding a real relation to, and a real dependence on, an efficient cause. Therefore, this sort of being, by which a thing is formally constituted in act outside its causes, is existence. But the minor proposition, namely, that that being by which a possible essence intrinsically and immediately is understood to become an actual essence constitutes an essence outside its causes or beyond nothing is almost self-evident from the terms, for by that being it is something in act. It has also been demonstrated from the principles laid down. For it has been shown[10] that an essence is formally constituted by this being outside the possibility which it had from eternity according to our way of thinking. Indeed, to be educed, so to speak, from possibility and to be constituted outside one's causes, are the same.

7.   *An objection is met.* Nor does it matter if someone were to say that this actual essential being depends on another distinct being, which others call actual existence, first because, although we may admit this dependence, it cannot be in the order of formal cause or term intrinsically constituting the essence in the order of actual essence. However, we have spoken of the being formally and intrinsically constituting the actuality of an essence in this way. And with regard to that being, we have shown it to have the true character of existence. We have proved what was assumed because we showed that that being by which an essence is constituted in essential actuality cannot be distinct in reality from it. Hence, if that other being, called existence by others, is distinct in reality from the essential actuality, it cannot formally constitute it in such an actuality. Hence, if there is any dependence of an actual essence on such an existence, it will not be dependent as on a formal, intrinsic constituent, but as on another cause or necessary condition. It does not matter for a further reason because, if this argument were carefully considered, it proves that no such distinct existence from actual essential being is given.

If, perchance, some condition is given or limit or necessary mode, in order for such an actual essence to exist, this cannot be, nor be called existence, but subsistence or inherence, unless this whole controversy be reduced to a question of words. But since the understanding of this whole problem depends largely on this point, it must be stated directly and explicitly and proved in the following section.

Notes

[1] See Section I, 13 and Sections II and III above.

[2] I read the *communicato* of the 1597 Salamanca and 1605 Mainz editions instead of the *communicatio* of the Vives text.

[3] See n. 1, this section, above.

[4] I read the *Propria* of the 1597 Salamanca edition instead of *Prioris* of the Vives text.

[5] See paragraphs 2 and 3, this section, above.

[6] See Section I, 3 and 11, above.

[7] See Section II, above.

[8] See Section V, 5 and 6, below.

[9] See Section III, above.

[10] See paragraph 4, this section, above.

Section V

Whether another being in addition to the real being of
the actual essence is required for a thing to exist formally
and actually. The function of existence is explained.

1.   It is certain for all concerned that existence is that by which a
thing formally and intrinsically is existing in act. For, although existence is not properly and strictly a formal cause just as subsistence or
personality are not, still it is the intrinsic and formal constitutive of
its own constitute, just as personality is the intrinsic and formal constitutive of a person, be this with or without composition. For constitution is clearly more inclusive than composition as the theologians
teach more at length in part 1, q.40[1] or in 1, d.26[2] and 33.[3] But this
constitute[4] through existence, to have it indicated by one word
which all would admit, is nothing else than existing as such, even
though in this word equal obscurity persists as to what that is, unless
there be a fuller clarification of the notion or character of existing as
such. Whatever that may be, it is still certain that existing as such is
formally constituted by existence alone, and that, in this order, akin
to a formal cause, it depends on that alone. Yet this does not exclude
an existing thing, in other ways and in other classes of causes, from
depending on other things in its actual existence. And this must be
carefully considered, for some Thomists[5] seem either not to have
known this or have misrepresented it, as was touched on in the arguments for the first position[6] and as we shall see in the answers to
them.[7] However, this is evident in their position. For, if existence
and essence are distinct in reality, and if an existing being *(ens)* is
compounded of them as of an act and a potency, that composite
must depend intrinsically in the order of existing being *(ens)* on both
an essential entity and on an existential entity, although on the latter
formally and on the former materially; and[8] indeed the very existential entity must depend on an essential entity in the order of material
cause, just as, conversely, the essence depends on existence in the
order of formal cause.

2.   Again, in every opinion the existence of a created thing must depend on the existence of something, at least in the order of efficient cause. But if the existing created thing be imperfect or incomplete in the order of being *(ens),* the whole actual entity, and even the existence of such a thing, must depend on another, either as on a subject, or, as on a support, or, as on a union with another, or, as on the ultimate term of a complete entity. It is proved by induction, and this can be done by different examples, according to the different opinions. For this is the case with the humanity of Christ: its created existence both depends on the Word as on a support, and on the Incarnation as on the union by which it is joined to the Word. So too the humanity of Peter: its existence also depends on subsistence as on an ultimate term completing a substance, just as a line too, however much it may be conceived of as existing in act, can be said to depend on a point as on its term. But one example is almost beyond all question. For an accidental form brings its own existence with itself; and this existence depends naturally on a subject as on a material cause and on a union or an inherence in a subject as on a mode by whose mediation it is supported by a subject. Now (what is more certain) a material substantial form brings its own existence with itself, and this depends naturally on matter, as a material cause. But there is a general argument, for every being *(ens)* which is imperfect and incomplete in its own order can depend on another being *(ens)* either as on an intrinsic cause or as on an extrinsic cause insofar as it has been adapted to its nature. For this involves no repugnance and is otherwise consonant with the imperfection of such a being *(ens).* But if this is readily admitted in an actual essential entity, and without question, there is no reason to deny it in an existential entity, since that too can be imperfect and weak for supporting itself, as is clearly the case with every accidental existence.

THE POINT OF THE DISPUTE.

3.   From these considerations, therefore, it is rightly concluded that an actual essence as such, even though it includes existential being in its intrinsic and formal being, as was proved, still can naturally be in need of some further term, or mode or union, for it to exist *in rerum natura* either absolutely or in a connatural way. The reasoning given clearly sets this forth and confirms it, as do the examples and arguments adduced in it. Hence, the proposed question derives from this. For some [9] say that, even if the essence is a true actual being *(ens)* by its own real essential being, it still needs another further distinct actuality so that it can be. And they call this existence.

RESOLUTION [10]

4.   Nevertheless, it must be said that a real and actual essence can indeed naturally demand a mode of subsisting or of inhering in order to exist, yet it must be said that this mode or further term is not the existence of the essence itself; nor can another besides these modes or terms be thought of which would be both distinct in reality from the actual essence and be its true existence. It is readily proved by running through the individual essences and their modes. And by beginning with the more evident examples, an accidental form, besides the actual entity essential to it, includes an actual union or inherence in a subject; the mystery of the Eucharist reveals clearly enough that this is distinct in reality from the entity of an accidental form. In this mystery the actual inherence is separated and destroyed while the entity of an accident is conserved. So too the same mystery manifests that the same actual inherence is outside the essence of an accident. But this inherence is not the existential being of an accident. For who ever said this! In the sacrament of the altar a new existential being by which the consecrated accidents may exist is not created, as almost all the theologians teach. Therefore, the consecrated accidents retain the existence which they had in the bread and do not retain the inherence. Hence, the inherence is not the existence of an accident but a certain mode of it, by means of which that existence naturally depends on and is conserved by a subject. God supplies this dependence in the separated accident. It is the same, with the proportion preserved, in the material form with regard to matter, and in the matter with regard to form, as we shall say below at greater length. [11]

5.   *Substantial existence something distinct from subsistence.* But a substantial nature which exists substantially includes, besides an actual essential entity, a certain ultimate term by which it positively subsists, as we shall mention below in its place against Scotus and others. [12] Now we also suppose that this term is distinct in reality from the actual entity of the whole nature or of the substantial essence. Also we deny that this term is existence but is rather the subsistence of the nature or supposit. Although it may be that those [13] who so speak as to call this term, or subsistence, substantial existence could be differing from us only in their manner of speaking, yet there can also be a real difference, and, should it be only in expression, they are not speaking correctly. For, should they call subsistence existence itself because they truly think that the substantial essence first and formally is constituted in the being of a being *(ens)* in act and is distinguished from a possible being *(ens)* by the very subsistence as such, it is plainly false, as even the Thomists [14]

more often think, and as we shall see below in the treatment of subsistence. [15] Conviction is possible from what we have thus far said. For we have shown that that being, by which first and formally an essence is constituted within the range of a being *(ens)* in act and distinguished from a possible essence, cannot be distinct in reality from an actual essential entity. Hence, this cannot be the formal effect of subsistence, since we suppose this latter to be distinct in reality. Furthermore, just as this mode is distinct from an essential entity, so an essential entity can be conserved when such a mode is destroyed. Then it retains that whole intrinsic being by which it is constituted in such an actuality or actual entity. Thus, it is not formally and intrinsically constituted in this actuality by subsistence. The antecedent is supposed from the mystery of the Incarnation and from those remarks which we shall express below on nature and subsistence. [16] But the consequence is proved first because numerially the same constitute cannot be conserved when an intrinsic and formal constituent is destroyed, just as the same person cannot endure when personality is removed, even if the same nature endures. Secondly, the consequence is proved from something similar, for we are right in proving that the formal constituent of an accident in the order of a being *(ens)* in act is not inherence, because, when inherence is removed, numerically the same accident is conserved in the order of a being *(ens)* in act; and so it is the same in the present case. Therefore, in this sense the mode of subsisting cannot truly be said to be the existential being of a substantial nature.

6. But in another sense, one could, of course, speak accordingly: because the actual entity of a substantial essence cannot exist in *rerum natura* without such a mode, and that for this reason that being, by which an essence is intrinsically constituted a being *(ens)* in act, would not be called existential being but essential being only, for, of itself, it is not adequate to constitute the existing thing, yet it is adequate to constitute the essence of a thing. But the termination or mode of subsistence would be called existential being because it completes the entity of a thing and, when this has been posited, it is sufficient for the thing to exist. Indeed, this manner of speaking differs from our opinion in the use of terms only. For above all we maintain this point and we judge that the whole matter is contained in this, that in created beings *(ens)*, besides an actual essential entity, and a mode of existing in oneself or in another, no other existential being distinct in reality from the actual entity of essence and from the mode of existing in oneself or of inhering in another would be imagined, and this is conceded to us by that opinion when explained in that way. Yet that manner of speaking is very displeasing. First, because of the abuse of terms, because by existential being no one

understands all that without which the actual entity[17] of the thing cannot be conserved, but that by which an entity of this sort is formally constituted in the order of a being *(ens)* in act and outside its causes. Hence, although the actual entity of a substantial essence cannot be without subsistence, if by it (subsistence) it does not formally have the status of existing outside its causes, it cannot be said to exist by it. Consequently, neither can it (subsistence) be called existence.

7.   Secondly, this manner of speaking is very displeasing because otherwise the subject of an accident would have to be called the existence of an accident, because it cannot exist naturally without a subject. Indeed, matter could be called the existence of a form depending on it in being, a form could be called the existence of matter. Further, if they speak consistently, they ought to call the actual essence the existence of its own subsistence. For subsistence cannot exist without a nature which it terminates and on which it depends. Hence, if all these must be denied, only because that dependence in existing is not as on a formal constituent of an actual entity, by the same reason it must be denied that subsistence is the existence of that nature which it terminates.

8.   Thirdly, this manner of speaking is very displeasing because, at least supernaturally, an existing nature is conserved when its own subsistence is removed, as is clear in the mystery of the Incarnation. You will say it is indeed conserved without its own existence but still not without[18] some other existence, which would take the place of its own and which also will be able to be called the existence of the nature. But against this is both the fact that it is still being controverted as to whether a created nature can be conserved without any subsistence, its own as well as alien; and Cajetan, along with others,[19] holds it can; and it is probable, as we shall see later.[20] And also against this is the fact that, even though its own subsistence is removed and another is substituted in its place, the nature always remains numerically the same in the order of such an existing entity. This would not be possible if it were to exist formally by subsistence. For when a formal constituent is changed, the constituent must change.

9.   Fourthly, this manner of speaking is very displeasing because subsistence is so related to a substantial nature as is inherence to an accidental nature. For in itself and in another, taken proportionately, are opposed to one another and in their own way they have to do with the same divided thing. Hence, just as actual inherence is a mode of an existing nature, so actual perseity, which is proper subsistence, is a mode of an existing nature. Therefore, it cannot be rightly called its existence. Nor do I see what reasoning influences

those who speak in this way, except to maintain, at least in words, that existence is distinguished in reality from essence, for in fact they are accordingly thinking only of subsistence.

THE MAIN CONTENTION IS URGED.

10. It remains for us to prove the second part that chiefly concerned us, namely, that, besides an actual essential entity, and that being by which it is constituted in it, and which is not really distinguished from it, and in addition to the mode of subsistence or inherence, no other existential being distinct in reality from these is involved. But there seems to be an adequate proof of this[21] truth because every other entity or real mode is superfluous and concocted without proof. Why then must it be multiplied? The antecedent is clear because the arguments offered to prove a distinct existence of this type either prove only in regard to the subsistence in a substantial nature and in regard to inherence in a accidental nature, or they are absolutely inefficacious because they suppose I know not what eternal essential being on the part of a creature which is truly nothing at all. Therefore, those arguments would equally prove that an actual and temporal essential being is distinguished in reality from the essence of a creature, which no one can claim who has a moderate concept of what these words mean.

11. From this it is also sufficiently agreed that an entity or mode of this sort is superfluous. First, indeed, because if there were any necessity or utility for it, it could be revealed and urged by some probable argument. Secondly, what, I ask you, is the formal effect of such an entity or mode for which it was conferred by nature or by God? For, it cannot be for an essence to become an actual being *(ens)* and be constituted outside its causes; it had this formally by an actual essential being, as we have often proved. Nor also can it be for an essential entity in act to be in itself or in another; for it has these modes of being *(essendi)* from subsistence or inherence. Accordingly, what does another existence contribute? You will say, "It confers existing or formally constitutes an essence, not in the order of essence but in the order of an existent." But this is to beg the question or to use the same to declare the same. Our question is, rather: what does existing add to actual being outside of causes, bestowed by the effecting of an efficient agent, by which an essence is truly constituted in the order of a being *(ens)* in act, since we suppose that the discussion does not concern subsistence or inherence? Similarly we ask: what does *existing* add to *a being (ens) in act* outside its causes on the supposition that it does not add a subsisting being or an inhering being? Hence, since no real reason, distinct from the above-

mentioned ones, can be conceived, we conclude that a being *(ens)* in act and existing mean the same thing and the same formal aspect. And so no existential being, distinct from that being, by which each thing is constituted in the actuality of its essence, can be conceived of.

12.   From this we make a further inference that this sort of existential entity, distinct in the way mentioned, is not only superfluous but quite impossible. In the first place, indeed, because this entity is not posited as having been added extrinsically by God for some greater perfection of things but as connatural and due, as well as entirely necessary, for a thing to be outside its causes. Hence, if it is not necessary, then it is also not possible in this way because nature does not desire or demand what is superfluous. In the second place and *a priori,* because where there is no formal effect, or it is not possible, neither is the form possible. But here there is no formal effect which such an entity can grant. This is readily clear from what has been said because neither to be [22] a being *(ens)* in act nor to be in a particular way, namely, in itself or in another, can formally derive from such an entity. However, besides these formal effects, no other befitting a created being *(ens),* insofar as it is a created and existing being *(ens),* can be thought of.

13.   On this score the obvious difference between subsistence and that existence which is considered to be distinct from actual essence is perceived; for, with regard to subsistence, a formal effect can be easily revealed on account of which it is necessary. For it is not posited to constitute a substantial nature in the order of a being *(ens)* in act, but to complete and to terminate its entity, and to render it existing in itself and by itself and as self-sufficient to sustain intrinsically its own being, so that it be rendered incapable of another's subsistence or of a union to that, so that by it it is sustained in its own being. Just as, conversely, in the case of an accidental form, the quasi-formal effect, which inherence has in the essence of an accidental form, is also easily revealed. This quasi-formal effect is not to constitute that accidental form in the order of a being *(ens)* in act, but it is to unite it to something by which it may be sustained. But then as to existence, it cannot be declared what formal effect it has on essence, except to constitute it in the order of a being *(ens)* in act. Yet this effect cannot be formally and intrinsically from an existence which would be an entity distinct from the being *(ens)* itself or from the essence which is constituted in act, as was shown, and will again be shown below. [23] So, although it is easy to understand a mode distinct in reality from an actual essence, this would be subsistence or inherence, but would not be existence, and it would not be distinguished as well from subsistence or inherence as from an actual essence.

SATISFACTION GIVEN TO AN OBJECTION AGAINST
WHAT WAS STATED.

14.   But someone objects, for it seems that this whole discourse supposes that the total actuality of the essence formally derives from existence. This is false, because, within the realm of essence, an inferior grade is an actuality with respect to a superior. Form is actuality in respect to matter, not by reason of existence but by the entity of essence, even though existence is the necessary condition for actuating it. The point is more fully revealed, for man to be is one thing, and another for man to be rational or to be an animal. One has the first from existence, the second from an essential entity, and in each there is its own proportionate actuality.

15.   I answer the objection by saying that there is an equivocation on the word *actuality* or *act*. For it can be taken either as opposed to an objective potency, or as it regards a receptive potency. We speak of *actuality* in the first sense, in which it is absolutely true that every actuality of a being *(ens)* derives intrinsically and formally from an existential being, because a being *(ens)* in act is formally the same as existing. The objection, however, proceeds in the second sense, for a form is the actuality of matter as an act received in it. But a difference only according to reason is the act of a genus because it is conceived of as if it were received in it. For there cannot be a real relation of act and potency between a superior and inferior grade since they are not distinguished actually in the thing. However, a first or entitative actuality is related to a second or formal act in such a way that it is sometimes distinguished really, sometimes only in reason. For that actuality is transcendent and is shared in not only by a formal act but also by a receptive potency whose entitative actuality is really distinguished from the actuality of form. But in a form itself, to be the act of matter at least aptitudinally and to be such a being *(ens)* in act are distinguished by reason only. For by one concept the proper relation to a receptive potency is disclosed which is not disclosed by the other concept. Thus it is not only true that a being *(ens)* in act, distinguished from a being *(ens)* in potency, is formally and intrinsically constituted by an existential being, but it is also true that every formal actuality, or rather actuation, so to speak, as it derives from some partial actual essence, so it derives from some existence. For a form does not actuate matter, except as it is such an actual entity. It has this from its own existential being. On behalf of confirmation it is replied that, in reality it is the same for man to be and for man to be a man, if in both propositions being expresses an act and not a mere aptitude or a propositional truth. Similarly it is really the same for man to be man and to be rational or an animal,

etc., for all these are the same in reality. Therefore from the same actuality and from the same thing all these predicates are derived, whether that thing be called an actual essence or its actual being. Only by the precisions and compositions of reason are all these distinguished. Thus, in one thing there is not more than one being by which it is constituted a being *(ens)* in act and that very being is existential being.

Notes

[1] See Gabriel Vasquez, *In Sum. Theol.,* I, q. 40, a. 1, Disp. 158, cap. 2; II, 204ab and Suarez, *DM* 31, XIII, 10; XXVI, 301. For a list of theologians, see Suarez, *In Sum. Theol.,* I, Bk. VII, cap. III, 4; I, 694b.

[2] Gregory of Rimini, *Super Primum et Secundum Sententiarum,* I, d. 26 and 27, Reprint of 1522 edit. (St. Bonaventure, N.Y.: Franciscan Institute, 1955); fol. 127r-129v.

[3] Thomas of Argentina, *Commentaria in Quatuor Libros Sententiarum* (Venetiis, 1564), *In I Sent.,* d. 33, q. 1, a. 2.

[4] I read the *constitutum* of the 1597 Salamanca edition instead of the *constitutivum* of the Vives text.

[5] See D. Bañez, *In Sum. Theol.,* I, q. 3, a. 4, dub. 4; 153. See *DM* 31, VIII, 11; XXVI, 256-257.

[6] See Section I, 4 and 7-9, above.

[7] See *DM* 31, XII, 38; XXVI, 294 and XI, 16-20; XXVI, 276b-278a.

[8] I read the *et* of the 1597 Salamanca and 1605 Mainz editions which is deleted in the Vives text.

[9] See Capreolus citing Giles of Rome, *Def. Theol., In I Sent.,* d. 8, q. 1; I, 315a. See *DM* 31, XI, 5; XXVI, 273a and *DM* 34, IV, 1-2; XXVI, 367a.

[10] I read this heading from the 1597 Salamanca edition. It is deleted in the Vives text.

[11] See Sections VIII and X below.

[12] *DM* 34, II, 8-20; XXVI, 355-359.

[13] Suarez cites Capreolus explicitly in *DM* 34, IV, 2-3; XXVI, 367.

[14] See *DM* 34, IV, 3; XXVI, 367-368

[15] *Ibid.*

[16] *Ibid.*

[17] I read the *entitas* of the 1597 Salamanca and 1605 Mainz editions instead of the *identitas* of the Vives text.

[18] I read the *sine* of the 1597 Salamanca edition which is deleted by the Vives text.

[19] See *DM* 34, IV, 22; XXVI, 373-374.

[20] See Section XII below.

[21] I read the *hujus* of the 1597 Salamanca and 1605 Mainz editions instead of the *hujusmodi* of the Vives text.

[22] I read the *esse* of the 1597 Salamanca and 1605 Mainz editions which is deleted in the Vives text.

[23] See Section VI, 1-12.

Section VI

What distinction can occur or be conceived between an essence and created existence. The real distinction between an actual essence and existence is excluded.

1.   If the things we have said have been sufficiently proved by us, it is not difficult to conclude therefrom what must be thought in the question set forth and of the positions cited in the first section. For, first, we must say that a created essence constituted in act outside its causes is not really distinguished from existence, so that there are two distinct things or entities. In this conclusion I suppose the meaning of the terms and the distinction already set down of an essence in potency and essence in act. I also suppose that the discussion is not of subsistence or inherence but of proper existential being. Hence, the conclusion explained in this way can be proved from Aristotle who everywhere says that being *(ens)* joined to things adds nothing to them. For the being *(ens)* that is man is the same as man. But, with the same proportion, this is true of a thing in potency and in act. Thus, a being *(ens)* in act which is properly a being *(ens)* and the same as existing, adds nothing to the thing or actual essence. This is taken from the opinion of Aristotle who speaks this way in 4 *Metaph.*, c. 2,[1] bk. 5, ch. 7,[2] bk. 10, ch. 1.[3] Averroes imitates him in the same places while taking Avicenna to task.[4]

2.   But it is especially demonstrated by reason because such an entity added to an actual essence, can neither formally endow it with the first (so to speak) actuality or the first feature of a being *(ens)* in act by which it is separated and distinguished from a being *(ens)* in potency. Also, it cannot be necessary under any aspect of cause, properly or reductively, for an essence to have its own actual essential entity. Hence, by no reason can such a distinct entity be imagined. The consequence is evident from a sufficient enumeration of parts for, up to now, no other function of such an entity has been thought of nor, indeed, can it be thought of. For, the first part of the division

laid down is both admitted by all the authors, even by those who make a real distinction of existence from essence; and it is clearly evident practically from the very explanation of terms already sufficiently propounded in the suppositions laid down. For it is repugnant for an entity to be constituted in entitative being by something mutually distinct from itself.

3.   I give a further proof of this in this way: every form, really distinct from the potency which it actuates, forms one composite with it. Hence, such an act can be called a formal cause either in relation to the composite, or in relation to the potency or the other quasi-component part, if it cannot be without such an act or form. Thus, in relation to the composite, it is best and most truly said that such an act formally and intrinsically constitutes it, yet it cannot be altogether mutually distinguished from it but must be included in it and be distinguished as a part from the whole, because such an act cannot be the total entity of a composite which must include another companion-part or another component. But, indeed, if an act be compared to another thing or a potency whose act it is, it cannot intrinsically and formally constitute its proper entity because that entity is not composite but simple. Otherwise, it would not be a second component part but the whole composite, which is certainly repugnant in a real composition of distinct things. Also, that entity or the part which receives [5] act would otherwise consist of that act and some other thing. Of this other thing, I shall again ask, whether it is intrinsically and formally constituted by that act. For, if this be affirmed, we shall proceed further to infinity. But if it is denied, the intended conclusion is made, of course, that a potency, properly compounding with a really distinct act, cannot be intrinsically and formally constituted by the very act with which it composes. Thus when an ultimate analysis to the first or most simple components is made, it is necessary that that entity which is related as a potency to the other not be intrinsically and formally constituted in its entity by the other, which is act, although, perchance, it may demand it in order to be, as matter demands form. So then, if they were distinct, one would have to philosophize about an essential entity and an existential entity; for they would compose a unit, for instance, this existent, in relation to which existence would have the status of an intrinsic and formal act. Still, in relation to the essential entity it could in no way intrinsically constitute or compose it, because one would be mutually distinguished from the other as a simple entity from a simple entity. Nor can it be said that an essential entity so conceived and distinct is not actual, for, otherwise it would not make a real composition since an entity in objective potency does not make a real composition with an act. So, then, it is clearly established that an

existential entity, distinct from an essential entity, cannot be required for it to constitute intrinsically the very essential entity in its proper actuality.

4.   However, the second member of the division, namely, that such a distinct entity is not required in any other genus of cause so that the essential entity could be in *rerum natura,* is proved sufficiently (as I judge) in the above sections when we showed that, besides an actual essential being and a mode of subsistence or inherence, there is no need for another existence. Or at least let it be shown to us or be clarified what that causality is and to what genus it is referred. Some say that that entity is a necessary condition without which an essential entity cannot remain *in rerum natura.* But, in the first place, this retort which is easy to state must not be admitted not only in this but also in many other questions, unless also a sufficient reason for the necessity be given, and the mode or causality of such a condition be clarified. Otherwise, anyone could gratuitously demand a number of such conditions for some effect inasmuch as no greater reason can be given for one than for many. Since, therefore, it was shown in the above sections that there is no utility, much less necessity, for this entity to be multiplied, it is gratuitously said to be a necessary condition. And it ought to be rejected with the facility with which it was stated. Further, drawing on what has been said above, I add that, even if that entity were a necessary condition, it could not be called on that account the proper existential being of that actual essence, because it would not constitute it in the order of a being *(ens)* in act. Otherwise, every other condition or thing without which the essence itself could remain *in rerum natura* would have to be called its existence, because there is no greater reason for this than for the rest. As to this, granted that that entity is in reality a necessary condition, since it is not a formal cause of the actual essential entity, why will it not be possible, at least with regard to the absolute power, for the essential entity in its actuality to remain and be conserved *in rerum natura,* so that it be truly a being *(ens)* in act, without that entity or necessary condition which they call existence? For, with intrinsic formal causality removed, no implication can be alleged. But if God can do this, then as a consequence that actual essential entity has a proper and intrinsic actual being by which it is *in rerum natura* and outside its causes. But what else is existing than to be accordingly? Therefore, that other entity is not absolutely necessary for existing. Hence, it is truly not existence.

5.   But it can be said finally that a formal cause has a twofold relationship. One is to the composite which it constitutes. And in this way it is true that an existential entity is not a formal cause of the actual essential entity, and this latter can be called an intrinsic formal

cause because it intrinsically composes its effect. But a formal cause has another relation to the subject which it informs, because, if in informing and actuating that, it contributes to its being, it can rightly be called the formal cause of that, and in this way in natural things a form is not only the cause of the composite but also of matter. And in the same way can it be said that an existential entity is a formal cause of an essential entity, for by constituting, along with it, an existing being *(ens)*, it actuates it, and thus formally makes it remain in being. A proportional argument can be given. For just as matter is a pure potency in reference to a formal act, so the essence of a creature is a pure potency in reference to existing. For this reason, just as matter requires form in order to be, although it does not compose it but rather composes with it, so essence requires an existential entity in order to be, although it does not compose it, but composes with it. [6]

6.   And this way of answering and clarifying this position is less improbable than the rest. But it really has the same difficulties and can give no sufficient reason why that formal act is necessary, if it is not necessary in order to constitute intrinsically a being *(ens)* in act and outside its causes. So we readily[7] admit that distinction of formal cause in the good sense according to what was said on causes above.[8] Also, it is quite true that existence cannot be a formal cause intrinsically constituting an actual essential entity. Nevertheless, we conclude from this that no constitute can be designated for which such an entity would be necessary; and we logically infer that it cannot be necessary as a formal act, as if it were something coming to essence and composing something else with it. The first inference was proved in the above sections. For something intrinsically constituted by existence could not be but existing. Existing, however, and a being *(ens)* in act, that is, not in potency, are absolutely the same. Thus, if that entity is not necessary to constitute intrinsically a being *(ens)* in act, then it is not also necessary to constitute intrinsically an existing being *(ens)*. Therefore, no immediate constitute can be designated for which it would be necessary. But from this also the second inference is clear. For a form through itself is primarily for the sake of the composite and, as a consequence of this, it can be necessary for the sake of another component part, if it be the sort that could not be outside a composite. So, if there is no composite for which a distinct formal act be necessary, it cannot be necessary for a second component part.

7.   Furthermore, it is certain from this that something false was assumed in the proportion claimed in the above argument. For, although the essence of a creature, before it comes to be, could be said to be in pure objective potency on its own part, still that essence

as it is now an actual entity by the effecting of its cause, is not in itself and on its own part purely a potency in reference to being. But, intrinsically and in an absolute identity, it has some real and actual being; and this being is true existence since it formally and intrinsically constitutes an entity outside its cause. All of which was proven in the above sections. Hence, it is said without any foundation that that entity depends on another formal and distinct act in order to be. This is especially so because the arguments, by which the necessity of a distinct existence is usually proved, are all based on the following: that to be in act is not of the essence of a creature since that essence could be understood in mere objective potency on its part and effective potency on the part of the creator. Therefore, if some actual and entitative being is now supposed by which that essence is outside objective potency, there remains no reason why another formal act is required which is distinct from the first being, since even that actual being cannot be of the essence of a creature; and since an existential entity itself can be now in potency and now in act, and logically it must also be granted in its regard that it is not of its essence to exist in act nor to constitute the existing thing in act. And we will press this reasoning further when solving the arguments and turning them about in the opposite direction. [9]

8.   Moreover, the argument already made is relevant here, to the effect that at least by divine power the actual essential entity could be conserved without that other formal cause, still He can supplant the dependence of one component part on the other, even if that part is a formal act. Just as He may not be able to supplant a material cause as intrinsically composing, still He can supplant the dependence of a form or of an accident on a material cause, as was said more at length in the above sections. But if God were to conserve an actual essence without a further act of distinct existence, that entity so conserved is truly existing. As a consequence, whatever can be thought to be added to it, cannot have the true character of existence, and without cause is it said to be naturally necessary for the formal effect of existing. For the force of this argument, a mere precision by our concepts suffices. By the very fact that we understand an entity of actual essence made by God, even if we do not understand that another entity has been added to it, we sufficiently conceive it as existing. Nor do we include in this objective concept something false or self-contradictory. But from this we rightly infer that no distinct and super-added entity can be necessary for the formal effect of existing, because not even mentally can a formal effect be prescinded from a formal cause. But if that entity is not necessary to constitute this formal effect, it can neither be truly called existence nor can a probable cause be rendered why it would be necessary, as a condition or as a second and, in some way, extrinsic cause.

The modal distinction between actual essence and existence is excluded.

9.   Secondly, it must be said that existence is not distinguished from the actual essential entity as a mode distinct in reality from it. This conclusion, in my judgement, follows clearly from the preceding. So I judge that they who admit this one in the present case, while denying the first distinction, do not speak consistently. For, although in common parlance, this distinction, which is minor, could happen where the first, which is major, cannot occur, still in the present case, the arguments which prove that existence is not an entity distinct from an actual essence plainly prove that such an existence is nothing at all. Or (and this is the same thing) that, besides an actual essential entity, nothing further can be formally required for existing as such, but only for subsisting or inhering or something similar. This will easily be established by applying all the arguments already made. For we have shown that that real being, by which an actual essence is immediately and intrinsically constituted a being *(ens)* in act, cannot be distinguished in reality from that essence insofar as it is an entity in act. In addition to the arguments made above in Section III, it is easily explained in this way: for, a positive distinction in reality on the part of each term cannot occur except between two terms of which one would be the mode of the other, in such a way that the thing, as prescinded from the mode would be a positive and real being *(ens)* is act; otherwise, the distinction will be one of reason or of the sort that can be between a being *(ens)* and a non-being *(ens)*. If, then, an essence as it is a being *(ens)* in act, were distinguished in reality from that being, by which it is primarily and intrinsically constituted in such an actuality, as a thing from its mode, that very essence, precisely conceived and mutually distinct from that mode, would be a true being *(ens)* in act. Therefore, as it is such an entity, it could not be intrinsically constituted in such an actual entity by that mode or by a distinct being, but rather it would compose with it a certain third composite. For, from what are distinguished in reality as a being *(ens)* and a mode, a true real composition results. But those terms from which a real composition is produced, and into which it is reduced, must be related in such a way that one does not compose nor intrinsically constitute the other, as was explained sufficiently[10] in the beginning of the previous declaration. Therefore, such a mode, distinct in reality, cannot be the primary and intrinsic real being constituting the actual entity of the essence itself. Hence, that being by which it is so constituted, whatever it be, cannot be distinct in reality from the very actual essential entity.

10. And I confirm. An essential entity in an Angel, for instance, precisely conceived without any real mode, distinct in reality from it, is still conceived as an actual entity since it is conceived as something temporal and outside nothing, and as sufficient to make a real composition with another thing or mode added to it; this cannot be understood except in a real entity. Therefore, an essence in its own entity is not intrinsically constituted by a mode distinct in reality from it. Otherwise, it could be analyzed into another entity and that mode, and thus there will be a procession to infinity until we should stop in a simple actual entity not composed of a thing and a mode distinct in reality. This we call an essential entity and, in the case of the Angel of which we speak, it is a simple entity; it is similar in matter and form, although in their case it is a partial entity in relation to essence or nature. So, of these is composed the integral essence of a material thing which in the same proportion and arrangement does not include in its essential[11] entity any being distinct from its total self or from the matter, form and their union taken together.

11. Moreover, we have shown that the real being itself, by which an essence is primarily constituted a being *(ens)* in act, is the true existential being; therefore, from this angle it has now been sufficiently proved that such an existential being is not distinguished in reality from the actual essence. But we add further that, besides this existential being, no other being is required for the thing to exist, because that intrinsic and entitative being suffices and to it alone can be added a mode either of subsisting or of inhering; every other entity or real mode ordained only for existing is certainly invented. So we are left with the proof that not only is there not given an existence which would be an entity distinct from the essential entity but also neither is there an existence which would be a mode distinct in reality. This is confirmed by the argument also insinuated above. For, if anything would compel one to this modal distinction, it would be especially so because the essence of the creature can exist and cannot exist. But even that mode which is said to be a distinct existence can be in act and in mere objective potency because it can exist and cannot exist. Hence, even in that mode there will be a distinction in reality between it and its actual being, which is impossible. Otherwise, the same argument will occur with the existential being of that mode, and thus there will be a procession to infinity. If, then, in the case of existence itself, it can be understood that now it would be and now it would not be, without a distinction in reality, why will it not be possible to understand the same in the actual essence?

12. I know certain Thomists[12] deny that the act of being *(essendi)*, by which created essence exists, is its own being. But speaking of its being only in regard to identity or indistinction, I do not see in what

sense it can be true, For, if it is not its own being, then it has being distinct from itself. Then it will be necessary to inquire of that whether it is its own being. For if such is the case, why is not the same thing said of the first act of being *(essendi)?* But if it is not, the regress will go on to infinity, unless they would happen to say that the act of being *(essendi)* of an essence is neither its own being nor has any being, but only is that by which another is. But this is to play with words rather than to solve the difficulty. For, although existence is not said to be or exist as a supposit, which is most properly speaking, yet there is no doubt that, more generally speaking, it exists as truly as accidents exist or parts and other incomplete beings. For, if this existence is a being *(ens)* distinct in reality from essence, then it has being in the manner in which it is a being *(ens);* for a being *(ens)* is named from being. Also, such a being *(ens)* before the creation of things was only in potency, and after creation is a being *(ens)* in act. Thus, it is outside causes or *in rerum natura.* So it must have a proportioned being or be its own being. Then, even if we thus speak, namely, that existence does not exist but is that by which an essence exists, in this very statement one may consider the difference laid down, namely, that sometimes such existence constitutes the existing thing in act, sometimes only in objective potency. So also one may argue that it is not of the essence of existence to constitute an existing thing in act because in the existence in potency is conceived all that which is of the essence of created existence, even if it is not conceived to exercise in act, or to be the act of existing, or to constitute the existing thing. Nonetheless, existence according to its essential character is not distinguished in reality from itself, as it exercises in act the function of existence, so that a distinction is conceived of between two members which would be something in act. Therefore, it is the same with the existing essence or the non-existing essence. In this way all the arguments by which some others try to prove a distinction in reality between essence and created existence are plainly enfeebled and made weak in the instance or example of created existence, as is sufficiently clear from what has been said and from what we shall insist upon often in the solution of the arguments. [13] Also with this is excluded the retort of others who say that existence does not need another existence by which it may exist. For, since it is the very feature of existing for another, logically it can exist by itself. Just as action comes to be by itself, by the very fact that a termination comes to be through it, both the duration of motion endures by itself and quantity is extended by itself. But this response takes its course as if the force of the argument presented were based on the fact that the formal principle of some effect could never of itself share in that effect in some way; and we do not say this nor is it universally true as the induction made correctly proves. Hence, the argument is not based on that, but rather on this: from the fact that something may now be and may now not be, a distinction in reality between that which exists and that by which it exists cannot be concluded. But if the conclusion is not drawn from this principle, there is no other from which it can be drawn. But in the examples cited either there is not always a distinction in reality between that *by which (quo)* and that *which (quod)* as perhaps between duration and what endures; or if there is such a distinction it must be concluded from elsewhere, and it must never be admitted without sufficient evidence, as was treated above. [14]

How essence and existence are distinguished.

13. I say thirdly that in creatures existence and essence are distinguished either as a being *(ens)* in act and a being *(ens)* in potency, or, if both are taken in act, they are distinguished only by reason with some basis in reality. This distinction will suffice for us to say absolutely that it is not of the essence of a creature to exist in act. To understand this distinction and the ways of speaking based on it, it is necessary to realize (what is most certain) that no being *(ens)* except God has its own entity from itself insofar as it is a true entity. I add this to remove the equivocation in regard to an entity in potency which is truly not an entity but nothing; and it bespeaks only nonrepugnance or logical potency on the part of the creatable thing. Hence, we speak of a true actual entity, whether it be an essential entity or an existential entity. For there is no entity outside of God, except by the efficient causation of God. Wherefore, no thing outside of God has its own entity from itself, for that *from itself* includes the negation of having from another i.e., it means the sort of nature which has actual entity or rather is an actual entity, without the efficient causation of another.

14. From this it is concluded in what sense it is most truly said that to exist in act is of the essence of God, and not of the essence of a creature. For, truly, God alone by virtue of His nature, has existence in act [15] without the efficient causation of another; but a creature by virtue of its nature does not have existence in act without the efficient causation of another. Yet in this sense too, it is not of the essence of a creature to have an actual essential entity because by the mere virtue of its own nature it does not have such an actuality without the efficient causation of another. Thus every actual being by which an essence in act is separated from an essence in potency will not be said to be of the essence of a creature because it does not befit the creature of itself alone, nor does it suffice of itself to have this

being, for it must come forth from the efficient causation of another. Whence it clearly happens that, for the truth of this way of speaking, a distinction in reality between being and the thing whose being is spoken of is not necessary. It suffices that that thing does not have its own entity, or rather that it is not, nor could be that entity, unless it comes to be from another; for by that way of speaking the distinction of one from the other is not indicated, but only the condition, limitation and imperfection of such an entity, which does not have from itself the necessity to be what it is, but only has it from the influence of another.

15.   From this it further happens that our intellect, which can make precisions in what are not separated in reality, can also conceive of creatures by abstracting them from actual existence. For, since they do not exist necessarily, it is not repugnant to conceive of their natures by prescinding from efficient causation and consequently from actual existence. But at the same time they are so abstracted, they are also prescinded from an actual essential entity both because they neither have this without efficient causation nor of themselves nor of necessity, and also because an actual entity cannot be prescinded from existence as was proved above. From this mode we have of conceiving, it happens that, in a thing so conceived of by prescinding from actual entity, something would be considered as altogether intrinsic and necessary and, so to speak, the primary constitutive of that thing which is the object of such a conception. This we call the essence of a thing because without it it cannot be conceived of. The predicates which are taken from it are said to belong to it with absolute necessity and essentially, because without them, it can neither be nor be conceived of, although, in reality, they do not always belong but they do when a thing exists. From the opposing argument, we deny that the very existing in act or being an actual entity is of the essence, because it can be prescinded from the above-mentioned concept and, in fact, it cannot belong to a creature insofar as it is an object for such a concept. All these apply differently in God, for, since He, of Himself, is a necessary being *(ens),* He cannot be conceived of in the manner of a potential being *(ens)* but only of an actual one. So, being in act is truly said of His essence, because being in act necessarily belongs to Him both in the thing itself and in every true objective concept of divinity.

16.   *How the distinction of reason between essence and existence*[16] *is explained by some.* From these remarks, therefore, the whole problem for the most part is explained in brief, and from the same doctrine the single parts of the statement made can be explained and can be proved. First of all there is not one of the theologians who would not admit a distinction of reason between essence and existence although not all

explain it in the same way. Some [17] say that existence means the individual nature but essence only means the specific nature prescinded from individuals. So they say that there is a distinction of reason between them of the kind which exists between a species and individuals. But these persons are out of touch with and do not grasp the sense of the question. This question is different from that of the distinction of the specific nature from the individual, for essence can be not only specific but also individual and singular as was the essence of man in Christ, of which there is the question how it would be distinguished from its existence. Similarly existence itself can be conceived of in general and can be singular. For the existence of Peter is one thing and that of Paul is another. Thus, existence does not signify the singular thing more than does essence, nor are essence and existence distinguished as common and particular. Hence, the distinction of existence from essence is not the same as that of an individual from the specific nature. Although, by way of example or similitude that distinction could be of service to explain how a distinction of reason between existence and essence can suffice for the denial that existence in act be of the essence of the creature. For a similar distinction of reason between an individual and the species suffices for saying that the specific nature alone, and not individuation, is the total essence of a thing.

17. *The explanation of some others.* — Others [18] say that the essence and existence of a creature differ by a mere relation to God. For an essence as such is not related to God as an efficient cause but as an exemplary cause only. However, existence adds to essence a relation to God as efficient cause from which it is shared. Nevertheless, this explanation either does not make the matter clear or includes many false statements. For, in the first place, on the matter of essential being, it either talks of an actual essence or what would include the true reality of essence, or of potential essence. In the first way it would be more than false to say that the essence of a creature is not from God as from an efficient cause, as was proved above. In the second way, it is gratuitously asserted that the essences of creatures are related to God as an exemplary cause, because, truly, essences so conceived of have no cause in act since they are nothing in act. But in potency or in primary and virtual act they not only have an exemplary cause but also an efficient cause. Indeed, when causality, or the relation or application to a causing is suspended, it is said that God has rather the structures of possible things than that He has exemplars. For the former indicate only speculative knowledge, but the latter denote more a practical relation on the part of a cause. Again, the essences of creatures are not for that reason such as they are or have such a connection of essential predicates because they

are related to such structures or divine exemplars, but rather God therefore knows each possible thing in such an essence and nature because such is knowable and producible, and not otherwise. Therefore, an essence taken in this way, although it has a structure or exemplar in God, is not called an essence from that mere relation to an exemplar as such. Add also that existence, created or possible, has an exemplar in God, although not distinct from the exemplar of the essence itself. For nothing can have an efficient cause in God which would not have an exemplary cause, since God does nothing except as an intellectual agent.

18.   Furthermore, in regard to the second part about existence which they say adds to essence only a relation to God as to an efficient cause, they either think existence consists in this relation or brings this relation with itself. The first is plainly false. For the existence of an absolute [19] thing is not a relation but something absolute. Further, it is false because that relation, as it is in act *in rerum natura,* is based on or attached to an existing creature. Indeed, if it be understood to be a real predicamental relation, it presupposes the creature already produced and existing. But if the discussion be about the transcendental relation of dependence on God, this is not the existence of a creature but its causality. Whence, it is distinguished from the existence of the creature not only in reason but in reality, as was shown in Disput. 18, [20] and will be touched on again below in Disput. 48 [21]. But the second is true, namely, that the actual existence of the creature has this relation to God conjoined to itself, but still an actual essence has this same relation conjoined to itself, which cannot be the case except by the efficient causation of God. Hence essence is not rightly distinguished from existence by this relation. Besides, if existence has this relation conjoined to it, then it is something distinct from it. Therefore, as to existence itself, as distinct from such a relation, it remains to be explained how it is distinguished in reason from essence. Indeed, that is what Henry [22] says rather obscurely to the effect that it is neither really distinguished nor is it distinguished in reason alone, but is so intentionally. For what is it to be distinguished in intention except in the mind's conceiving? Finally, in that relation of a creature to God, essence can be distinguished from existence, as distinct in reason, and not by relation; this is self-evident.

19.   *The explanation of others.* Others make a distinction of reason between existential being and essential being because one is conceived in a concrete way, the other in an abstract way. So thinks Lychetus in 2, d.1, q.2, [23] where especially he says, concerning the mind of Scotus, that existential being and essential being are the same and altogether inseparable, although Scotus, there § *As concerns that*

article, does not say they are the same but that essential being is never really separated from existential being. Nevertheless, with sufficient probability this is from the mind of Scotus; for since he there says that an essence is not separable from existence and in 3, dist. 6[24] explicitly teaches that the humanity of Christ could not have been or have been assumed without a proper existence, he obviously thinks it is not distinguished in the thing itself. Hence, Lychetus, above in a marginal note, which is his gloss adds: "Essential being and existential being bespeak one and the same reality, and they are the same really and formally, and are distinguished as concrete and abstract which are distinguished only in reason." [25] Nevertheless, in this opinion it is still obscure how a distinction of concrete and abstract is relevant in this case. For, were we to speak of essence and existence, as they are signified by these names, both are conceived in an abstract way, just as matter and form or as act and potency. But the concrete will be a created being *(ens)* consisting of being and essence. Yet were we to use these names *essential being* and *existential being,* both have the same manner of signifying and are subordinated to the same way of conceiving. And sometimes, according to the use of philosophers, this expression *being,* is usually taken in the sense of an abstract name for the very act of being *(essendi),* which they also call existence. This expression is not found among the Latins, but sometimes it is taken in the sense of an infinitive which is more proper and the Latin use of that expression, and so it is not properly concrete nor abstract yet comes closer to the signification of the concrete because it signifies a formal effect of that act of being *(essendi),* indeed, the very act alone as exercising that effect, just as running and being wise and the like.

20.   From this one could take the opportunity to say that essence and being are distinguished in reason so that the former is abstract in the manner of a form, but the latter concrete, so to speak, in the manner of an exercised formal effect. But being *(ens)* would be properly concrete, as constituted of such a form and a formal effect, just as is the case with a run, running, and a running, and just as also wisdom, being wise, and a wise being are related. According to this manner of distinction, essence is properly abstract, for it is a form, so to speak, whose formal effect is being. But what is constituted through it and being is[26] the being *(ens)* itself, which constitution is not by a real composition but by identity. This manner of speaking can have a basis in Augustine, Bk. 12, *On City of God,* ch. 2, saying: "Just as *wisdom* gets its name from that which is *being wise, essence* gets its name from that which is *being.*" [27] And Bk. 2, *On Morals of Manichees,* ch. 2: "The nature itself (he says) is nothing else than what is understood to be something in its genus. Thus, as we now call

essence by a new name from that which is being which we also commonly call substance, so the ancients who did not have these names
were using the name *nature* for *essence*.." [28] Hence Calepinus, [29] citing
Augustine, says that the expression *essence* has been adopted by the
philosophers for the very being of anything whatever. But according
to this peculiarity of words, although essence and being or existing
are distinguished in reason in the above-mentioned way, still essence
and existence are not mutually distinguished in reason just as being
and existing are not mutually distinguished. For being, simply and
substantively taken, is the same as existing, as was said in the above
sections [30] and this is established from the common usage of these
words themselves because it is impossible to set forth a diversity both
in the things signified by those words and in the ultimate concepts to
which they are subordinated. So, therefore, will also essence and
existence be the same, and will differ only in names, because, just as
essence was derived by the Latins from the word *I am* and *to be,*
because by it a thing is or because it is that by which something is, so
from the verb *I exist* and *to exist* the name of existence, by which a
thing exists, is taken by the philosophers. And for the same reason it
must in consequence be asserted that essential being and existential
being, if both be properly taken for true, real being, do not differ
even in reason but only in name because essential being and existential being are so mutually related as essence and existence are mutually related. And in this way does it seem that Gabriel, in the place
cited, [31] thought of these words and concepts, where he says *being, a
being (ens), essence* do not differ according to the thing signified but only according to the grammatical modes as verb, participle and noun;
and that similarly *being* and *existing* signify the same thing, and so
also *essence* and *existence* are the same. Others of the authors cited, [32]
adopt the same manner of speaking, and the position is quite probable. It is necessary only to show some greater difference or distinction of reason between essence and existence according to the meaning given by many philosophers to these words, by reason of which it
is truly denied that existence is of the essence of a creature, because
it cannot be denied of essence itself.

21. *The thinking of others in this matter.* Thus, others [33] add that
essence and existence differ in this: that essence does not signify a
thing outside its causes, but absolutely, whereas existence signifies a
thing with being in itself and outside its causes. And Fonseca [34] rejects this manner of speaking because it does not explain what it is
for a thing to be outside its causes. For, either this is to be related to
causes, and this is not to exist, as was proved against Henry; or it is
to have received being from causes and not to have lost it and this,
indeed, is, so to speak, previous to being, but it is not properly and

formally being itself; or finally, it is for a thing not to be only objectively in an intellect or in the power of causes. This surely declares what it is not, but not what existence itself is, or how it is distinguished from essence. But an answer can be given that for a thing to be outside its causes is nothing else than to be in itself a being *(ens)* in act. But 'outside its causes' is used to make it clear that it does not have that actual entity from itself but from another. Indeed, there is a greater difficulty in that opinion, that being and non-being outside causes is common to essence and existence. For essence also is outside causes when a thing is made, just as existence, and existence was only in the potency of a cause and objectively in an intellect before the thing was made. Hence, the difference between essence and existence cannot be constituted here. Yet, to this, according to the distinction posited, we must say that it is one thing to speak of essence and existence according to the peculiarity and rigor of these expressions, but it is another to stretch the above-mentioned expressions to the same or similar meaning. For this expression *existence* does not strictly signify existence (as they say) in signified act or as conceived of and in potency only, as even Capreolus, in the place cited, indicates. [35] But, it does signify that only in exercised act, or as actual. For there is no repugnance in this state of existence being signified by some expression, and it seems that to this end the word *existence* was invented. Hence, by the very fact that the thing is abstracted from existing in exercised act, existence is not now conceived of as is signified by this word. And because this state or this exercise of existing is not of the concept of the essence of a creature, as it is signified by this word, it is for this reason right to say that existence adds to essence the act of being *(essendi)* outside its causes. Nevertheless, this state does not really differ from the actual essential entity itself. But if the name *existence* be extended to that which is only in potency or objectively, it must be acknowledged that the difference posited is not relevant. But, with proportion maintained, existence in potency is entirely identified with essence in potency and existence in act with essence in act.

22. But [36] according to this doctrine and way of distinguishing essence and existence, it plainly follows that essence is only distinguished from existence taken in the strict sense as a being *(ens)* in potency from a being *(ens)* in act. And thus it is distinguished not only in reason but also really privatively as a being *(ens)* and a non-being *(ens)* because a being *(ens)* in potency as I have said above is simply a non being *(ens)*. But the conclusion seems false because we distinguish at least in reason between essence and existence as between two real and positive extremes. You will say that, indeed, these extremes are conceived of as positive and real yet not as actual,

rather by abstracting to that extent wherein being *(ens)* abstracts from a being *(ens)* in act and a being *(ens)* in potency. But this is opposed because we conceive of essence under the proper character of essence not only as potential but also as actual. And so also we distinguish the latter in reason from existence. For when we say that a thing in act has its own essence and its own existence, we do not say the same thing twice. Hence, they are not synonymous words. So the significations of these words are distinguished at least in reason. Hence, in Christ we suppose that there are two essences and we ask whether there are two existences. In humanity there are two partial essences, namely, soul and body, and it is controverted whether there are two existences. Hence, it is necessary to add something for making this distinction of reason clear.

23. *Explanation of the author.* Therefore, it must be said that essence and existence are the same thing but that it is conceived of under the aspect of essence, insofar as by its character the thing is constituted under a particular genus and species. For essence, as we have explained above, disp.2, sect.4, [37] is that by which something is primarily constituted within the realm of real being *(ens)*, as it is distinguished from fictitious being *(ens)*. In each and every particular being *(ens)* its essence is called that by whose character it is constituted in such a grade or order of beings. As Augustine said, 12 *On City of God,* cap. 2: "The author of all essences gave more being to some and less to others and thus ordered the natures of essence in grades." [38] Under this aspect the essence is usually signified by the name of quiddity. For that is what is expressed by a definition or by some description by which we manifest what a thing is or of what nature it is. But, indeed, this same thing is conceived of under the aspect of existence insofar as it is the aspect of being *(essendi) in rerum natura* and outside its causes. For, since the essence of a creature does not necessarily have this from its own power that it be an actual entity, then when it receives its own entity, we conceive of something to be in it, which would be for it the formal character of being *(essendi)* outside its causes. That, under such an aspect, we call existence, which, although in reality it is not other than the very essential entity, is still conceived of by us under a diverse aspect and description; this suffices for a distinction of reason. But the basis for this distinction is that created things do not have being of themselves and can sometimes not be. For from this it happens that we conceive of the essence of the creature as indifferent to being or non-being in act. This indifference is not in the manner of a negative abstraction but of a precisive one. So, although the character of an essence be absolutely conceived of by us even in a being *(ens)* in potency, still much more do we understand it to be found in a being *(ens)* in act, although in

that we prescind that whole which necessarily and essentially belongs to it from the very actuality of being *(essendi)*. In this way do we conceive of essence under the aspect of essence as potency, but we conceive of existence as its act. Hence, for this reason we say that this distinction of reason has some basis in reality, which is not some actual distinction which occurs in reality. But it is the imperfection of a creature which, from the very fact that it does not have being of itself and can receive that [39] from another, affords the occasion for this conception of ours.

24.   From this the last part of the conclusion is also clear. In this expression, by the name *creature,* a real actual or actually created entity must not be understood. For, if an expression is made with this reduplication or composition, truly the creature essentially demands to exist in act in order to be a creature. In this sense, just as whiteness is of the essence of a white thing as it is a white thing, so existence is of the essence of a creature as it is a thing created in act. For it constitutes it equally or more formally than whiteness constitutes the white thing. Hence, just as whiteness is inseparable from a white thing unless a white thing is destroyed, so existence is inseparable from a creature unless the creature is destroyed. For this reason it is not rightly inferred that, if existence is of the essence of a creature taken in the way mentioned, the creature cannot be deprived of existence, because it only follows that it cannot be deprived of it unless the creature is destroyed and ceases to be. The very great truth of this is established from what was said and will be confirmed further from what is to be said. [40] Still equivocation in that expression, *of the essence,* must be guarded against. For, as I was saying in the beginning of this section, sometimes to have being of its essence means to have that from oneself and not from another, in the way that no creature, even if it be in act, has being of its essence. Nevertheless, we do not now say it that way, but insofar as that which is the prime and formal constituent of a thing is said to be of the essence, as whiteness is of the essence of a white thing as such, it does not have that by itself, however, but from another. Hence, in this way existence can be truly said to be of the essence of the creature constituted in act or created, as it is such. But when it is denied that to exist in act is of the essence of a creature, *creature* must be taken as it abstracts or prescinds from a created or creatable creature, whose essence objectively conceived abstracts from actual being or actual entity. In this way to exist in act is denied to be of its essence, because it is not included in its essential concept so prescinded. Sufficient for all these things is a distinction of reason or a real negative distinction which is between a potential essence and an actual essence.

Notes

[1] Aristotle, *Metaphysics,* IV, 2, 1003b23-35. The Vives reference to "3 Metaph." is incorrect. The 1597 Salamanca edition carries the correct one. See *Aristotelis Metaphysicorum Libri XIV* (Venetiis: Juntas, 1574), IV, c. 2; Vol. 8, 66r-67v.

[2] *Ibid.,* V, c. 7, 1017a35-1017b9. In the Juntas edition cited in n.1, above, see 116v.

[3] *Ibid.,* X, c. 2, 1054a14-19. In the Juntas edition, see X, c. 4; 257r.

[4] Averroes, *In Libros Metaphysicorum Aristotelis* (Venetiis: Juntas, 1574), IV, c. 2; Vol. 8, 67r-68v; V, c. 7; 116r-118v; X, c. 1; 257r-258v.

[5] I read the *recipit* of the 1597 Salamanca edition instead of the *incipit* of the Vives text.

[6] See *DM* 31, XIII, 5; XXVI, 299-300.

[7] I read the *facile* of the 1597 Salamanca and 1605 Mainz editions instead of the *facillime* of the Vives text.

[8] *DM* 15, VII, 1-5; XXV, 522-523.

[9] *DM* 31, XIII, 9-10 and 28; XXVI, 301 and 307.

[10] I read the *satis* of the 1597 Salamanca and 1605 Mainz edition which is deleted in the Vives text.

[11] I read the *essentiae* of the 1597 Salamanca and 1605 Mainz editions which is deleted in the Vives text.

[12] See D. Bañez, *In Sum. Theol.,* I, q. 44, a. 1 ad 4, (Salamanticae, 1584), I, col. 647 where he states: "Ad secundum probationem respondetur quod actus essendi quo essentia creata consistit, est ens per participationem et non per essentiam et non suum esse, quicquid dominus Cajetan dicat, quoniam ipse non subsistit proprie loquendo."

[13] See *DM* 31, XIII, 9-10 and 28; XXVI, 301 and 307. Also see VI, 1-12; XXVI, 241-246.

[14] See paragraph 11, this section, above.

[15] I read the *actu* of the 1597 Salamanca and 1605 Mainz editions which is deleted in the Vives text.

[16] I read the *et existentiam* of the 1597 Salamanca edition which is deleted in the Vives text.

[17] See Michael de Palacios, *In I Sent.,* d. 8, disp. 2; fol. 82vb-83rb.

[18] Henry of Ghent, *Quodlibet* I, q. 9; fol. 6v-7r.

[19] I read the *absolutae* of the 1597 Salamanca edition instead of the *absolute* of the Vives text.

[20] *DM* 18, X; XXV, 680-683.

[21] *DM* 48, II, 16-19; XXVI, 878-879.

[22] Henry of Ghent, *Quodlibet* I, q. 9; 6v-7rv.

[23] See Scotus, *Opus Oxon., In II Sent.,* d. 1, q. 2; T. 2; 66a.

[24] Scotus, *Opus Oxon., In III Sent.,* d. 6, q. 1; T. 14, 305-314.

[25] There is no such marginal gloss or note in the Vives or Wadding edition of Scotus. Earlier editions evidently carried it but the authorship of Lychetus is disclaimed. See the disclaimer of Alonso Briseño, *Celebriorum controversiarum in primum Sententiarum Joannis Scoti* (Matriti, 1638), Appendix Metaphysica; T. I, 9-10, who ascribes the gloss to Cardinal Constantius Sarnanus. Another disclaimer is to be found in B. Mastrius, *Disputationes in XII Arist. Stag. Libros Metaphysicorum* (Venetiis, 1646), Disp. VIII, q. 2, a. 4; T. 2, 123b, who exclaims "...legitur tantum in nota marginali ibidem ab aliquo rudi adjecta..."

²⁶ I read the *et esse est* of the 1597 Salamanca and 1605 Mainz editions instead of the *est esse et* of the Vives text.

²⁷ St. Augustine, *De Civitate Dei,* XII, c. 2; *PL* 41, 350. The Vives reference to "cap. 1" is incorrect.

²⁸ St. Augustine, *De Moribus Manichaeorum,* II, c. 2; *PL* 32, 1346.

²⁹ Ambrosius Calepinus, *Dictionarium Octolinguae* (Lugduni, 1663), 567a. For *ens* see 649a.

³⁰ See Section IV and esp. Section V, 11, above.

³¹ Gabriel Biel, *In III Sent.,* d. 6, q. 2, a. 1; fol. 253va-254rb.

³² See Durandus of St. Pourçain, *In I Sent.,* d. 8, q. 2; fol. 35ra-36rb; Hervaeus Natalis, *Quodlibet* 7, q.8; fol. 139rb-140rb; Alexander Achillinus, *De Elementis,* Bk. I, dub. 23; fol. 103vb-104.

³³ See P. Aureolus whom Suárez has cited according to Capreolus, *Def. Theol.,* I, 317b-320b. For Aureolus directly, see *Scriptum super Primum Sententiarum,* I, d. 8, q. 21, ed. E.M. Buytaert (St. Bonaventure, N.Y.; Franciscan Institute, 1956), Vol. II, 884 et seq. See also Gerard of Carmel as cited by Capreolus, *Def. Theol.,* I, 315b-317a.

³⁴ P. Fonseca, *In 4 Metaph.,* cap. 2, q. 4, sect. 3; col. 754.

³⁵ Capreolus, *Def. Theol., In III Sent.,* d. 1, q. 3, ad 1 Aureoli; III, 71a.

³⁶ I read the *vero* of the 1597 Salamanca edition instead of the *veram* of the Vives text.

³⁷ *DM* 2, IV, 6-7; XXV, 89.

³⁸ St. Augustine, *De Civitate Dei,* XII, c. 2; *PL* 41, 350.

³⁹ I read the *illud* of the 1597 Salamanca edition instead of the *aliud* of the Vives text. J. Gómez Cafferena, "Sentido de la composición de ser y esencia en Suárez," *Pensamiento* 15 (1959), 138 n. 12 calls attention to this reading without citing any source.

⁴⁰ See Section XII below.

Section VII

What the existence of a creature is.

1. *The opinion of some.* Now that the distinction has been presented and it is understood what essence is, it will be easy to explain what existence properly is. The explanation of this topic will further confirm the doctrine put forth. Thus certain authors so speak that they say that the existence of a creature is its accident. Avicenna says as much in Bk. 5 of his *Metaphysics* where he says that being *(ens)* is accidentally said of creatures,[1] because being signifies formally that which happens to them. St. Thomas imitates him in *Quodlib.* 2, third article, citing Comment. 5 of the *Metaphysics*.[2] Some of those who think existence is a thing or mode distinct in reality from an actual essence, consider this to be true in every respect. For they claim that existence is a certain accident belonging to a particular predicament, namely, to the predicament of When or of Quantity, of course.[3] There is a basis for these, because duration and existence are the same, for to endure seems to be nothing else than to exist. But duration is an accident of the thing which endures and is properly located in the predicament of Quantity under the species of time if the duration be successive, or in the predicament of When if it be of another sort.

2. *It is rejected.* But this opinion is rejected by almost all the Doctors, for being is as equally unrestricted as being *(ens)* itself, since being *(ens)* is said from being. Hence, just as being *(ens)* does not belong to a particular genus but transcends all the predicaments, so being equally transcends them. In addition, it is rejected because of itself it is unbelievable that the existence of a substance is a proper accident. In the first place, this is so, for otherwise it would not be being simply, but relatively. Hence, also, the generation of a substance would not be generation simply but relatively, because it would be terminated to a certain accident. For it is terminated to being, as is said in the 5th Bk. of *Physics,* Chapt. 1.[4] Secondly, for the reason that if existence were an accident, it must be either a common or a proper accident. Not the first, because a common accident can be absent without the corruption of the subject and comes from without to a pre-existing subject. Nor can it also be a proper accident, because the proper accident is consequent on, and results from, an already existing thing. So it does not primarily and directly come to be by generation or creation, but results from the thing produced by generation or creation. Thirdly, for the reason that otherwise existence would have to be inhering in a subject and dependent upon it, hence it would be necessary to suppose that subject as existing. The fourth reason is that an act must be proportioned to a potency, but substantial essence, especially according to this opinion, is in substantial potency to be actuated by existence. Hence, existence cannot be an accident but rather its substantial act. The final reason is that otherwise every existing substantial essence would be an accidental unit and not a substantial one, which is utterly absurd. And these arguments prove also that the existence of each and every accident cannot be a thing belonging to another predicament but that the existence of quantity shares the same character of quantity, since it has extension essentially proportioned to quantity and essentially pertains to the completion of the formal effect of quantity which is to be so much. And it is the same, with the proportion maintained, in quality and in the others. But as to duration, either it must be denied that in reality it is altogether the same as existence, or, if they are altogether the same, it must be denied that in reality duration is an accident save only according to a certain mode of our predication or denomination which would suffice to distinguish the predicaments. Of this we shall speak below[5] when treating the predicaments.

3. *The position to be taken.* Therefore, those who have a better opinion, even with a distinction of essence from existence supposed, say that existence is a certain act or termination of the essence of the same predicament with it, even though it is not located in it directly but reductively. Such is taken from St. Thomas, quest. 5 *On Power of*

God, art. 4, ad 3 [6] and at length from Capreolus, in 1, dist. 8, quest. 1, conclus. 3 [7] and from Cajetan, *On Being and Essence,* cap. 4 just before q.6 [8] and cap.5, quest. 10, to 8. [9] This opinion, with the distinction supposed, can be easily defended. For the objection some raise that, if existence has a proper entity or mode of being *(ens)* there is no reason why it is not a complete being *(ens)* or why it is not directly located in some genus, this objection (I say) is easily dispatched. And in a similar question it must of necessity be solved by all. For, otherwise it would equally prove that subsistence is an accidental mode directly set up in some predicament and that the mode of inherence sets up its own predicament also. Hence, it must be said in this opinion that existence is not a complete being *(ens)* because it is essentially ordained to be the act of an essence which constitutes with it a substantial unit. And for the same reason it must be said that existence belongs to the same genus with essence, yet not directly but by reduction. For, existence is in the manner of a part or act of the same genus and of something composing a substantial unit with it. So, against the above-mentioned distinction of essence and existence, we have not used this kind of argument that existence either is or is not an accident.

4. *The objection is answered.* It could only be objected that when something is reduced to some predicament as a constitutive act, it is at least necessary that the very thing constituted be directly located in such a predicament. But the existing thing, as existing, is not located in some predicament because the list of predicaments abstracts from actual existence. For things are located in a predicament only according to those predicates which necessarily or essentially belong to them. Hence, existence cannot belong to a predicament even reductively; thus we can also argue from the contrary. For complete things are set up in a predicament according to the total fullness which they have in their genus. But they are not set up as they are existing, hence, existence does not belong to their fullness. Therefore, it will be an accident of theirs and will not make a substantial unit with them but an accidental unit. For what makes a substantial unit belongs to the fullness of that being *(ens)* which it constitutes. Some say (perhaps to avoid these and similar arguments) that the existence corresponding to the essence of each and every predicament is not so much reduced to that predicament as it is beyond every predicament, and it is shared in by each and every predicament as something more perfect than every thing and every essence located in a predicament. But I think that existence as exercised in act is not properly located in a predicament, not on account of its excellence, of which we shall speak below, [10] but because such an existence is not properly other than potential existence or exis-

tence conceived of in designated act which is located in a predicament. As it is in act, it signifies a certain state not at all related necessarily to the list of predicaments.

5.   Thus, the arguments presented rightly explain how actual existence cannot add a thing or a real mode beyond the whole individual essential entity insofar as it is a created substance both entirely complete and directly located in the predicament of substance under the last species. The reason is that singular things alone exist essentially and primarily. Thus, the thing existing in act adds no reality beyond the whole individual substance located in a predicament. The consequence is clear because that thing neither is an accident, as was proved, nor is a partial or incomplete substance. Otherwise it would further complete the substance to which it would be joined. This is impossible because substance was taken to be complete in every way in its genus, and as such located in the predicament of substance. Hence, it must be said that an existing substance is located in the predicament of substance. Still, because to be located in a predicament is not something real but of reason, for this reason it must be said that it does not need actual existence exercised in act to be located in a predicament. Yet, nevertheless, it must be said that it is located insofar as it is something existing in designated act or as existing possibly. From this it necessarily follows that existing in act itself does not add a new thing or new mode beyond that whole substance as possibly existing, so that there would be an addition of one thing or actual mode beyond another actual thing. But rather it adds (so to speak) the whole substances itself. For, when it was only in potency it was nothing and when it is in act the whole substance is something.

6.   From this it also comes about that existence could not be some incomplete being *(ens)* such that it be distinct in reality from another real and actual being *(ens)*, of which it would be the mode or act and with which it would compose one complete being *(ens)*. For, every composite or complete created being *(ens)* can be conceived of with its total fullness and its every mode, as prescinding from the actual exercise of existence or as including it in possible being or in designated act. Hence, because the Doctors cited call existence in this sense an incomplete substance and the mode or act of a substance, for this reason this opinion[11] of theirs is not proved to us. But if they were speaking only according to the metaphysical abstraction of reason, then it could very well be conceded that existence, as we conceive of it to be distinct in reason from essence, is something incomplete and that it is conceived as a mode or act of an essence. Just so do we call incomplete beings *(ens)*, the differences by which a genus is contracted or the "thisness" *(haecceitas)* by which a species is limited

to the being of an individual, and the modes by which being *(ens)* is limited to its inferiors, all of which are distinguished, not really but in reason, from the things which they contract or constitute. Truly many authors cited from the second position in only this sense say that existence is a mode of essence. Fonseca, [12] who compares this mode with the modes determining being *(ens)* to the highest genera has especially explained this, only differs from us in that he calls a distinction of this sort a formal distinction and distinction in reality. But we call it only a distinction of reason with a foundation in reality. Fonseca cites for his position Alexander of Alexandria, 7 *Metaphys.*, text. 22 where in the last small question [13] he explicitly treats the present question and expressly teaches our opinion and he explains it better and more clearly than the rest of the authors.

7.   *In what sense existence is said contingently of the creature.* According to this same sense, an explanation must be given of what is sometimes said by serious authors, namely, that existence or existing is said of creatures contingently or accidentally. For it is said contingently of a creature absolutely taken, because of itself it prescinds from this, that it be created or only creatable. The name of creature in this expression, as I have said, must be accepted in this realm. For, if a creature be taken only for the thing created in act, being does not belong to it, such as it is, contingently, but necessarily. But that necessity is not absolute but conditioned according to what Aristotle has said: "a thing when it is, is necessarily." [14] But existing is said accidentally of the creature, not according to the thing which is predicated but according to the form of a predication because existing or nonexisting can belong to the creature conceived of in itself, although, when it does not exist, then, indeed, it is not a creature except only objectively or rather as creatable. But this contingent or accidental predication is not the sign of a real distinction or distinction in reality between an actual essence and existence. For predications come about according to the mode of our conceiving and, thus, when it is said that existing is predicated contingently of the essence of a creature, an essence is not conceived as actual. Just so also, a difference dividing a genus is said to be predicated accidentally of that, and similarly individuation is predicated of the species. It could be said to belong to it contingently, although, in the thing itself, the individual is not distinguished from the species or difference from genus, because our mode of conceiving and prescinding suffices for these expressions.

8.   *Why Aristotle wished that the question "Whether a thing is" be distinct from the question "What is it".* And from this, by the way, one understands how Aristotle distinguished the twofold question about things, namely, whether they are and what they are. [15] From this

some conclude that he had distinguished existence which is at issue in the question, "whether it is", from the essence which is sought by the question, "what it is". But this is no conclusion, for Aristotle has distinguished these questions not only in created being *(ens)* but in being *(ens)* simply. And we distinctly ask of God whether He is and what [16] is He. Hence, for this a distinction of reason suffices. But there is a difference in this regard between God and creatures because in God these questions are distinguished only according to our way of conceiving of the relation or connection of the predicate with the subject, namely, confusedly or distinctly. For we sometimes conceive of some predicate to belong to some subject by not distinctly conceiving how it may belong: whether essentially and primarily, or secondarily, or accidentally. And so of God Himself we can first come to know that He is, and then question how being may belong to Him and whether it is of His essence. And, for this reason, we distinguish the questions, whether God is, and, what God is, although in reality being itself is of the quiddity of God. But then in creatures the basis for distinguishing these questions is greater if the question, whether it is, be about actual existence. For the meaning of the question, whether a thing is, can be twofold. On the one hand, we can ask whether it actually exists, while on the other hand, whether it is true real being *(ens)* which could be. In this second sense the question, whether it is, truly does not differ from the question, what is it, except as a common query from a particular one. For, being taken in potency, being *(ens)* insofar as it signifies that which is able to be, is an essential predicate or of the quiddity of a creature, as was demonstrated in the above sections, [17] even though, because it is transcendent, it is not posited in the definition of things, as Aristotle said in 8 *Metaphys.* text.15, [18] because it is included in all genera as well as differences. So, when being *(ens)* is taken in this way, the question, whether it is, in which the precise character of being *(ens)* is included, is distinguished from the question, what is a thing, in which the proper essence and definition of a thing is sought. But the question, whether a thing is, can be understood in another sense, of actual existence. So with a much greater reason, based in some way on the thing itself, the question, whether it is, is distinguished from the question, what is a created thing, namely, because existing in act, absolutely speaking, does not concern the quiddity of a creature. Nevertheless, just as this is true without a distinction in reality between existence and an actual essence, so also those questions can be justly distinguished without a distinction of realities.

Notes

[1] Avicenna, *Opera Philosophica* (Venice, 1508), *Metaphysica,* Bk. 5, c. 1; fol. 87rb (Louvain: Edition de la Bibliothéque S.J., 1961).

[2] *Quaestiones Quodlibetales,* ed. Spiazzi, q. 2, a. 1; 24.

[3] John of St. Thomas cites the same doctrine and names Molina. See *Philosophia Naturalis,* ed. B. Reiser (Turin: Marietti, 1933), I, q. 7, a. 4; T. 2, 115.

[4] Aristotle, *Physics,* V, 1, 224b9.

[5] See *DM* 50, I-II; XXVI, 912-922; 50, XII, 13-15; XXVI, 969.

[6] *De Potentia,* ed. Pession, q. 5, a. 4; II, 139.

[7] Capreolus, *Def. Theol., In I Sent.,* d. 8, q.1; I, 321b.

[8] *In De Ente...,* cap. 4, q. 5; 88-89. The Vives reference to "just before question five" is incorrect. The 1597 Salamanca edition reads correctly, *proxime ante q. 6.*

[9] *Ibid.,* cap. 5, q. 10 ad 8; 159.

[10] *DM* 31, XIII, 21-23; XXVI, 305-306.

[11] I read the *sententia* of the 1597 Salamanca and 1605 Mainz editions instead of the *substantia* of the Vives text.

[12] *In 4 Metaph.,* c. 2, q. 4; col. 755-758.

[13] Alexander of Alexandria, *In 7 Metaph.,* text 22; 207vaD.

[14] *On Interpretation,* c. 9, 19a23.

[15] *Posterior Analytics,* II, 1, 89b25.

[16] I read the *quid* of the 1597 Salamanca and 1605 Mainz editions instead of the *quod* of the Vives text.

[17] See *DM* 31, II, 10; XXVI, 232; *DM* 2, IV, 13-15; XXV, 91-92.

[18] *Metaphysics,* VIII, 6, 1045b1-7. The Vives reference to "text 19" seems in error; the 1597 Salamanca edition also carries it. See Juntas edition, (Venetiis, 1562), 224r, where it is text 15.

Section VIII

What causes, mainly intrinsic, created existence has.

1.   Although the nature of existence and its identity with actual essence seems sufficiently explained and proven from what has been said,[1] still for the completion of this matter and the greater confirmation of its truth and for the solution of the bases of the other opinions set forth in the first section,[2] we must treat with precision many other matters which can be looked into and desired concerning created existence. Among these a knowledge of the causes, which we investigate here, holds first place.

2.   In this matter, all philosophers, especially Catholics, agree on this, that every being or existing outside God needs an extrinsic efficient cause and, consequently, a final cause. For an efficient agent, is not essentially operative except on account of an end. Nor is it necessary, even according to Aristotle, to distinguish in this case between corruptible and incorruptible being, material or immaterial. Whatever it may be, if it is not divine, it necessarily has come to be, even according to the mind of Aristotle, as we have shown above, in treating of causes and the first being.[3] From what was said there[4] it is also established that this efficient cause of created being itself must be God, either alone or with another. For, since He alone has being of Himself, others cannot have it except as shared from Him and consequently by His effecting. St. Thomas explains this argument at length in q.3, *On Power of God,* art.5,[5] following Aristotle, 2 *Metaph.,* cap.1,[6] and Avicenna, Bk.8, *Metaph.,* c.7[7] and Bk.9, c.4.[8] Hence, on this, all agree. But they disagree on the other causes, namely, material, formal, and proximate efficient. And the disagreement arises from the already treated diversity of opinions about the distinction of existence from essence.

On the material cause of existence.

3.   Therefore, in regard to material cause, those who[9] think that existence is really distinguished from actual essence, assign some material cause to it, not understood, of course, as corporeal or quantified matter, but generally for a receiving subject and contributing in that way to the coming to be and being of something. For, in this way, they say that essence is a proper recipient of existence outside of which it can neither become nor be. But should you object that then it happens that the existence of nothing is created by God, because the cooperation of a material cause is repugnant to creation, they reply that, indeed, it is not created but it is concreated in the creation of the existing supposit. In this way, it is not repugnant for something incomplete and quasi-partial to come into being, or rather, to be co-produced with the concursus of a material cause. For, this is the way the form of the heaven is concreated. But, surely, with the removal of a distinction in reality between existence and essence, this material causality is not necessary for the effecting of existence. Where there is no distinction, there cannot be a true and real subjective potency as recipient and a received act, and consequently, neither can there be true concursus of a material cause. Nor is a metaphysical distinction[10] of act and potency distinct in reason sufficient for this, because material causality is physical and real. For this reason no one has ever said that a difference comes to be from a genus as from a material cause, or something similar.

4.   Nor, absolutely speaking, can that type of causality be adequately understood, because it cannot be attributed to an essence as considered in mere objective potency. For thus, as I have often said,[11] it is simply a non-being *(ens)* and nothing. But what is nothing, according to this prescinded state cannot have real influence, nor receive something, nor can another adhere to it. For how will it adhere to that which is nothing?[12] Nor can that causality be ascribed to the essence as already produced and constituted in the order of a being *(ens)* in act. For, as such, in itself, as receptive or as mutually distinguished from a second act, it intimately contains some actual being outside causes. This possesses the whole essential character of existence, as we have proved above.[13] Hence, in respect to this, an essence cannot be related as a recipient potency because an act which is received in a potency is not intrinsically contained in the potency itself or in the entity which it requires in order to be receptive, as was also made sufficiently clear in the above sections.[14] Therefore, created existence, as such, does not require this type of causality on the part of the essence. Hence, since one essence has but one existence, as we have also proved above,[15] no created existence requires this causality on the part of the essence.

5.   Consequently, some existence can only require a material cause when an actual essence has called for it. For, since they are really the same, it is necessary that they arise from the same physical causes. So it happens that the existence of immaterial substances has no material cause. But the existence of material substances has one, in the way in which their essence has one. Hence, if the discussion be about a complete substance, its being has a material cause composing it intrinsically. But the being of the material form similarly has a material cause, not composing it, of course, for that is always simple and partial, but supporting and receiving it. In this way, too, every being of the accidental form, be it spiritual or material, by its own nature possesses a material cause by which it may be supported. But the being of a substantial spiritual form, of the kind that only the rational soul is, does not have a material cause, not because that being is a complete existence, as some say. [16] For if existence is not a thing other than essence, since the essence of a rational soul is not complete in the order of substance, neither can its existence be complete. But the reason it has no material cause is that that being is spiritual and hence independent from matter. Since in other respects it is substantial, it is both independent from a subject and by its nature apt to subsist with at least an incomplete subsistence. Finally, the being of matter itself has no proper material cause just as neither can matter itself have a material cause, since it is the primary subject.

On the formal cause of existence.

6.   On the other hand, the formal cause of existence must be discussed. On this point, almost all [17] who distinguish in reality existence from essence, say the form is a formal cause of existence. They think that this is the opinion of Aristotle in 5 *Metaph.,* cap. 8, text 15, when he says: "There is another substance in things which is the cause of existence as the soul in the animal;" [18] and in 2 *On Soul,* c.4, text 36, where he says that the soul is the cause of being itself or why it is an animal; [19] and in 2 *Phys.,* c.1, text 12, he says that a thing is in potency through matter and is in act through form; [20] and Boethius in the *Book on Unity and One* says that every being flows from form. [21] St. Thomas, too, often says as much as in part 1, quest. 48, a.1; [22] 2 *Against the Gentiles,* c.54 [23] and 55; [24] the Commentator in 2 *Phys.,* text 12 [25] and in 2 *On Soul,* text 8 [26] and in the same place Themistius, cap. 1 and 6 of his *Paraphrase.* [27] Finally this axiom is such a commonplace among philosophers that it does not seem to be able to be denied in the least. For a thing is constituted in act by a form, and every act is from a form. But existence is the supreme act. Further, generation is

the change from non-being to being. But generation is toward form. Hence, being also is from a form. Indeed, for this reason, generation is toward being because it is toward the effect of form. But other authors[28] use a distinction, for being is twofold. The one they call entitative, the other formal. They say that the latter is from a form and thus they understand the references made to Aristotle.[29] Yet they deny that the former is always from a form, because matter has its own proper existence which it does not have from a form.

7. However, though I myself judge that the latter position is true in the sense in which it is presented by the authors, still, I think that, in a true and proper sense, it must be said simply and without distinction that every being either is of a form or from a form in its own order of cause. In order to make this clear, I assume that the question concerns the substantial existential being, for it is certain that accidental being, in relation to a subject or a whole composite, is from the accidental form. For, in regard to the form itself, such being is not properly from it by a proper and real causality. In reality, such being is the form itself; and in it there is the same order and relationship concerning substantial form, as we shall say.[30] Next, I assume that the discussion concerns being in material substances. For in spiritual substances there is properly no substantial form which could have formal causality. For, although these substances are usually called subsistent forms, they do not get their name because they are[31] informing forms but because they are perfect essences, with a perfect and complete essential being as a result of their formal differences. Hence, in these substances, existence does not have a physical formal cause. But whether it can be said that being issues formally from that very essence, will be established from what is to be said.[32] On the other hand, one can understand in four ways that a form is the cause of the total existence in material causes. The first is because a form formally completes the proper recipient of existence. The second is because existence results from form as from an intrinsic formal principle. The third is because form intrinsically composes the existence of a whole substance in the manner of an act. The fourth is because every substantial being in some way depends on a form.

8. Therefore, those who think that existence is some simple entity really distinct from matter, and from form, and from the nature composed of both, do not say, nor can they say, that a form is the formal cause of existence in the third way cited above. Nor can they say also that existence is the primary formal effect of a form, not only because such an effect is inseparable from an informing form, yet, in their position, existence is separable, as in the case of the humanity of Christ; but also because this effect must necessarily be in some

way composed of the form itself and include it intrinsically. Hence, it cannot be distinguished from it as a simple entity from a simple entity, but as whole from part. So they say that essential being or the constitution of an essence is the primary effect of a form, but that existence is a secondary effect, in the second of the first two ways cited above. The first of these is more accepted among the Thomists, as is clear from Capreolus, 1, dist. 8, quest.1, art.3 to 3 Henr.,[33] and to 3 Gerard[34] against the first conclusion; and from Soncinas, 7 *Metaph.,* quest.22[35] especially in the solution to the arguments; and from Cajetan in the references cited above in *On Being & Essence*[36] where he compares form and existence to diaphaneity, or clearness, and to light, for by diaphaneity air is formally constituted in its character of being immediately receptive to light. In this way form completes the essence in an order immediately receptive to existence. This is immediately received in the whole essence and not in the form alone, and this is what they understand when the form is material and inexistent. For, if it be spiritual and subsistent, as a rational soul, the nature first receives a proper existence in itself and then communicates it to the whole composite. Hence, such a form not only completes the recipient of existence, but also it is itself the primary recipient of existence according to the mind of St. Thomas, 1 p., quest.76, art.4[37] and in *On Being and Essence,* cap.5[38] at the end where Cajetan[39] defends it at length. This is how it happens that angelic forms by themselves are much more receptive of existence.
9.   Nevertheless, this manner of speaking does not really explain formal causality but rather the material causality of the form in relation to existence. For, to be receptive of existence is not to be its formal cause but rather its material cause. Hence, what completes a recipient of existence, even if it completes it formally, cannot be called the formal cause of existence. Likewise, a rational soul or an angelic essence, by reason of the fact that of itself it is receptive of its own existence, is not called its formal cause. Therefore, much less can a lesser form, by reason of the fact that it may be a part of the essence receptive of existence and formally completing it, be called it formal cause. Besides, who ever said that quantity is a formal cause of all material qualities by reason of the fact that it would formally constitute their proximate recipient? Or who ever said that clearness or light is the formal cause of the sensible species whose proximate recipient it constitutes? In these examples and in countless others which could be presented, a form which constitutes a recipient is reduced either as a proximate recipient potency or as a disposition to a material cause. Consequently, this is what has to be said in the present case, and although this could appear to be focusing on a manner of speaking, still it is quite important for explaining the

matter. For at this point it is established that this manner of causing existence is no different than the preceding with regard to a material cause, and consequently, that it is no more possible or true than the preceding. Hence, from the argument by which we showed that an essence cannot be the material cause of existence, one can conclude that form cannot be its cause in this manner. It happens that what is assumed in this type of causality, namely, that form, with a natural priority, in the thing itself, is united to matter, and that it has in the thing itself its own primary formal effect before it would have existence. This is as unintelligible as that a thing would be or conceived of to be *in rerum natura* when existence has been prescinded, of which I shall speak again later.[40] Finally, although we might grant that form is related in this way[41] to the integral existence of the whole essence, still up to now it has not been proved that a partial existence cannot be granted or any part of the essence cannot be by itself receptive to its own accommodated existence. Just by itself it is capable of its own proper essential being and its own proper actuality. For this reason, then, I think it is false for a form to be a formal cause of existence in that first way.

10.   Therefore, some other Thomists[42] also add a second way which they insist is true for no other reason than that, since being inseparably accompanies form, it is consonant with reason that being emanate from it. But the arguments made against the preceding can be more forcefully directed against this second way. First, because this type of cause is not formal but efficient. Likewise, even though passions flow from the form, it is not their formal cause, but efficient. Similarly, a substantial nature, even though subsistence may result from it, is not its formal cause but its efficient cause by natural emanation; and it is the same in all similar cases. Second, from this it is more clearly established that it is impossible for a created essence, being understood to be naturally prior to the existence provided, to be understood to have a sufficient being for this type of causality. For, conceived of in this way, either it is being *(ens)* in potency, and thus it cannot be an efficient principle nor reduce itself to act; or it is conceived of as a being *(ens)* in act and thus it is already conceived of as including an actual being outside causes, which is existential being. Finally, St. Thomas in 1, *Against the Gentiles,* cap. 22[43] and in other places,[44] and all his disciples,[45] professedly prove that a creature cannot be an efficient cause of its own existence. The arguments of these men, if they were carefully weighed, prove as well of every efficient causality, even by way of natural emanation because even this type of causing supposes existence in its principle. So it is no less repugnant that the same thing be the cause of itself in this way than by proper action and by essential effecting. Finally, although we

should admit this type of emanation of existence from actual essence, by no means has it thus far been proved that a proper and accommodated partial existence cannot emanate from some partial essence.

11.   Therefore, due to some of these reasons some Thomists[46] now deny absolutely that a form is a formal or an efficient cause of existence; this is because neither of those two types are approved by them, nor are the other two, posited by us, pertinent when the real distinction of existence from essence is supposed, which distinction they defend. But when the contrary opinion is supposed, it is very well said, and logically, that form formally constitutes and intrinsically composes the existence of a nature or supposit consisting of matter and form, because it formally completes and composes its actual essence and its total entity. To make the expressions formal, it is necessary to distinguish in reason essence from existence in the form itself. For when form is said to compose existence in this way, it must not be understood of the form's essence precisely conceived, for as such, it causes nothing in act but it is conceived of as being able to cause. Therefore, it must be understood of the essence of an actual form and inasmuch as it is its very own existence. In this way it is easily established how form is a cause, in its own order, of the total existence of natural things. On this matter, the sayings of Aristotle[47] and other authors[48] could be suitably explained, for only this existence is simply being, about which they speak.

12.   *Whether form causes the existence of matter.* However, a form cannot, in this way, be a formal cause of the proper and intrinsic existence of matter, because it is not a part of that matter. Nor does it compose that intrinsically in its actual entity and essence in which existence must be included, as was shown above.[49] But, nevertheless, a form is in some way a formal cause of the existence of matter, because, for matter to be, it needs informing by a form, and it depends on it in the way explained above in *Disp.* 15[50] and 18.[51] So there is no existential being in the composite, neither integral nor partial, which would not be either the being of a form itself or would not depend in some way on a form. For the very partial being of a form does not depend on it in the order of a formal cause, because it is not a formal cause of itself, speaking physically and according to the propriety of a formal cause. So I have not said absolutely that every being derives from a formal cause, but that it is either the being of the form itself or depends on it as upon a formal cause. Metaphysically, though, or according to reason, a form can be called a formal principle of its own proper existence, because by itself or by its own entity it formally has that, even though it has it from another as an efficient cause; in this way also angelic forms exist by their own formal entity. And

according to these points, we can interpret also the evidence generally brought out above. [52]

13. *Justice is done to an objection.* You will say, "Consequently, also
every existence of a material substance either is of matter or is from
matter in its order of cause. Hence, there is no reason why this is
properly ascribed to form." An answer is given by conceding the first
consequence, understood formally of the existence of a material substance, as such, or of material existence. The reason I add this is
that, although the existence alone of a rational soul does not depend
on matter, still it is not a material substance. Insofar as it is a form of
matter, it also depends on it in regard to actual union. But the being
of the total composite is intrinsically composed of the being of matter, and the being of all other forms depends on matter. In this way
is matter a cause in its own order of every existence of a material
substance. But still, the second consequence is denied. For being is
ascribed to form for a special reason because it is an act completing
and perfecting being absolutely. In the same way, also essence or
essential being is especially ascribed to form, even though matter is
also a part of the essence. For form is what completes an essence and
what determines matter so that it is a part of this essence, since of itself it is indifferent to being a part of this or another nature. Further,
if Aristotle be read carefully in the reference given, in 2 *On Soul,* [53] he
speaks more clearly of essential being than of existential being. For,
when he said that the soul is the cause [54] of the being of living things,
he adds, "But living is the being of living things." [55] But it is agreed
upon that living in primary and basic act (and the discussion is
about this in that place) is the essential being of living things. It is
agreed upon also that a body is the material cause of the life of living
things. Hence, living is ascribed to the soul itself because it completes it and distinguishes it from other being, not because it excludes the cooperation of the material cause. Consequently, the
same must be said, even if by being we understand existing, and I do
not deny that Aristotle understood this. Further, I conclude from
this reference, that, according to Aristotle's opinion, actual essential
being and existential being are really the same. For Aristotle speaks
only of being in act, as St. Thomas [56] and all explain, [57] and this is
obviously the same as existing, and yet he says that living in living
things is this sort of being which is essential to the very living thing.

14. *Whether essence is a final cause of existence.* But finally, someone will
object. For, from what has been said it follows that essence is in no
way the cause of an existence proper and adequate to itself, by which
it immediately and formally exists. We have excluded every feature
of an intrinsic cause and yet it is agreed also that being cannot be an
extrinsic cause. To this some Thomists [58] grant that essence is not a

formal cause nor an efficient nor final cause of existence. But they except material cause. In this instance, they speak logically, given the distinction they maintain, but they do not speak logically in those arguments they use for excluding the order of efficient cause, because even essence, for it to be a truly recipient cause, requires actual essential being. Next, I do not see why they exclude final cause, since existence is for nothing else but to constitute the essence *in rerum natura.* Hence, these very persons say that existence is not a being *(ens)* because it is not that which is, but it is that by which an essence is. Hence, it is (if I may say so) a being *(ens)* of a being *(ens)* and, as a result, it is because of that, namely, because of an essence at least as existing. But in the principle posited by us, [59] it must be granted, of course, that essence does not have true real causality in regard to its own existence. For, where there is no real distinction, there can be no real causality. Nor is this anything improper, for there is no necessity for the existence of a creature to have an intrinsic principle in it except insofar as the essence itself can have such a principle, namely, matter or form. But it is enough that it be from an extrinsic efficient cause. This alone remains to be discussed, and in the following section we shall present the matter so as to move forward with greater clarity.

Notes

[1] See Sections II-VII above.

[2] See Section I above.

[3] *DM* 20, I, 24-26; XXV, 751b-753a.

[4] *DM* 20, II-III; XXV, 754-769.

[5] St. Thomas, *De Potentia,* ed. Pession, q. 3, a. 5; II, 48-49.

[6] Aristotle, *Metaphysics,* II, 1, 993b23-30.

[7] Avicenna, *Metaphysica,* Bk. 8, c. 7; fol. 100v-101v.

[8] *Ibid.,* Bk. 9, c. 4; fol. 104v-105r.

[9] See Section III, 5 above, esp. nn. 17-18. Also see D. Bañez, *In Sum. Theol.,* I, q. 3, a. 4, dub. 4; 153-154. J. Urraburu, S.J., *Ontologia* (Rome, 1891), 741, n.1 lists Dominic of Flandria and Blasius a Conceptione along with Bañez.

[10] I read the *distinctio* of the 1597 Salmanca and 1605 Mainz editions instead of the *constitutio* of the Vives text.

[11] See Sections II-III above.

[12] See Section III, 5 above.

[13] See Section IV above.

[14] See Sections III-IV above.

[15] See Section V, 15 and Section VI above.

[16] See *DM* 14, XIV, 1-12; XXV, 455-459.

[17] See *DM* 15, VIII, 2; XXV, 525.

[18] Aristotle, *Metaphysics,* V, 8 1017b15.

[19] Aristotle, *De Anima,* II, 4, 415b8.

[20] Aristotle, *Physics,* II, 1, 193a10-193b8.

[21] Boethius, *Liber de Unitate et Uno, PL* 63, 1075. This is a spurious work. See P. Glorieux, "Pour Revaloriser Migne," *Melange de Science Religieuse* (1952) Cahier Supplementaire, 43 and M. Alonso, S.J., "El Liber 'De Unitate et Uno'," *Pensamiento* 12 (1956), 179-202.

[22] *Sum. Theol.,* I, q. 48, a. 1; T. 4, 490-491.

[23] *Sum. Cont. Gent.,* II, 54; T. 13, 392.

[24] *Sum. Cont. Gent.,* II, 55; T. 13, 393-395.

[25] Averroes, *In Libros Physicorum Aristotelis* (Venetiis: Juntas, 1562), Bk. 2, c. 6-7; Vol. 4, fol. 52rv.

[26] Averroes, *In Aristotelis De Anima* (Venetiis: Juntas, 1574), Bk. 2, c. 1; Vol. 6, fol. 53r.

[27] Themistius, *Paraphrasis In Libros de Anima* (Venetiis, 1499), c. 1 and 6; fol. 78a and 79a.

[28] See *DM* 13, V, 1-6; XXV, 414-415.

[29] See nn. 18-20, this section, above.

[30] See paragraphs 9-12, this section, below.

[31] I read the *sint* of the 1597 Salamanca and 1605 Mainz editions instead of the *sunt* of the Vives text.

[32] See paragraphs 8-11, this section, below.

[33] Capreolus, *Def. Theol.,* I, 321-322.

[34] *Ibid.;* I, 322-323.

[35] Soncinas, *In 7 Metaph.,* q. 22; 152b-154a.

[36] See Section VII, nn. 8-9 above.

[37] *Sum. Theol.,* I, q. 76, a. 4; T. 5, 223-224.

[38] *De Ente et Essentia,* ed. Roland-Gosselin, c. 5; 42.

[39] Cajetan, *In De Ente...,* c. 5; 142, 162-169.

[40] See paragraph 11, this section, below as well as Section XIII.

[41] I read the *hoc modo* of the 1597 Salamanca and 1605 Mainz editions instead of the corrupted reading of *ali-hoc modo* of the Vives text. The latter seems to derive from the *aliquo modo* reading of the 1751 Venice edition.

[42] See J. Urraburu, S.J., *Ontologia,* 743 n.1 where he cites a text of Blasius a Conceptione. Also see Capreolus, *Def. Theol.,* I, 326a.

[43] *Sum. Cont. Gent.,* I, 22; T. 13, 68-69.

[44] *Sum. Theol.,* I, q. 2, a. 3; T. 4, 32-34.

[45] See Sylvester of Ferrara, *In Sum. Cont. Gent.,* I, 22; T. 13, 69-70 and Cajetan, *In Sum. Theol.,* I, q. 2, a. 3; T. 4, 32-34.

[46] See D. Bañez, *In Sum. Theol.,* I, q. 3, a. 4, dub. 4; 153.

[47] See nn. 17-19, this section, above.

[48] See nn. 20-26, this section, above.

[49] See paragraph 8, this section, above. Also see *DM* 13, IV, 8-17; XXV, 411-414 and *DM* 15, VIII; XXV, 525-532.

[50] See *DM* 15, VIII; XXV, 525-532.

[51] See *DM* 18, II, 3; XXV, 599. The Vives reference to Disp. 28 seems incorrect.

[52] See paragraphs 8-9, this section above.

[53] See n. 19, this section above.

[54] I read the *esse causam* of the 1597 Salamanca and 1605 Mainz editions which is deleted in the Vives text.

[55] Aristotle, *De Anima,* II, 4, 415b13.

[56] St. Thomas, *In De Anima,* II, 7; #319, 113.

[57] See *Conimbricenses, In II De Anima* (Lugduni, 1604), cap. IV; 149-150 and *Complutenses, In III De Anima* (Lugduni, 1637), Disp. III, q. I-III; 40-57.

[58] See D. Bañez, *In Sum. Theol.,* I, q. 3, a. 4, dub. 4; 153-154.

[59] See Section I, 13 above.

Section IX

What the proximate efficient cause of created existence is.

1. There is no question about the efficient cause of the existence of those things which come to be by creation only, because we assume that God alone is the cause of it, since He alone is the creator of all things. Concerning the existence, though, of those things which are generated and corrupted, embracing under theses all those things which come to be by a change from a presupposed subject, be they substances or accidents, the problem is whether this existence too comes to be from God alone. I find three opinions on this point.

THE FIRST OPINION, ATTRIBUTING TO GOD ALONE THE EFFECTING OF EXISTENCE.

2. Some new commentators on St. Thomas, part 1, quest.3, art.4,[1] claim that God alone, without the effecting proper to any second cause, principal or instrumental, effects the existence of all things. And they cite St. Thomas, part 1, q.8, art.1;[2] q.45 art.5,[3] 2 *Against the Gentiles*, c.21[4] and Bk.3, c.66.[5] These are their reasons. First, because only God is a being *(ens)*[6] by essence, and all creatures possess a participated being. Hence, it is God alone who produces being. The consequence is proved, because a power causative of existence assumes the very being in the agent cause. But a creature does not essentially have being but from an extrinsic cause. Consequently, it is not essentially causative of existence, just as water, since it is not essentially hot, is also not essentially warming. Second, because every creature in its action assumes something produced by God alone, because acting from nothing is impossible, but from a presupposed subject is possible. Hence a creature's action assumes being; therefore, it is not a cause of being itself. Third, because only God gives existence to prime matter, because by Him alone can it come to be and be conserved. Therefore, second causes

do not produce the existence whereby prime matter is conserved and exists. For otherwise they would produce it and corrupt it. But matter exists only by the existence of the whole. Consequently, second causes do not effect the existence of the total substance. Fourth, because we cannot explain with another argument that God is the cause of the whole being *(ens)* if not because He alone causes the being of both the form as well as the matter of the whole. Even if creatures effect this very thing, they also will be called the causes of the whole being *(ens)*.

3.   But were you to ask what then, do second causes effect, if they do not impart being, or how do they generate, since generation tends to being, they answer that second causal agents complete the recipient of being itself by inducing a form in matter; and because such a form is always determined, so, accordingly, they determine and limit the existence or the action of God. The result is that He grants existence of a certain quality and (if I may say so) quantity, for every received act is limited by what is receptive. A further consequence of this is also to effect a union of existence with essence because they ultimately dispose and determine the essence for the reception of such an existence.[7] So, finally, even though second causes do not effect existence, they do effect the existing thing, just as a man generates a man, even though he does not effect the soul, because he gives it union.

THE SECOND POSITION WHICH, BESIDES GOD ALONE, GRANTS AN INSTRUMENTAL CAUSE OF EXISTENCE.

4.   There is a second opinion that existence is produced by God alone as a principal cause, but with the cooperation of a second cause as an instrument only. Ferrara says as much in 2 *Against the Gentiles,* c.21[8] whose opinion can be understood in two ways; one way: as a broad use of the name, *instrument,* just as every inferior cause, subordinated to another, and needing the influence of that other for its every operation, can be called its instrument. Ferrara speaks in this way in the reference above, and thus in reality does not differ[9] from the true opinion to be explained immediately. So he there criticizes Scotus for burdening St. Thomas with the statement that second causes do not effect being.[10] That opinion about a proper instrument can be understood in another way, as it is distinguished from a principal cause, even second and proximate; and in this sense this opinion is usually reported as claiming that a second cause, as principal and efficient cause by its own power, effects an essence like itself, but it effects existence only as an instrument and in God's power, although in this sense I do not remember reading

any advocate of this opinion. [11] It is usually based on certain expressions of St. Thomas, part 1, q.45, art.5; [12] q.5 *On Truth* art.9, to 7; [13] quest. 3, *On Power of God,* art.1, [14] where he says that no thing gives being except insofar as it has a share in divine power; and he cites the third proposition from the *Book of Causes* where it is said, "A noble soul has divine operation insofar as it gives being." [15] In the same reference he also says that only God grants being as such, but second causes determine that being as such to this or that being. And he cites the eighteenth proposition of the *Book of Causes* where it is said, "God grants being to all by way of creation; but second causes give living and sensing by way of informing." [16] Finally, in 3 *Against the Gentiles,* c. 66, he proves professedly that a "second cause does not grant being except insofar as it acts by divine power." [17] The arguments which can be given for this opinion are reduced to the arguments produced for the first opinion.

THE THIRD OPINION ATTRIBUTING TO SECOND CAUSES A PROPER EFFECTING OF EXISTENCE.

5.   The third opinion is that, when existence happens through generation, it is produced by a proximate cause as by a proper and principal cause in its own order, essentially subordinated to God as to a first cause. St. Thomas intends this opinion in the references cited and in 3 *Against the Gentiles,* c.13, [18] and part 1, quest. 104, art.1, [19] and quest.7, *On Power of God,* art.2. [20] And so do all the old Thomists understand and think, especially Cajetan [21] and Ferrara [22] on St. Thomas in the references given. Also Scotus, in 4, dist.1, quest.1 [23] professedly maintains this, although he falsely thinks that St. Thomas thought the opposite. And this opinion is quite true, and, as I think, can be demonstrated by most evident reasoning.

RESOLUTION OF THE QUESTION AND CONFIRMATION OF THE LAST OPINION.

6.   Hence, it must be said first that second causes, truly and properly effect the existence of their effects insofar as they come to be from them. I am presenting this conclusion first by demonstrating the weakness of the arguments which prove the opposite. For, if there is no reason why this effect be denied to second causes, no one (I believe) will deny that it is to be ascribed to them. God created them with every power to communicate themselves and to produce perfectly their own effects, of which they were capable by their nature. What reason, then, is there why a creature would be incapable of the power to produce existence? Or is it because it does not

have existence of itself but from God as an extrinsic agent? But, indeed, it does not have essence of itself but from God as an extrinsic agent, and so neither will it be able to produce essence. What then does it produce? Therefore, what it would not have of itself matters nothing, if only it has it in itself wherever it may have it from. Thus, a retort to the first argument of the first opinion [24] could be made in this way: Only God is his own real essence essentially. But all creatures have an essence imparted by God. Thus proposition 18 in the *Book of Causes* is stated in this way: "All things have essence because of a primary being *(ens)*." [25] Therefore, only God produces every essence. Just as, therefore, there is no consequence here, because a creature by the participated essence it has from God is the effector of a similar essence, so, in a similar form applied to existence, it has no force, but only concludes that a creature cannot effect being except by means of being received from the first cause; and this is altogether true.

7.   But (they say) the creature at least does not essentially effect being, just as hot water does not heat essentially. On the contrary, for although heating is not essentially attributed to water, still it both truly and properly heats. And insofar as it is hot, it heats essentially even if it heats by a heat received from an extrinsic agent. Thus, a creature, insofar as it is existent, will truly and essentially be able to effect existence, even if it has its own being from another. Hence, in this case we grant the comparison, but in another sense, between water in relation to heat and a creature in relation to its being; for water not only of itself does not have heat, but also in no way includes it, nor does it require it, for there to be water, nor does it have it as an essential attribute, but entirely accidentally; and so the action of heat is said accidentally to belong to water absolutely speaking. But, then, a creature, although it does not have being of itself, still, to be a creature in act, it necessarily and essentially includes and requires it; however, a creature in potency does not effect existence, but a creature in act does. Therefore, it causes as an essential cause, and in virtue of a proper and connatural entity received from God. There is confirmation, for here also can the argument used be applied, [26] that a creature would not essentially cause essence or essential being in its effect because neither does it effect this by an essence which it would have of itself, but which it receives from God. However, other authors [27] also do not deny that this is false. Therefore, it is established that the first argument for the denial of this effecting to a creature is entirely without validity.

8.   *The second argument is faulted.* Indeed, the second argument is just as ineffective. First, because at most it concludes that a creature does not effect that being which is supposed for its action. Also it is rightly

concluded from this that a creature cannot effect every being, for it has to be supposed that something has been made by God alone. But that a creature would not effect some being, that, namely, at which its action is terminated or which belongs to the effect produced by it, can in no way be concluded because of that argument; this is because that being which terminates the action is diverse from that which is presupposed for the action. Thus a creature can effect the former although it presupposes the latter. This argument is further explained. For one can understand that a twofold subject is supposed for the action of a creature. The one is remote, which does not remain in the terminus of action and has the character of a terminus from which, as is the wood from which fire is generated. The other is proximate, remaining under both termini, as is prime matter. Of the first it is true, speaking naturally, that its existence is presupposed for the action of a second cause. Yet that existence is destroyed by the action of the same cause. Therefore, this presents no obstacle to the existence of the begotten thing in coming to be by the same cause. Indeed, one follows naturally from the other, for the terminus from which is the corruption of one is usually the generation of the other, speaking essentially. But as to the second subject precisely considered, as it is essentially supposed for the action of an agent, the authors[28] of that argument cannot say that, in it, some existential being is presupposed for the action of a natural agent, but only essential being. For they think that prime matter, as it is in the moment of generation, has no existence naturally prior to receiving form by the action of an agent. But that it would have had that existence during the whole preceding time inasmuch as it was under the form of a corrupted thing, not only is no obstacle, as was explained in the first member, but also is accidentally required for the effection of substantial existence which takes place in the moment of generation. Therefore, in their opinion also it is not true that every effecting of a second cause essentially and directly supposes some existential being on the part of the subject. So if we were to imagine that God in one instant creates prime matter and in the same instant a second cause induces a form in it, with God concurring (as perhaps happens in the generation of worms or in the nourishment from the consecrated species), then that substantial generation (according to their opinion) does not suppose existence in matter neither with temporal priority nor with a priority of nature. Therefore, the fact that such an action supposes a subject is no obstacle to existence coming to be by it.

9.   *The objection is met and a response is given to the third argument.* Perhaps they will say that there is another obstacle connected with the third argument,[29] surely, that then prime matter would have exis-

tence from a second cause by which it exists. But this, on their principles, is no incongruity because matter (as they say) does not have existence immediately by the action which creates it but by the action by which the whole composite receives existence, be that created or generated. For it does not exist by a proper existence but by the existence of the whole. Therefore, there is nothing incongruous in its having existence from a second cause, by which the whole composite is generated, seeing that for the effecting of that existence matter is already supposed as an adequate subject from which a second cause can do something. They say that it follows that prime matter is generated and corrupted by second causes because it acquires and loses existence by their action. But, I ask you, why do they not proportionately infer the same thing about God, if that existence be from God alone, that, of course, by God Himself is matter corrupted and generated, because by the action of God it acquires and loses existence? But both are established to be equally false, since matter is ingenerable and incorruptible. They answer that the argument limps, because the terminus of the divine action is only being which is never lacking to matter. But particular causes determine this being into which something else is changed. But this is both[30] irrelevant and false. For if, to corrupt and generate a thing, it is sufficient to change the existential being, it makes no difference that this come about in one way or another and by this or that action. But if that does not suffice, as long as being in common be not broken but, in quasi-continuity, the same essential being remain under both existences, even if that change of existences takes place through the action of a natural agent, then, not for that reason will there be generation and corruption of matter. Very especially, for the reason that in that opinion it cannot be denied that, at least dispositively, this change of existence takes place through the action of a natural agent, because it destroys the proximate recipient of one existence and composes or disposes another; therefore, just as this argument says that it corrupts one existing thing and generates another, it will also say that it generates and corrupts prime matter. Or if this cannot be said because the same essential being of matter, enduring always, stands in the way, for an equal reason, that will not follow even if a second cause effects existence. It is also false that the action of God is only terminated at being as such and not at a determinate being. For, although the effective power of God is not of itself limited to this or that being, but extends itself to every being, still when He works in a particular instance, He truly effects a determinate being and changes one into another; and all by Himself He can corrupt one and generate another. So, although according to the above-mentioned opinion, the determination to such a being in the order of material and dispositive cause proceeds from a second cause, still, in the order of efficient cause it is essentially from God alone, because He alone effects existence and such an existence. Therefore, He alone will also generate and corrupt prime matter, if that argument amounts to anything. Hence, these arguments are neither sound nor logically drawn in their teaching.

10.   Nonetheless, simply speaking, it is true that, in a proper subject of generation which remains under both terms and which is prime matter, some existential being made by God alone is supposed for every action of a natural agent, because there is supposed prime matter, created and with its own proper essential being in itself and outside its own efficient cause. Without existential being this cannot be understood, as was proved above.[31] By the same reasoning, it is impossible for prime matter to change a proper and intrinsic existence without changing the proper entity and actuality of its essence; and consequently it would not only be generated and corrupted but also annihilated and created, or transubstantiated. Now from this true principle it can only be concluded that a second cause cannot effect the total existence of a being *(ens),* or of a composite with respect to all its parts. Yet it will be able to effect the existence of a form in matter and generate the being of the whole, not, to be sure, by supposing no part of it, for this would not be generating, but creating, but by composing that, in uniting the parts of which it consists, and in adding to it the ultimate and formal complement.

11.   *Fourth argument is refuted.* So too it is also established that the fourth argument[32] is unsuccessful. For, although second causes effect existence by generating the whole, yet they do not [do so] by creating nor by directly effecting the total being in regard to each of its parts while presupposing none. This is proper to God as it is said to be proper to Him to effect the total being *(ens),* as we shall explain at length later.[33] Therefore, by no probable argument is the power to effect the existence of their effects denied to second causes.

12.   Secondly, the conclusion is chiefly proved by showing that the way is false in which the above-mentioned opinion explains that second causes concur unto being. For, what it says—that a second cause effects a determination to such a being, but not being—either means that a second cause effects in being itself some difference or intrinsic mode by which such a being is determined, and this is impossible except by effecting the whole being itself, because physical action does not extend to a mode or a metaphysical difference, but to the very thing itself as it is in itself—nor do the mentioned authors intend this meaning; or the meaning is that only on the part of a subject do second causes determine being by preparing a subject which is receptive of such a being and not of another as the men-

tioned authors plainly seem to intend; and this too is shown to be false. For that doctrine supposes that, as often as some effect results from a creature, two actions occur there: one which is from a second cause inducing a form into matter only according to essential being; another, that of God alone granting existence. But this I show to be false in many ways. First, by that [34] commonplace axiom, that just as things, so also actions are multiplied in vain when reason or necessity does not demand. For here there is no reason for multiplying these actions, as is sufficiently established from the preceding discussion. Secondly, because if that action of a second cause be considered precisely, which is said to precede, in the order of nature, the action of God by which existence comes to be, it is necessary that through that [35] some existential being be given, because through that there is given some real being by which the thing, which immediately comes to be by that action, is constituted outside its causes; and this can only be existential being, as is clear from what was said above. And it must be granted by the authors cited, with whom we are disputing. For they say in the same place [36] that existence is that by which formally a thing is understood to be actually outside its causes. And they think it probable that the "existence" used is from "to stand outside" *(extra sistere),* because by existence a thing stands outside the potentiality of its causes.

13.   It can be explained and confirmed in this way. For by that first action which is said to be proper to a second cause, a form is educed from the potency of matter. For this is the function and the action of a natural agent, as is fully established from I *Phys.* [37] and from what was said in *Disp.* 15 [38] and 18. [39] However, an eduction from potency cannot be understood unless that which is educed be, so to speak, extracted from the potentiality in which it was previously, and be reduced to act. But it is not reduced to act except through being, as was shown above. [40] So generation as generation is terminated at being, as was said in 5 *Phys.,* c.1. [41] Therefore, by virtue of that action of a second cause, some existential being is imparted to its effect. Thus another action of God by Himself is superfluous. The consequence is clear, not only because the prior action of a second cause must also be from God, because every action of a second cause depends essentially on a first cause, (hence it happens that also that being which is imparted by such an action is made by God; why then is it necessary for God to bestow another being?); but also because it is not repugnant for God to suspend every other action which was about to be done all by Himself. For if those actions are distinct, why will not God be able to suspend the second action? For certainly (whatever the case may be as to possibility), although we conceive of its happening thus, nevertheless we understand that, by virtue of the

first action, a form is educed from the potency of matter and informs it in act, and that consequently another form is excluded and the total existence of another thing is corrupted. Hence, even if we understand that every subsequent action is suspended, we shall still understand that, by virtue of this first action, a thing is produced in act and outside its causes. There, it is also understood, by virtue of the same action, to have received existence. So every other action is redundant.

14.   Finally, it is explained in this way, for either an effect receives some real being by that action or not. If it receives none, how can it be a real action, since every action tends to being? For where there is no being-made *(esse factum)*, there can be no coming-to-be *(esse fieri)*. But where there is no coming-to-be, neither is there a making, and, consequently, neither is there a real action. Nor is it enough if it be said, in the same instant in which that action is, that being is imparted to an effect by another action. For from this it only happens that, concomitantly with the first action, being is given to an effect, but not because some being would be granted by it; for it is not of the nature of real action that some being be given with it, but that some being be given by it, because, otherwise, by it nothing will come to be or will be made. But if some real being comes to be by that action, I ask again whether that is existential or essential being? If the first, the point is made. If the second, I further ask whether that being is in potency only; and this cannot be said because this being is nothing in the thing produced, nor is it a denomination from an action but from a potency to action, as was shown above.[42] Therefore, that being is actual and new or temporal, because, again, an effect has that in itself and outside its causes; hence nothing is lacking to it to be existential being. And this is confirmed and insisted upon further. For it can be asked of that very action which derives from a second cause, whether it is something existing *in rerum natura* or not, as it proceeds from a second cause? For action has its own proportionate existence, just as the other accidents. But it cannot even be conceived of mentally that an action would have come from an agent and not be in its own way something existing, because neither can the actuality of action be greater than its causes, nor can it be understood to be outside its causes in another way. Furthermore, it is inconceivable because otherwise one must imagine another action of God by Himself, through which existence would be given to that action, and this is utterly absurd. For, just as for an action there cannot be another action, so neither for the being of an action; and because an action and the being of an action bespeak a relation to the same principle, just as, generally an accident and the being of an accident bespeak a relation to the same subject, since a form and the

being of a form maintain a mutual relationship. But if that action, as it comes from a second cause, is something existing, from that we then gather in the first place that some existential being flows from a second cause, namely, the existence of its action. Secondly, we conclude that by that action, existential being comes to be in its term, because an existing action as such is terminated at the existing thing as such. For, the total being, which is in action, whatever kind it be, tends toward a terminus; and the particular being, such as it is in an action in process, corresponds in the terminus actually produced. Hence, if a second cause exercises true, real and an existing action, through that action it communicates existential being to an effect; and, consequently, that other action, which is said to be from God alone, is redundant.

15. These arguments must be noted in passing. For, to my mind, a general conclusion is to be clearly drawn from them: every real action and effecting most formally tends to impart some existential being to its intrinsic terminus. For if these arguments are applied correctly, they apply equally to every action. Therefrom is a further confirmation of the identity between existence and actual essence. What are posited and destroyed at the very same time by the same formal action are in reality the same, as was treated in the above sections.[43] Yet existence and essence are related in this way, consequently, they are not really distinguished. Secondly, it is indicated by the same arguments that it is impossible for some cause to dispose effectively a subject to the reception of some existence, while not giving it some existence, because first, it was indicated in general that there cannot be a real action which does not give existence; also because that disposition, which was previously in potency, is in act through that action. Therefore, it has its own essence in act, and this is to exist. This argument is effective against the authors cited, not only in itself, but also *ad hominem.* For they say[44] that a proper passion can emanate from essence because it supposes the essence in act, but that existence cannot emanate from essence because one would have to suppose an essence in act. This is repugnant to existence. So we, in a similar fashion, say that it is repugnant for an essence to be disposed effectively toward existence, because one would have to suppose an essence in act. For an effecting does not have to do with an essence in potency but with an essence in act.

16. Finally, that doctrine on the part of the other action, which is ascribed to God alone, so that by it He alone effects existence, I show to be false. I ask whether that action is a proper creation or an eduction of the act of existing from the potency of a subject or an essence. For no medium between these can be conjured. But it cannot be said that that action is a proper creation. First, because therefrom it fol-

lows that every created existence is subsisting, and independent in
being and becoming from everything receptive. But the previously
mentioned authors think this is generally impossible, and at least it
is established as false in the existence of accidents and of material
forms. Secondly, because if existence is not distinguished from
essence, it is clear that it cannot be created, if essence is not created.
If it is distinguished, it is at least certain that existence cannot be
produced naturally nor exist except in its essence and by actuating
it. Thus, it depends on it in becoming and in being; consequently,
when it is produced in a connatural way, it is not produced by creation. Thirdly, because otherwise one would have to add a third action by which existence would be united to an essence, just as in the
generation of man, because the soul is properly created, but besides
its creation and another accidental action by which a body is disposed or organized, a third substantial action is required by which the
soul is united to the body, and this is generation proper. But this
multiplication of actions in the present case is proved *a fortiori* to be
imagined and superfluous from what was said, and because no
philosopher, up to now, has thought them up.

17.   But if the other part be chosen, to be sure, that that action is
not a creation, but an eduction, it is ascribed to God alone without
reason, and not to a second cause as well. The consequence is proved, because such an action does not surpass the power of a created
agent, neither in the way it comes to be, nor in the term to which it
tends. The first is clear because the action is from a presupposed
subject. But this mode of acting does not exceed the powers of a
created agent. The second is clear because whatever is in the term or
effect of that action does not exceed the perfection of a created agent.
But what some[45] say, that existential being is something absolutely
perfect and therefore impossible for it to be produced by a created
agent, is of no moment. For, although existential being, as such and
in its own order, is perhaps a supreme perfection, (a point we shall
see later),[46] still this existential being, which is produced in fire or in
water, for example, is not absolutely perfect nor is it more perfect
than a similar being would be in the generating fire or water. Therefore, on no score does an action productive of existence exceed the
perfection of a created agent. There is confirmation, for otherwise a
created agent would not produce the existence of its own effect nor
the union of existence with essence, as the first opinion[47] was saying.
The sequence is proved, because when a form or an act is produced
by an eduction from the potency of a subject or of a receiver, it is
produced and united by the same action. For it is not produced without the material cooperation of a subject, and a subject cannot
cooperate except by way of a union, as was explained at length in the

above secions[48] and in the first tome, on the third part.[49] Therefore, if existence is not produced by creation but by eduction, it is united by the same action by which it is produced. Hence, if a second cause does not produce existence, then it does not unite it either.

18.   *Our assertion is presented directly.* And finally from these considerations, by which both the bases of the first opinion and the way of explaining it are rejected, the direct proof of our assertion is easy. First, because by a unique and identical action an existing thing and its existence are produced, as was shown;[50] for second causes produce their own real and existing effects. Therefore, they produce the existences of their effects. Secondly, because every true effecting is terminated at some existential being, as was also proved.[51] But second causes truly produce something, hence, they truly effect existential being in their own effects. Thirdly, and especially *a priori,* because existence is not distinguished in reality from actual essence. But by their effecting, second causes draw out the forms or essences which they produce from potency into act, and so they give them actual being or actual essential entity. Hence they give them existence.

19.   I say secondly that the existences of things which are generated and corrupted, are not only produced by second causes as instruments, but also as by proximate principal causes, and universally are existences produced in this way by these causes, just as essences. Along with us, the authors of the first opinion teach this proposition in part, inasmuch as they deny that second causes are instruments, properly so called, for producing existence. This part must be understood in regard to those[52] causes which are the principal ones in producing effects with regard to essential being. For, if in this, they be only instruments, as is heat, for example, for the production of fire or seed for the production of the animal, it is no wonder that they be also instruments for producing the existences of such effects. Rather, that is necessarily the consequence according to the last part of the conclusion, and so I have proposed the conclusion under those words, namely, that second causes in producing existences are not only instruments but also principal causes, so that these be attributed to different causes and that there be something like a suitable distribution (as the Dialecticians say). For the same causes do not have each feature but different ones do. Thus, when explained in this way, this part is given no other proof by the cited authors[53] other than because it appears ridiculous for a second cause to be a principal and an instrumental cause of the same effect. Then they add that it is said arbitrarily that God bestows the fluid and instrumental power on second causes by which they produce existence. But I do not see why they can judge that first item to be ridiculous, since they say that there are essence and existence in the same

created effect, and that the former comes to be from a second agent, as from a principal cause, but that the latter is produced by God alone. If then there are distinct things in the same effect which are said to be produced by God in different ways, namely, either by Himself alone or through a second cause, why then could they not be produced in different ways by a second cause, namely, as by a principal agent and as by an instrument? Or if the actions by which essence and existence are produced are different, what is ridiculous about the same proximate agent, which by its proper and principal power produces another, being assumed as an instrument to produce another, if it does not have a similar principal power for working that out? For, it is not unusual for natural agents to work instrumentally when they cannot do so principally.

20.   Therefore, when that doctrine is supposed, this other on instrumental action cannot be attacked effectively enough. Yet, from the principle posited in the preceding assertion, this second is clearly inferred. For an action by which an effect of a second cause is produced is the same one which is terminated at the existential being of that effect. Hence, whenever a second cause, in its own order, is principal with respect to its own effect, it must, in the same way, effect its existence, because it cannot, with respect to one and the same action and terminus, be the principal and the instrument. Secondly, because a second cause effectively cooperates toward the existence of its own effect, as they grant who admit that it is an instrument, for an instrumental cause truly effects; but such an effect does not exceed the power of such a cause, as was already proved.[54] For neither in the perfection of the thing produced nor in the way it is produced does it surpass it. Therefore, it produces as a principal cause and not as an instrument, for that is called a principal cause which acts by a proper power, adapted and proportionate to the effect. Thirdly, because, for example, fire, due to no other cause, produces fire as a principal cause according to essential being or according to the form of fire, and does so for no other reason than that the effect does not exceed the power of the cause either in itself or in the way in which it is produced by the agent. But it is the same in the case of the existence of such an effect. Therefore. Consequently, even when a real distinction between existence and essence is posited, I do not see with what probability this assertion can be denied. But it is much more evident when the identity of existence and actual essence is posited, on which the last part of the conclusion[55] is based, because if these are in reality the same, they cannot be produced in different ways by one and the same cause at the same time and by one action, and also, as was fully explained,[56] because to produce a thing or actual essence is nothing else than to give it

existence. Hence, a proximate agent cannot be a principal cause of the one and an instrumental cause of the other.

THE PARTICULAR REASON WHY THE EFFECTING OF EXISTENCE IS ATTRIBUTED TO GOD.

21. I say thirdly: in the effecting of existence, God possesses something proper in which He surpasses creatures; yet He has the same eminence in effecting the essence of the creature. The first part is posited for grasping and reconciling different passages in St. Thomas cited above.[57] It is explained in this way. For, especially, the adequate object of divine power is created being *(ens)* to the extent it is such; and this cannot be the adequate object of some created power, since it cannot effect itself nor one more excellent than itself. But the proper and adequate act of a being *(ens)* is being, and, for this reason, God properly and directly imparts being as such, while the creature only produces this or that being. The reason is not that God does not effect in every being every definite characteristic of it, or that, when a creature produces some being, He does not effect in it every common feature of being *(essendi)* which can be abstracted by us. For these are impossibilities, as is self-evident. But the reason is that the characteristic under which God achieves that effect, and which is adequate to His power, would be being itself as such; but with regard to the creature, it would be such or such being.

22. There is a second difference, because God can impart total being to a creature, and totally, so to speak. But the creature cannot so much give total being, as completing or perfecting an unfinished being by adding partial or accidental being. Cajetan mentioned this difference, part 1, quest. 8, art. 1.[58] But because he does not admit in substances a partial or total being, but only one simple being of the whole supposit, for this reason he explains it by causes or conditions required for existing. For God alone effects in the thing that whole which is necessary for existing. For, if the thing be immaterial, God alone produces the whole substance of the thing. But if it be material, God alone at least produces the matter. This explanation has truth. But we add, logically, that in every created thing there is something of existence, or some total or partial existence, which is produced by God alone. But there is no existence which would be produced by a creature without God; and in this way do we say that God effects total existence totally. We also say that God alone posits in every thing the first foundation of existence, without which the creature cannot produce something of existence. The reason is because every effecting is terminated at existence, as I have proved. But in every effect by a creature, some effecting by God alone is sup-

posed. Hence, some existence is also produced by God. The minor is proved by a similar induction. For in order for a creature to effect the existence of an accident, it supposes the existence of the substance which, if it be spiritual, is produced by God alone. But if it be material, it at least has matter from God alone. Then, were a creature to effect substantial being, it also supposes the matter effected by God alone and consequently subject to some existential being, to which that effection of God alone is terminated.

23.   A third difference is drawn from this, that God produces existence from no pre-existing created thing; yet a creature never gives being except from the presupposition of a second being. Then it happens that even for this reason God is said, essentially and directly, to produce being as such, but the creature only as the being is such. For, as we said with Aristotle when discussing the causes,[59] the effect is said to be produced essentially and directly, according to that character of a being *(ens),* which is not presupposed on the part of the effect itself. For example, when fire is generated from air, fire is essentially and directly produced, but not an element or a body, because these features were already presupposed in the air. Consequently, according to those features proper to God, St. Thomas sometimes says that God is the proper and essential cause of being itself,[60] but he does not exclude the proper effecting of second causes in regard to the particular existences of their effects as was made clear from the other references to his doctrine cited[61] above.

24.   *Creatures concur in the production of essence in the manner they concur in the production of existence.* But it is clear from these arguments, if they were correctly considered, that these differences not only enter into the effecting of existence but also into the effecting of essence, even if we should imagine they are distinct. It is proved, for also God alone is the effector of every creatable essence, and, consequently, He alone regards the producible essence, as such, as an adequate object and as essentially and directly producible by Him. Similarly, God alone as a proper and principal agent can produce the total essence of a thing, totally or according to that whole which intrinsically composes such an essence or constitutes it in some way in actual essential being, as is clear from the same induction. For if an essence be spiritual, God alone produces it; but if it be material, at least in regard to the matter is it produced by God alone, and according to that is it supposed for the action of a second cause. This, at most, adds the other part to an essence, and thus completes it. You will say: granted it is the case in substances, still it is not so with accidents. For the subject is not a part of the essence of an accidental form, and so a second cause totally effects the total essence of an accident. The answer is that the same can be said of the existence of an accident,

for also the subject or the existence of the subject is not a part of it. Then, indeed, one must say that the discussion is both about essence and complete existence, for that which is incomplete either cannot be produced by a natural agent, as prime matter cannot, or, if it can be produced by a natural agent, it supposes another part of the essence produced by another, as substantial form; or, certainly, if it be a question of a lesser entity, as is an accident, it supposes the substantial essence, on which it naturally depends; and although it is not of the essence of such a form taken abstractly, it still pertains to its essence in some way. But the second statement is that, just as the substantial form is not properly generated but the composite is, so neither is the accidental form, in the abstract, properly produced, but the concrete thing is, which is intrinsically composed of subject and form. And in this way such an effecting supposes something of which the effect itself intrinsically consists, whether it be considered in essential being or in existential being.

25. From this other differences have easy application. For God alone produces an essence, without presupposing any essence. Consequently, He alone essentially and directly produces a created essence, as it is such. They will say, perhaps, that although God produces existential being from no existence, because He produces from nothing, He still does not produce an essence from no essence or from nothing of essence; for, unless the essence is supposed, one cannot know that a thing would be producible by God. The ones who answer in this way plainly labor under an equivocation, for, if by essence were they to understand a thing in mere objective potency, we are not dealing with that, because that, as such, is nothing, nor is it truly produced or is it the terminus of effecting, unless perhaps[62] it be called the terminus from which; and this is of no significance, because in the same way will it be said that existence is produced by God from non-existence in act and from existence in potential and objective being. For if existence were not possible and not as such pre-known by God, it would not be able to be produced by Him. But were we to speak of an actual essence which would be truly some entity outside of God, it is altogether false that God does not produce a created essence simply and absolutely from no essence, because He does not even produce a created essence from His very own essence, since that is impossible. For essences are at once different. Nor does He produce it from another essence outside of His own, since all that must be created by Him. Hence, it is established that God has the same pre-eminence and singular character in effecting essence as He has in effecting existence. This is also a necessary consequence of the identity of an actual essence and existence, according to the last part of the preceding assertion.[63] For, just as there we were inferring

from that principle that essence and existence are produced by a second cause in the same way, so it must be said here that they are produced by the first cause in the same way. The reason is absolutely the same. This same doctrine of the same efficiency for existence and created essence confirms the doctrine of their mutual identity put forth above. [64]

Notes

[1] See D. Bañez, *In Sum. Theol.,* I, q. 3, a. 4, dub. 4; 152-158.

[2] *Sum. Theol.,* I, q. 8, a. 1; T. 4, 82.

[3] *Sum. Theol.,* I, q. 45, a. 5; T. 4, 469-470.

[4] *Sum. Cont. Gent.,* II, 21; T. 13, 312-314.

[5] *Sum. Cont. Gent.,* III, 66; T. 14, 188-189.

[6] I read the *ens* of the 1597 Salamanca and 1605 Mainz editions which is deleted in the Vives text.

[7] I read the *existentiae* of the 1597 Salamanca and 1605 Mainz editions instead of the *essentiae* of the Vives text.

[8] Sylvester of Ferrara, *In Sum. Cont. Gent.,* II, 21; T. 13, 314-320.

[9] The 1597 Salamanca and 1605 Mainz editions both read "...supra et ita in re non ita..." instead of the Vives text reading:"...supra, et non ita in re differt..."

[10] See n. 8, this section above.

[11] A modern advocate of this position would seem to be J. Owens, C.Ss. R., *An Elementary Christian Metaphysics,* (Milwaukee: Bruce, 1963), 201. However, no brief is held for an *esse essentiae.*

[12] *Sum. Theol.,* I, q. 45, a. 5; T. 4, 469-470.

[13] *De Veritate,* ed. Spiazzi, q. 5, a. 9 ad 7; 107-108.

[14] *De Potentia,* ed. Pession, q. 3, a. 1; 37-41.

[15] *Ibid.,* 39.

[16] *Ibid.*

[17] *Sum. Cont. Gent.,* III, 66; T. 14, 188.

[18] *Sum. Cont. Gent.,* III, 13; T. 14, 35-36.

[19] *Sum. Theol.,* I, q. 104, a. 1; T. 5, 463-464.

[20] *De Potentia,* q. 7, a. 2; 190-193.

[21] Cajetan, *In Sum. Theol.,* I, q. 104, a. 1; T. 5, 465-466.

[22] Sylvester of Ferrara, *In Sum. Cont. Gent.,* III, 13; T. 14, 36.

[23] Scotus, *Opus Oxon.,* IV, d. 1, q. 1; T. 16, 12-99.

[24] See paragraphs 2-3, this section above.

[25] See *Liber de Causis,* prop. 18, ed. R. Steel, in *Opera hactenus inedita Rogeri Baconi,* fasc. 12 (Oxford: Clarendon, 1924), 175. The variant reading for line 20 must be heeded. See also O. Bardenhewer, *Die pseudo-aristotelische Schrift uber das reine Gute, bekannt unter den Namen Liber de Causis* (Freiburg: Herder, 1882), 17, 1. 19; 179.

[26] See paragraph 6, this section, above.

[27] See n. 1, this section, above.

[28] See paragraph 2, this section above.

[29] *Ibid.*

[30] I read the *Sed hoc et est impertinens* of the 1597 Salamanca and 1605 Mainz editions instead of the Vives text which deletes the *et*.

[31] See *DM* 13, IV; XXV, 409-414.

[32] See paragraph 2, this section, above.

[33] See paragraphs 21-25, this section, above.

[34] I read the *illo* of the 1597 Salamanca and 1605 Mainz editions instead of the *illa* of the Vives text.

[35] I read the *ut per illam* of the 1597 Salamanca and 1605 Mainz editions instead of the *ut propter illam* of the Vives text.

[36] See D. Bañez, *In Sum. Theol.*, I, q. 3, a. 4, dub. 1; 142-145.

[37] Aristotle, *Physics*, I, 184a-192b.

[38] See *DM* 15, II-IV; XXV, 505-517.

[39] See *DM* 18, I; XXV, 593-598.

[40] See Section VIII, 6-14 above.

[41] Aristotle, *Physics*, V, 1, 224b9.

[42] See Sections II-III above.

[43] See *DM* 7, II, 9-28; XXV, 264-271.

[44] See D. Bañez, *In Sum. Theol.*, I, q. 3, a. 4, dub. 4; 157-158.

[45] *Ibid.*, 155.

[46] See Section XI, 9-10 below.

[47] See paragraph 2, this section, above.

[48] See *DM* 13, IX, 9-16; XXV, 431-434.

[49] See Suárez, *In Sum. Theol.*, III, q. 2, a. 8, disp. 8, I, 1-7; XVII, 328-331.

[50] See paragraphs 10-14, this section, above.

[51] See paragraph 15, this section, above.

[52] I read the *earum* of the 1597 Salamanca and 1605 Mainz editions instead of the *omnium* of the Vives text.

[53] See D. Bañez, *In Sum. Theol.*, I, q. 3, a. 4, dub. 4; 152.

[54] See paragraphs 6-18, this section, above.

[55] See paragraphs 19, this section, above.

[56] See paragraphs 6-18, this section, above.

[57] See paragraphs 2-5, this section, above.

[58] Cajetan, *In Sum. Theol.*, I, q. 8, a. 1; T. 4.

[59] See *DM* XII, II, 1-4; XXV, 384.

[60] See references in paragraph 2, this section, above.

[61] I read the *citatis* of the 1597 Salamanca and 1605 Mainz editions instead of the *satis* of the Vives text. See paragraph 5, this section, above, for the other texts of Aquinas.

[62] I read the *forte* of the 1597 Salamanca and 1605 Mainz editions instead of the *fortasse* of the Vives text.

[63] See paragraphs 18, this section, above.

[64] See Section VI, above.

Section X

What effects existence has and in what it differs from essence on this score.

1.   Now that the causes of existence have been explained, it is fitting for a treatment of its effects to follow, since also from them some[1] are wont to draw indications of some real or modal distinction between essence and existence. But we, on the contrary, think that the doctrine of their identity can be confirmed from this.

THE TITLE OF THE QUESTION IS EXPLAINED.

2.   Now existence can be compared in the causal order either to an essence whose existence it is or to other things. Here we are not concerned with the first comparison but with the second, for there was a satisfactory discussion of the first above,[2] and all agree on the point that existence in respect to an existing essence has the character of an act, and acts like a formal cause. All teach alike that it is not properly and strictly a formal cause. Yet we explain this with very little difficulty, because a proper formal cause is distinguished in reality from the subject in which it has its formal effect and along with it makes a true and real composition. But existence is not distinguished in reality from essence and so it cannot be a true form nor a physical act, but a metaphysical act and mode so intrinsic that it is not distinguished from the thing which it modifies, just as difference is the act of the genus and is not properly its form. But those[3] who think that existence is distinguished in reality from essence, explain this with more difficulty. Yet those[4] who say it is not really distinguished but only modally, can say that the mode of the thing is more inclusive than form, although it is related after the manner of act or form.

They have the example of subsistence by which to explain it; for subsistence is a mode of a nature distinct in reality from it, yet not properly a form, since it is neither an accident, nor can it be a substantial form, since it supposes an integral and complete substantial nature which it modifies, as we will mention more at length below. [5] Hence, these authors should speak of existence in this way. But the ones who think that the act of existence is a thing really distinct from essence find greater difficulty in being able to give a reason why it is not properly a form. Still, they can also use the argument already given, because it is not an accidental form, as was shown, [6] and it cannot be a substantial form, since it supposes a perfect and complete form. Likewise, there is a theological argument, because, according to this opinion the act of existence can be furnished without information. [7] For thus do they say that the Word furnishes the existence of Its humanity, although it still does not inform it. Hence, the existence of the created nature, by virtue of its manner of actuating it, does not seek to be a true form. Nor, indeed, does it have that by reason of its own entity, because it is not an accident; hence it is not properly a form but is a certain ultimate term and act of the essence. Yet it is said to act like a form because it is that by which an essence is constituted under such an aspect, and because it ultimately terminates it and reduces it from potency to act, just as it can be said that a point is compared to a line like a form insofar as it constitutes it as terminated; and under this aspect is actuates it. Yet it is not properly a form.

3. But it can be objected that essence is the material cause of existence. Hence, existence is the formal cause, for these two are related as correlative. The answer in our opinion is to deny the antecedent. But others logically ought to say that, with the same proportion, the essence certainly does act like a material and receptive cause, Yet it is not properly and strictly matter or a subject. Still, what this formal effect is, or what this formal actuality is which existence gives to another thing distinct from itself, always remains for them to explain, since it cannot be the entitative actuality itself and every other actuality superadded and distinct from subsistence or inherence can neither be necessary, nor intelligible, as was shown at length above. [8]

4. Hence, the proper meaning of this question has to do with the effects and causality which existence can have in regard to other things, or rather, an existing thing can have by reason of existence. And the question can be at issue in all types of causes. But for now, let us pass over the final cause inasmuch as its causality is quite intentional; it is accordingly a philosophical tenet accepted by all, that for the end to cause, it does not require actual existence, because it moves metaphorically as known. So objective being in an intellect is

sufficient for that. And yet, the end truly would not cause except in line with its own existence, and for that reason final causality could be ascribed to the existence of a known good; to the existence (I say) not now exercised, but known in the good itself, which has the character of an end; and this because the good moves only as it is in reality, whether it is known to be or about to be or able to be; this matter we discussed amply above in *Disp.* 23.[9]

Whether existence can cause something by formal or material causality.

5. *First opinion.* Therefore, in regard to material and formal causality, almost all who distinguish existence from essence really or modally say that existence formally and properly never performs the function of a formal cause or a material cause in regard to another thing.[10] Indeed, they say that neither is it an essentially necessary condition and naturally prior to the causalities of these causes, although according to temporal duration it is a necessary condition and, according to the natural order, it is consequent upon the above-mentioned types of causes. These are stated and proved at the same time. For, prime matter, as an example, does not receive form by its own existence but by its essential entity, rather does it, by means of a form, receive existence; and similarly substance does not receive accidents in its existence but in its essential entity. Just as in the humanity of Christ, if we should understand it to be existing by the uncreated existence of the Word, then we understand that the accidents of the humanity are received[11] in it according to the essential entity and not in the uncreated existence of the Word. This can be proved by reason because existence as such signifies the order of act and not of potency. Consequently, it is called an ultimate act by many. Hence, existence as such cannot be the reason for receiving something because this is the function of potency. Therefore, neither can it be the reason for some material causality. From this the other part about a formal cause is established, for these two causes are mutually related and preserve a mutual proportion. Therefore, if matter does not cause or receive by existence but by essence, neither does a form inform by its own existence but by essence.

6. A further necessary consequence of this is that these causes, neither formally nor naturally, need existence for causing, because matter has being only by form. Hence, it receives the form naturally prior to existing. Then, too, the form informs naturally prior to existence being given to matter or to the whole composite by reason of that. Therefore, then, it does so naturally prior to its having existence, because it has that only in the whole composite. And this at

least is true in the case of material forms. For the rational soul certainly has existence naturally prior to its informing; yet that is not because of the necessity of informing, but on account of the excellence of such a thing. There is confirmation in the case of accidental forms, which are dispositions toward a substantial form, for they dispose to that naturally prior to its existing; [12] for they dispose matter and exist in the composite, and yet it belongs partly to a material cause to dispose inasmuch as it is a certain determination of matter; partly to a formal cause inasmuch as the restriction of matter to this form comes about by the information of heat or a second similar ultimate disposition.

7.   *The Refutation.* This doctrine cannot stand along with the foundation set down about the identity of essence and existence; and so, to declare the truth, we must take note that it is one thing to speak about the thing itself according to itself, and another as it is signified by the expression *existence* and as it is conceived of by an abstract and precise concept corresponding to that. Again, it must be noted that it is one thing to speak of existence as such, another to speak of this or that existence. For, in the first manner of speaking, it is clear that existence as such does not of itself call for material or formal causality in regard to another thing. Rather, to the degree that existence is more perfect, to that degree it abstracts more and is more separated from causalities of this sort, as is determined to be the case not only with the existence of God but also with angelic existence and with any complete substantial existence. Hence, we are concerned with existence in its total scope to see whether, namely, within that there be some existence which could share a causality of that sort, and consequently, whether the nature of existence as such, though it does not require it, at least allows for this type of causality.

8.   Hence, I say first: actual existence is altogether necessary to perform material and formal causality, not only in the duration of time but also in the precedence or order of nature. Indeed, to be inwith, all agree on the temporal duration, because the causality of matter or form, if it be related to the composite, consists in its actual and intrinsic composition. But if there be a mutual relation, it consists in this, that matter sustains form and form actuates matter, and thus they mutually support and maintain each other in being. But it is impossible to understand that they would exercise this function reciprocally or compose the whole unless they be existing in act. Otherwise, neither will the composite exist in act, but it will be possible or will be in objective being; and similarly, the causality will not be in act but in potency and objective being.

9.   This same argument, were it rightly pondered, proves that the existence of a thing, which is actually a formal or material cause, is a

prerequisite because of the intrinsic character of such actual causality. Consequently, it proves that it is required not only in the same duration but also in the priority of nature. First, indeed, because if the cause actually causes, the causality itself must exist in reality; therefore, it must derive from an existing cause as such. Hence, not only according to temporal duration, but also according to the order of nature, is existence a pre-requisite in a cause for actual causality to derive from it. The first antecedent is proved, because if causality is already in act, precisely because of this is it outside its causes insofar as it can be. Therefore, from this fact also, it is existing. But the rest of the consequences are evident because something cannot be existing unless it be really caused by an existing thing.

10.   Secondly, because a creature can really cause nothing unless, according to the order of nature, it itself first be caused and produced by some efficient cause. But it was shown above [13] that every effecting is terminated at some existential being, because it is terminated at some being outside its causes. Hence, even according to the natural order, the existential being of a material and formal cause is supposed for their causality. The major seems to be self-evident, because a creature, while it is not understood as caused or effected, cannot be understood as a being *(ens)* in act but only in potency. But as such it cannot be understood as causing in act. Because if it is not outside its causes but in their potency, how can it constitute something else outside its causes? To speak in particular and to make the matter clearer, how can matter actually be united to form or sustain that, if it itself is not in act but only in potency? But it itself cannot be in act, if it be not effected in act. Similarly, form cannot actually inform matter unless it be created or educed from the potency of matter. I know that the usual reply is that to be created or to be educed is naturally prior with regard to essential being. But I have already demonstrated above [14] that this essential being, since it is not potential only but actual and outside its causes, is also true existential being; and that neither does the created being *(ens)* formally require another being for existing.

11.   Thirdly, because the actual existence of matter (and it is the same with regard to form) is necessary to it for causing, at least in the same instant of time, as all acknowledge; and it is not required as following upon its causality. Otherwise, it would cause itself, for it would cause its own being; hence, it is necessary as preceding its causality in the order of nature. The consequence is clear, because this necessity is not accidental and from mere coincidence. Otherwise, it could be blocked at least by divine power, and then it could happen that matter would be actually united to form and form to matter outside an efficient cause, and yet that they would have no existence. But one cannot conceive of this even in the mind.

12. *The existence of the matter and the form in a thing is that by which they cause.* I say secondly that the existence of matter (and it is proportionally the same with form) in the thing itself is that by which matter causes in its own order. But according to the way of signifying and conceiving it is recognized as a necessary condition, or as a mode constituting a thing in a state adequate for causing. The first part of this conclusion is well enough established from what was said about the identity of existence and actual essence. For matter causes only by its actual essential entity, for in keeping with that, it is in potency to form and receives that in it. But in reality the actual essence of matter does not differ from its existence. Hence, it really receives form in its own existence or in itself existing as it is an existent. There is confirmation and explanation, because neither of these causes performs its function or causality except insofar as it is a being *(ens)* in act as, namely, a being *(ens)* in act is distinguished from a being *(ens)* in objective potency. But this kind of being *(ens)* in act is formally and intrinsically constituted by existential being, as was proved above.[15] Hence, each of these causes actually causes as it is constituted by actual existential being. But that constitution is had through a complete identity in reality, as we have shown.[16] Thus, each causes as it is its own existence.

13. *Justice is done to an objection.* You will say that matter does not cause inasmuch as it is a being *(ens)* in act, but inasmuch as it is a being *(ens)* in potency. The answer is that there is a great equivocation in these words, ranging both from a receptive potency to an objective potency and from a being *(ens)* simply or complete to a being *(ens)* relatively or partial. Therefore, matter causes to the extent that it is in receptive potency to form and consequently causes to the extent that it contains the material form in some way, namely, in passive potency. For this reason, it can even be said to be a being *(ens)* simply and complete, not in act but in potency. But, of course, it does not cause to the extent that it has material being (which is partial and relative being) in potency, but in act; and so it does not cause as it, in its own order, is a being *(ens)* in objective potency, but as it is in act. To be a being *(ens)* in act in this way, that is, outside causes and outside nothing, and to be in receptive potency to a second act, are not opposed, but rather they are essentially subordinated. For potency cannot be in proximate readiness, or in a state in which it would be ready to receive its act, unless it itself has some actual entity, since real potency itself ought to be a real being *(ens)* and outside its causes; all of these things have been discussed at length above in Disp. 13.[17] This part is finally confirmed. For a cause should be proportioned to its effect and its causality. But the causality of matter or form, in that way in which it derives from it, is

something existing outside its causes and is terminated at a thing as it is something outside causes, as was shown above. [18] Hence, it itself also causes as it is existing. Therefore, it causes to the extent that, in reality, it is its own existence.

14.   *We do not conceive of existence except as a mode required for causing.* The second part of the conclusion, which looks only to the way of conceiving and signifying, is to be explained from what was said above about the distinction of reason between essence and existence. [19] For existence is signified by this word as prescinded and as distinct in reason from essence. But, as such, it is not conceived of as a sufficient reason for causing something outside the essence whose existence it is, but it is conceived of only as the character or mode of being *(essendi)* of the very essence itself. For neither form nor matter can cause except by imparting its very own essence; so, existence, as precisely conceived of, is not the proximate and physical reason for receiving or informing, but the existing essence is. Consequently, for this reason, existence as such is rightly said to be conceived of and signified as a condition or a mode constituting a thing in a state sufficient for causing than as a cause or a proximate reason for causing. There is confirmation, for causality is exercised by physical entities as they are in reality and not by grades or modes metaphysically conceived of or prescinded, just as the formal cause physically constituting man is not rational but a rational soul, although metaphysically it be said to constitute it. But existence is metaphysically conceived of as a mode constituting an essence in entitative act. Thus, under this prescinded concept, it is not apprehended as a physical reason for causing but as a mode or condition of the causing essence. When existence is called a necessary condition of matter or form for causing, it must be understood correctly lest one think it is one of those conditions which, though necessary, yet do not essentially contribute to an effect, just as, for example, are nearness or closeness; hence, this condition, considered in itself, is customarily called an accidental cause. Yet existence is not only necessary in this way but as constituting intimately and indivisibly (so to speak) the thing, which by itself is a formal and material cause. So, not accidentally, but essentially does it pertain to the order of causing.

15.   The reply to the basis of the opposing opinion is that it is false that a substantial or accidental form is received in an essential entity prescinded from an existential entity, just as it is also false that it is received in an existence prescinded from an essence. But it is received in the essence of the existent subject, as it is existent. For the proof about matter, it is denied that matter, properly speaking, receives existence by means of form; but just as it is immediately created, so [20] it immediately receives existence, although depen-

dently on form; so, in that way in which it is supposed, in its causal order, to form, is it supposed as existent, because it is supposed as created, and consequently outside its efficient cause; and this is to exist. But to the other part about an accident, I reply that it is false that an accident does not inhere in a substance as existing and, in reality, in its existence. Otherwise, the inexistence of an accident would not essentially and intrinsically suppose the existence of a substance but only accidentally. Nor would the existence of a substance support or be the basis for supporting the existence of an accident; these are falsities. Nor does the example of the humanity of Christ help matters, for it assumes something false. That argument can be turned around to be evidence that the humanity of Christ does not lack a proper natural existence, but only subsistence, as we have treated at greater length in its place. [21] Nor also is it unfitting that one existence in the thing itself be actuated through another, because this means nothing else than that one existing thing be a potency to receiving an existing act. But how existence is called an ultimate act and how some receptive potentiality is not repugnant to it we will disclose in the following section. [22] Finally, on behalf of ultimate confirmation (for all the rest have been taken care of) the reply is that something false is being assumed in it, for dispositions, if they are preparing matter or a subject, just as they dispose with a natural priority, so also do they exist with a natural priority. But if they be only consequents, preserving or adorning the composite, just as they do not exist with a natural priority, so neither do they dispose with a natural priority; nor are they properly the cause of the form or composite, but are its properties.

ON THE EFFICIENT CAUSALITY OF EXISTENCE.

16. It is easily established from these points what must be said about efficient causality. For what we have said about a material and formal cause [23] can and ought to be referred to an efficient cause, for they have more pertinence in that instance. Yet a few things are to be added. For the authors, who think essence is a thing distinct from the existence of a creature, say that existence through itself has no influence in efficient causality, yet is required as a necessary condition. [24] Certain of them [25] teach that existence is one of those conditions which, in the order of nature, must necessarily precede its very efficiency. But others [26] deny this to be universally necessary. Indeed, those who deny that existence is produced by second causes, but is produced by God alone, [27] speak logically when they deny that the existence of a second cause essentially has influence on the effect of the second cause itself, for if a second cause only produces essence

in its effect, it will be by its essence an adequate source of that. But these persons can offer no sufficient reason why they would claim that existence is a necessary condition for acting. Much less can they prove that, according to the order of nature, it would be antecedently necessary, although Bañez also still maintains that in part 1, where he was cited above, conclusion 5. [28]

17.   In his proof, indeed, he rightly says that an efficient cause operates as it is in act by existence, yet he cannot show this very thing by a consistent argument. Hence, the reasons he adds are surely sound, yet they clearly destroy his opinion. The first is that a cause not actuated by existence is only in potency; therefore, it cannot grant act to an effect, unless that be considered to be subject to a similar act. Indeed, he makes a correct inference. But, I ask, when he takes it that, "a cause not actuated by existence is only in potency," [29] whether it is a question about a cause not actuated in the order of temporal duration or in the order of nature. He cannot say in the first way, otherwise he would not correctly prove what he proposes, namely, that existence cannot emanate efficiently from an essence. For, in this case, a natural priority in essential actuality would suffice. Therefore, the proposition ought to be taken in the second sense already offered, in which case, then, it is most true, clearly proved (as I think) by us above. [30] But then I ask a further question. If a cause not actuated by existence is only in potency, how does it actually materialize or inform? Again, if a created cause contributes only an essential act to an effect, why is it not sufficient to consider it under a similar act in order for it to produce its effect? Hence, if it is subject to an essential act naturally prior to being subject to an existential act, as they say, without basis do they pre-require, in the order of nature, an existential act in a second cause for it to produce. But by supposing (which we have shown) [31] that nothing is in essential act naturally prior to being in existential act, it is best to conclude that it needs an act of existing for effecting, not only in the order of temporal duration but also in the order of natural priority.

18.   But then I do not see on what basis those who concede that a second cause influences the existential being in its effect can deny that the existence of a cause essentially influences and produces existence in an effect; because neither from the character of existence as such is it repugnant to be effective, nor is it repugnant even to such existence inasmuch as it is such. So we must say the same thing about this causality as we have said about material or formal causality. [32] For, in reality, the very existence of an active form is the very reason or essential source of acting. First, because, in reality, there is the very actual essence of a form which is a source of acting. Secondly, because a like is produced by its like in the best and most fitting

fashion according to that in which it is like; just as, therefore, the existential being of an effect is the formal terminus at which production is terminated, so a similar causal being will be the formal principle of such efficiency. Thirdly, because God is supremely effective for the reason that He is, by essence, being itself, supreme and most perfect. Hence, a creature will be effective by reason of some perfect sharing in such being, therefore, created existence can very well be a source of effecting. For why will this be repugnant to it? Surely not because it is existential being, since God's existential being is active. Nor because it is finite existential being, both because also the essential being of a creature is finite, and also because an infinite perfection is not required for acting on the part of a presupposed subject. Nor because it is being received in an essence, both because also material form is received in matter, and an accident in a subject, and nevertheless they are active; and also because, in reality, being is not properly received in an essence, but only according to reason; about this we shall speak below. [33] Or, finally, because being is such an imperfect act that it cannot be a source of acting. They, who think existence is a distinct thing, and the most perfect act of an essence, cannot say this. For if a thing acts insofar as it is in act and is constituted [34] by existence in most perfect act, then it will be constituted by existence in the order of an active principle. Indeed, according to our opinion, existence, as it is found in the thing itself, is not so much the act of an essence as the very essence in act. So, due to the imperfection of an act, it cannot be repugnant to it to be, in the thing itself, the principle of effecting.

19.   According to reason, existence as such, abstractly and precisely [35] conceived of, is not signified as the formal principle of effecting, but as constituting the form in a state suitable for effecting or operating. But the proper principle of acting is the existing form or the form which would be an actual entity, as was explained in the other causes and more at length above, Disp. 18. [36]

20.   It is understood from this that created existence, according to its common and abstract nature, does not arrogate to itself some determinate type of causality, but is repugnant to none of them. However, according to the determinate grade of existence or according to the perfection of the essence to which the existence belongs, it can partake of this or that type of causality. Thus, because the essence of matter is very imperfect, even if it be constituted in act by existence, it is still not effective but receptive only. So its existence does not share in the genus of an efficient cause, but of material cause only. But it is otherwise in the case of the existence of a form, and thus one must philosophize about the rest.

Notes

[1] See D. Bañez, *In Sum. Theol.*, I, q. 3, a. 4, dub. 1; 142-145. Also see Dominic of Flandria, *In Duodecim Libros Metaphysicae Aristotelis* (Coloniae, 1621), IV, q. 3, a. 4; 172.

[2] See Section V-VI above.

[3] See Capreolus, *Def. Theol.*, *In I Sent.*, d. 8, q. 1; I, 312-313.

[4] See Fonseca, *In 4 Metaph.*, c. 2, q. 4; col. 755-758; *In 5 Metaph.*, c. 7, q. 5; col. 533-534.

[5] See *DM* 34, III-IV; XXVI, 359-379.

[6] See Section VII, 1-7 above.

[7] See D. Bañez, *In Sum. Theol.*, I, q. 3, a. 4, dub. 1; 143-144.

[8] See Sections V-VI above.

[9] *DM* 23, VII-VIII; XXV, 875-882.

[10] See nn. 3 and 4, this section, above.

[11] I read the *recepta* of the 1597 Salamanca and 1605 Mainz editions instead of the garbled *rept a* of the Vives text.

[12] I read the *existat* of the 1597 Salamanca and 1605 Mainz editions instead of the *existant* of the Vives text.

[13] See Section IX above.

[14] See Section IV above.

[15] See Sections III-IV above.

[16] See Section VI above.

[17] *DM* 13, IV-V; XXV, 409-420.

[18] See Section IX above.

[19] See Section VI above.

[20] I read the *ita* of the 1597 Salamanca and 1605 Mainz editions which is deleted in the Vives text.

[21] See *DM* 34; XXVI, 347-424.

[22] See Section XI, 22, below.

[23] See paragraphs 5-6, this section, above.

[24] L. Lossada, S.J., *Cursus Philosophici Regalis Collegii Salmanticensis* (Barcelona: Subirana, 1883), Pt. 3, T. 10, 74; 151-152 cites *Collegium S. Th. Complut.* In any case, see Martin Meurisse, O.F.M., *Rerum Metaphysicarum Libri Tres ad mentem Doctoris Subtilis* (Paris, 1623), Bk. I, q. XVIII, concl. 4; 207-208. Also Franciscus Oviedo, S.J., *Cursus Philosophicus* (Lyons, 1651), *Phys.*, Controv. II, Punct. 1; T. 1, 137b cites Francisco Araujo, O.P.:"Secundo respondet Arauxo lib. 8, Metaph. quaest. 1 art. 2 in fine et art. 3 ad 3 #10 et 11....".

[25] See n. 24 immediately above.

[26] D. Bañez, *In Sum. Theol.*, I, q. 3, a. 4, dub. 4, ad 4; 157b.

[27] See D. Bañez, *In Sum. Theol.*, I, q. 3, a. 4, dub. 4; 150-158.

[28] *Ibid.*, 153-154.

[29] *Ibid.*, 153.

[30] See paragraphs 8-11, this section, above.

[31] See Sections II-III above.

[32] See paragraphs 8-11, this section, above.

[33] See Section XIII, 14-17, below.

[34] I read the *constituetur* of the 1597 Salamanca and 1605 Mainz editions instead of the *constituitur* of the Vives text.

[35] I read the *praecise* of the 1597 Salamanca edition instead of the *praecipe* of the Vives Text.

[36] *DM* 18, II; XXV, 598-615.

Section XI

To what things existence belongs and whether it is simple or composite.

1. Now that the common character of existence, both its causes[1] and effects[2] have been explained, there follows what must be said about the many types of existence of created things. At the same time, in the process, we shall solve the fourth argument proposed in Section I in favor of the first opinion.[3]

Whether existence belongs only to singular things.

2. *The superior grades of a thing exist by absolutely the same existence as the inferior grades.* Thus, one can ask at once whether existence belongs only to singular things or also to common natures. For some[4] say that even though common natures do not exist outside singulars, they still have in them their own peculiar and partial existences by which they formally exist and from which, along with the one existence of a singular thing, or rather its singularity, there comes about one singular existence by which the individual itself adequately exists. This manner of speaking would be probable enough, if the common nature were distinct in reality in the thing itself from the individual. But because this is impossible, as we have shown above,[5] for this reason too, it is impossible to distinguish the existence of a common nature from the existence of a singular thing by some distinction found in the thing itself. And this is so self-evident that it needs no proof.

3.   But I add next that the actual and exercised existence of the
common grades existing in a singular thing neither should nor can
be distinguished even in reason from the particular existence of such
an individual. Indeed, a common nature can be conceived of as abstracted from individuals; yet, as such, it cannot be conceived of as
existing in act, unless it be conceived of erroneously or as something
imaginable, but not as something possible. And although it can be
conceived of as suited for existing, it still cannot be conceived of as
having immediately and in itself such a relation to being, but as having it by means of the individual in which it exists. So it happens that
actual existence cannot be conceived of and exercised in the thing
itself as immediately actuating a common nature as such, but only as
contracted and made individual. There is proof, because a common
nature, with individuation prescinded, is not proximately capable of
existence, indeed, according to that state, actual existence is repugnant to it. Therefore, by conceiving of existence as an act of an
essence, it cannot be conceived of according to reason as having an
immediate relation to a common nature as common, but only to an
individual thing; but it has a relation to the common nature only as
it is made singular in the individual thing. Hence, in Peter, for
example, no twofold existence can be distinguished even according
to reason, one of Peter and the other of man. But there is only one by
which Peter immediately exists, and man mediately, according to
reason.
4.   *Objection: Refutation.* You will say, "The existence of man as such
can be abstractly conceived of just as man himself, and can be distinguished in reason from the individual existences of singular men.
Therefore, in this way, can the existence of a common nature be distinguished in reason from the existence of the individual." A reply is
given by denying the consequence absolutely, because, when existence is conceived of abstractly and universally, it is not taken as
actual and exercised, but only in signate act. I explain this as
follows. For man cannot be conceived of as existing in act by human
existence in common, but by this or that existence; so, when he is
conceived of with a relation to existence in common only, he is conceived of as something abstracted from the actual exercise of existing. Hence, actual existence, which exercises this function in the
thing itself, ought to be conceived of intrinsically as individual and
singular, and consequently as having an immediate relation to an
individual and singular essence; in this way there is no existence,
even distinct in reason, which would have an immediate reference to
a common nature, but only as it is existing in an individual and
made singular in it. Consequently, it must be said simply that existence belongs properly and immediately only to singular things; for

which reason Aristotle said [6] in the proem of 1 *Metaph.* [7] that effecting has to do only with singular things because effecting tends to being which is had only by a singular thing. So also in the chapter on Substance [8] he said that second substances are only in first substances. The argument is established from what has been said, [9] because there can be no being *(ens)* in act except an individual and a singular one. But existence in reality is nothing else than the very actual entity of an individual thing. But, then, if in one and the same individual thing we distinguish in reason the specific individual from the generic individual, then shall we also be able to distinguish in reason the existence of the one from the existence of the other. Yet both existences will be conceived of as the existence of a singular and individual thing to which it bespeaks an immediate relation according to reason. Hence, every existence, both in reality and according to the true order of conceiving, is immediately the existence of some singular thing.

WHETHER EXISTENCE BELONGS TO THE SUPPOSIT ALONE OR TO THE INDIVIDUAL NATURE AS WELL.

5.   But then a further question can be asked, that is, whether existence in created substances belongs to the supposit alone or also to the nature? For all the philosophers and theologians, who think existence is not distinguished from an essential entity, logically think that not only the supposit but also the substantial individual nature has its own proper existence. [10] So, in Christ the Lord, they think that His humanity retained the proper existence of the nature even if there were no proper and created supposit in it. But then the disciples of St. Thomas think the contrary. Yet they are split, for Capreolus [11] and others [12] surely teach that substantial existence belongs immediately and essentially to the supposit alone, but in such a way that existence does not suppose, as naturally prior, a constituted supposit and actuates that in the order of existing, but that it itself formally constitutes the supposit. So it happens that, according to this opinion, if we prescind from that which is the quasi-subject or receiver of existence, truly it is not the supposit but the nature itself. For the supposit is rather the composite or the constitute of nature and existence. So existence will belong to the supposit as to the constitute, but to the nature as to the actuable potency. This opinion is false in this because it confuses existence with subsistence and does not grant existence its proper formal effect which is to constitute a thing in act in the order of actual being *(ens)*. We have touched upon this matter above [13] and we intend to speak of it more at length below when treating of nature and supposit. [14]

6.   But then Cajetan [15] and others [16] teach that existence supposes a supposit constituted in the order of supposit and actuates it, and immediately and essentially constitutes a being *(ens)* existing in act. Their basis is because only the supposit is that which is, properly speaking, just as only the supposit is that which operates; for operation belongs to that to which being belongs. Hence, existence is immediately and essentially an act of the supposit. But, as a consequence, it is communicated to the nature and its parts. This opinion, indeed, would certainly be probable if existence were a thing distinct from the substantial nature, although what subsistence would do in regard to the substantial nature, precisely considered as it is an essence and is [17] naturally prior to existing, could be explained with difficulty. But we will discuss this in the cited disputation dealing with supposit. [18] However, absolutely speaking, this opinion is not speaking of accidental existence, as is self-evident; rather it can be understood concerning substantial existence, either concerning every existence of every and any actual substantial entity, or only concerning every existence partially complete. Hence, one can grant in this case that existence would belong to the whole supposit alone, as we will soon explain. [19] But this cannot be true of every existence. For it was shown [20] that the actual being of a nature or essence is true existence. But suppositality cannot terminate and modify a nature except by supposing in it some being, actual and outside its causes. Hence, it necessarily supposes some existential being in it; therefore, every existence cannot be the act of a supposit, but some existence is given, which would be the act of the nature. Moreover, suppositality is distinguished in reality from actual essence, as we will show below. [21] But the proper existence of the nature is not distinguished in reality from it as it is a certain actual essence. Hence, some existence must be proper to the nature itself, namely, that which is not distinguished in reality from the same nature.

7.   For this reason existence is correctly divided. A certain existence is entirely complete in the order of substance, which is usually called substantial existence, and it includes not only the actuality of an essence or a nature, but even the mode of such a nature, which is called subsistence, and its actuality. Hence, such existence belongs to the supposit alone, not as its simple act but as composed of the existence of the nature and the existence of the suppositality itself; of this we will speak below. [22] By reason of this existence a thing is said to be simply that which is or a complete being *(ens);* and so it is proper to a supposit, and this is supposed, essentially speaking, for operation; so to-operate is properly ascribed to the supposit or to the subsisting thing. But there is another substantial existence not entirely complete and terminated in its order, because it can still be

terminated by subsistence. This is the existence of the nature as it is a nature, more immediately congruous to it than to subsistence; for just as a substantial nature, even though it be complete in the order of nature, still simply in the order of substance, is not entirely complete until it is subsisting. Such a nature can exist before subsistence with a natural priority, just as in the mystery of the Incarnation the nature exists before its assumption; for everything assumed is presupposed to its assumption, as St. Thomas said in part 3, quest. 4, art. 2 [23] and 3. [24] So in quest. 6, art. 4, reply to the third, [25] he says that the humanity of Christ was a being *(ens)* naturally prior to its being united to the Word. But he speaks of a being *(ens)* in act, for it has been a being *(ens)* in potency from eternity; it is constituted, however, a being *(ens)* in act by existence. Hence, this existence, which is understood as prior to subsistence, must influence the nature proximately and immediately, and not the supposit.

WHETHER EXISTENCE IMMEDIATELY ACTUATES THE PARTS OR THE INTEGRAL NATURE ONLY.

8.   Thirdly, it can be asked what this existence of the nature is like and whether it is immediately the act of only the complete substantial nature or also of its parts. In this matter, omitting the opinion of those who distinguish existence really from essence and who should speak logically according to what was said in the above section, [26] we must say that existence, generally speaking, is not the act of the complete essence alone. But just as essence is distinguished into total or partial, or complete and incomplete, so also must existence be distinguished within that order. Therefore, partial existence is immediately congruous to a part of an essence, although the integral existence of the nature looks immediately to the complete essence. This clearly follows from the stated principle that existence is not distinguished in reality from an actual essence; for, just as the total essence is an actual being *(ens)* so also its parts are actual beings *(entia)*, although partial. Hence, they include proper partial existences which are not distinguished in reality from the very parts of the essence. Further, because prime matter, as it is supposed to form, when conserved or created by God, is an actual entity including some existential being, as was shown above. [27] Hence, it has a proper partial existence because under that aspect and as it is supposed as naturally prior to form, it cannot exist by the existence of the whole, as is self-evident. Again, form, since it is more actual than matter, brings with itself its own proper existence to a much greater extent; and this, when added to the existence of matter, will complete the integral existence of the whole nature. For neither can the existence of a form by itself

alone be integral and total, not only because a form alone is not the total essence of a thing according to the truer opinion, but also because, since the existence of a form supposes the existence of matter, and since it must be united to that, it must not be total but partial so as to be able to compose a substantial unit with it.

9.   A conclusion is drawn from this that existence is not always a simple entity nor always composite, but that it is such as the essence demands. So if an essence be simple and at the same time be complete and integral, existence similarly will be simple and total in its own order, or within the order of nature; and the substantial existence of an angelic nature is of this sort. But if an essence be simple and partial, existence similarly will be simple, and incomplete or partial in that order; and the existences of matter and substantial form are of this sort. If an essence be composed of form and matter, and be complete and integral, in a similar way existence will be composed of the existences of matter and form, and integral and total in its own order. Finally, if an essence is indeed composed of matter and form and yet be not a total essence but an integral part of another, it will have a similar or proportional existence. For thus does the head, for example, or the hand, have a partial essence composed of matter and form; and so it is partial because it consists of partial matter and of form, either partial or at least partially (so to speak) and inadequately informing that part of matter. Hence, according to the mode of essence, such is the existence of each and every thing, which [is] what clearly follows from the foundation set down, that an actual essence and existence are the same in reality.

10.   Against this solution, many objections are customarily made, but they can be reduced to three principal points. The first includes the authorities and arguments by which it is usually proved that matter has no existence but receives it all from form, [28] because of itself it is pure potency and next to nothing. If, though, it were to have existence of itself, it would have actuality of itself and that most perfect, for existence is perfect act and a perfect participation of divine being, according to Dionysius, chapt. 5, *On Divine Names*. [29] A further point is because it follows that form causes nothing in matter, because it bestows neither essence nor existence on it. A final point is that otherwise matter could be without form, at least by the absolute power; and St. Thomas [30] often teaches the opposite of this. There was a long discussion of all these points above in Disp. 13 [31] and 15. [32] So it is briefly stated that in two ways one can understand that matter has no existence of itself but receives it all from form. First, that matter does not have existence without being dependent on form by its nature; and we agree that in this sense matter receives existence from form, as was sufficiently explained in Section 9. [33] Another

meaning is that matter would contain no proper existence in its actual entity, but would obtain it entirely from form, with the result that by the form itself or by something which, by reason of form, is given to matter, it formally and intrinsically exists and is constituted in the being of actual entity; and this sense is false. So, in the opposite sense we grant that matter has its own proper existence which it does not formally have from form. This was sufficiently proved in the above sections.[34] In the same place it was also explained how matter is a pure receptive potency in relation to a formal act, but not to an entitative act or to an act of existence. However, it is said to be next to nothing because it holds the lowest place in perfection among substantial beings. Still, by the very fact that it is said to be next to nothing, it is logically said to have something of entity by which it recedes from nothing; and thereby it has something of existence. But even though being itself as such be said to be most noble, still not every being is most perfect; but in it are found degrees according to the diversity of things and essences. So, even though matter has some proper being, nevertheless, because it is most imperfect in the order of substance, for that reason, matter can be imperfect and next to nothing, such being notwithstanding. Further, though matter has a proper existence, it still has that as dependent upon form; and in this way form is said to confer being on it, as was explained in the above sections.[35] But just how great and of what sort this dependence on form is, was extensively explained in the reference cited.[36] So there is no need to say more about these objections here.

11.   The second chief objection is taken from the angle of form, and especially from the rational soul whose being is the same as the being of the whole man or humanity. But that is a simple and non-composite being, because it remains in the soul alone and is, in consequence, wholly spiritual. Consequently, though humanity is a composite essence, its being is still not composite; therefore, for the same reason proportionately the same will have to be said of any composite substantial nature. The antecedent is very well received in the School of St. Thomas on the basis of his teaching in part 1, quest. 76, art. 1, reply to the fourth[37] and in *On Being and Essence,* c. 5.[38] And in these passages Cajetan supports and explains it at length[39] and Ferrara in Bk. 2 *Against the Gentiles,* c. 63, near the beginning.[40] And it can be urged by reason in this way, because the being of the whole man cannot be material, otherwise a soul could not exist by that being. Hence, it must be spiritual, for there is no middle ground between these two. Therefore, in itself, it is incorruptible and everlasting; and it is befitting, essentially and immediately, to the soul, remaining in it after the separation. Secondly, because as long as the soul is in a body, it exists by the being of the whole,

therefore, it does not have being distinct from the being of the whole. Otherwise, it would simultaneously exist by two beings, and this is redundant and impossible. Consequently, the being of the soul and of the whole composite is the same.

12.   An answer to this objection is that the ones who think that existence is a thing distinct from essence, think, logically enough of course, that this being in man is immaterial, and, logically, immediately befits the soul, and through it is imparted to matter and the whole composite. But, then, given the contrary principle, of course, that existence is not distinct in reality from actual essence, it must be said that the being of the rational soul is related to the being of man or humanity just as the soul, in its essence, is related to the essence of man or humanity. The soul is not the whole essence of man, nor is it even fully distinguished from it so as not to be included in it, but it is distinguished as a part from the whole. So, then, the being of the soul is not the whole being of man or humanity, nor is it so fully distinguished from it as not to be included in it. It is intrinsically composing it and it is that which is foremost in the very being of man, even though it could not be the whole, because the body itself has some proper being which it also imparts to humanity in its own order of cause, namely, material. And Scotus in 4, dist. 43, quest. 1[41] and in *Quodlib.*, quest. 9[42] also thought this.

13.   Nor did St. Thomas teach at any time that the being of the soul alone is the total and integral being of the whole humanity. But in the reference cited, *On Being and Essence,* c. 5,[43] he says rather that one being in one composite comes from the soul and body, and he is clearly speaking about existential being. Then, if the being of man were not other than the very spiritual being of the soul, imparted and, so to speak, extended to the body, it would not be proper to say that that being results from the soul and body. What St. Thomas[44] adds at once, that that being, as it belongs to the soul, is not dependent on the body, does not mean that the whole being of man would endure in the separated soul and be independent of the body; because neither the words themselves manifest this meaning, nor is there anything to compel us to this interpretation. For the best meaning is that that being, *as it belongs to the soul,* that is, in regard to the part of it which looks to the soul, does not depend on the body. St. Thomas[45] places the differences between the being of a rational soul and other forms in the fact that other forms have being only as they inform matter and depend on it. But the soul has independent being and imparts it to matter when it informs it. Not because the matter formally exists by that being, but because it is actuated, perfected and supported or conserved by it. When the soul is separated, it can keep that same being in itself, because it is spiritual and sub-

sistent, though not wholly complete in the order of substance. Also, for this reason, St. Thomas was sometimes able to say that the be- ing, which belonged to the composite, endures in the separated soul, as is clear in the references given, 2 *Against the Gentiles,* c. 81, reply to the third,[46] *Quodlib.* 10, art. 3[47] and 6.[48] He never says in these refe- rences that the being of the soul is the whole being of the composite, but only that which comes to be or is the being of the composite when it is imparted to the body. However, it can be called the being of the composite as its act and principal perfection, although it is not its integral and total being. If anyone make a final contention that St. Thomas thought that that very immaterial being which endures in the separated soul is the integral and total being by which the whole man exists, which he inserts into the passages cited and else- where, as one can see in 1, d. 8, quest. 5, art. 2, reply to the second[49] and third[50] and dist. 15, art. 3[51] and many times elsewhere,[52] he, in consequence, ought to say that St. Thomas goes on to say in that opinion that being would be a thing distinct from essence; we are not now defending that.

14.   The first argument is answered by denying that the being of man is entirely immaterial, but rather it must be termed absolutely material just as the essence of man is material. However, the nature of man[53] is material, not because all the parts which make it up are material, but because one is material. For a thing is called immate- rial which does not consist of matter, since the negation included therein excludes a compostion of matter. So every thing which con- sists of matter, although from another source it is constituted by a spiritual and immaterial form, exists as simply material and must be termed so. Consequently, in like manner, the total being of man is material, not because every partial being which makes it up is mate- rial, but because it derives from the being of the body, which is material, and the being of the soul. But when an objection is made because the soul cannot exist by material being, the answer has to be that it cannot exist adequately and as by a proper act by that sort of being, and yet also, that is can exist inadequately or partially by that sort of being, not insofar as it consists of a material part, but insofar as it includes another spiritual part, proper and proportioned to the soul itself. Accordingly, this integral being of man is adequate to the whole man, but inadequate to its particular parts, that is, exceeding them; and so it does not actuate single parts according to its whole self, but according to something of itself, while maintaining a pro- portion with the single parts. Hence, the argument could be refuted, for also a material body cannot formally and intrinsically exist by immaterial being, because a body itself is an actual entity, material and extended, which is intrinsically constituted by some actual being

and which must also be material and extended; this being is true existence, as was proved in the above sections.[54] Consequently, a body itself cannot exist intrinsically by immaterial being; therefore, the being of the whole man must be material, as composed of the material being of the body and the immaterial being of the soul.

15.   Also, there is a ready response to the second argument from this, which can be made in regard to matter itself and to every part existing in the whole. So one must say that a part existing in the whole exists by the being of the whole, and by a proper being, yet[55] in a different way; and thus it does not exist by two beings, but by one and the same, considered under different aspects. For the being of the whole and the part are not properly two, but are related as container and contained. Therefore, just as the part is included in the whole, so does it exist by the being of the whole mediately and inadequately or (so to speak) excessively. However, it exists immediately and adequately by a proper being, which is partial and included in the being of the whole. Consequently, it does not exist by the being of the whole except by reason of that partial being which it includes. As a result it does not exist by two beings but by one and the same.

16.   The third principal objection was set forth above in section one, in the fourth argument for the first opinion.[56] It aims to prove that the being of a composite nature cannot be composite, and in its proof many things are touched upon which have already been explained. The first is, because otherwise matter would have proper partial being, and thus it would not be pure potency. An answer has already been given[57] to this, that it is indeed pure potency in relation to a formal substantial act, because of itself it has none, and that thus it is a pure receptive potency, yet not an objective potency, because it must have some real entity; otherwise it could not have even a real receptive potency.

17.   The second was, because otherwise a substantial unit would not result from matter and form, for a substantial unit does not come forth from two beings *(ens)* in act. The answer to this is as follows. If the discussion be about beings *(ens)* in act as they are distinguished from beings *(ens)* in potency, (for we are now speaking of a being *(ens)* in act in this sense, for thus through existence is it formally and intrinsically constituted a being *(ens)* in such an actuality), then speaking in this way about a being *(ens)* in act, it not only is not repugnant for a substantial unit to be constituted of two beings *(ens)* in act, but it is even impossible for it to be constituted except of beings *(ens)* in act. For a being *(ens)* in potency, since it is nothing, cannot constitute something in act, but only in potency, as was quite frequently noted in the above sections.[58] Further, that axiom taken

in that sense cannot be based on any probable argument. For why would it be impossible to constitute a substantial unit in such an order out of two beings *(ens)* which would be partial in their own order, even though they would have partial entities in act, that is, outside their own causes, and would be united by them for composition? Besides, even in the opinion of the opponents, it cannot be denied that matter and form would have some proper actuality in essential being by which they are united for composing an essence, which, in essential being is an essential unit, even though it consists of two beings *(ens)* in act in the same essential being. Consequently, it will be the same case with the same proportion in existential being. Indeed, in reality it is entirely the same, because actual essential being is true existential being. Likewise, in material beings *(entibus),* in regard to composition out of integral parts, it cannot be denied that just as a form is extended and divisible, so too is existence. For who would believe that the existence of a stone or a tree is so indivisible that it is wholly in the whole and wholly in whatever part? Hence, such an existence of a whole stone or tree consists of integrating parts. Consequently, these parts are united as partial actual beings *(entia),* and yet out of them is composed a substantial unit. Therefore, that inference must be denied in this sense. For the principle by which it is proved, taken in the same sense, has no evidence or probability.

18. Therefore, when it is said *a substantial unit does not come forth from two beings in act,* it must be understood about complete beings *(ens),* of which one is not related to the other as potency to an act of the same genus, nor as a part to the whole, or to a complementary part, according to statements above[59] about being essentially and accidentally. And it amounts to the same thing, were we to say that that axiom is understood about beings *(entibus)* simply, which are beings *(entia)* essentially and not set up for composing other beings *(entia).* In this sense, that proposition is not correctly applied in the present case and the inference is not made correctly, because matter and form are not beings *(entia)* simply, nor complete, but by their own nature set up to complete a being *(ens)* simply. So, even though a proper entitative actuality be understood in them, out of them is very well composed a substantial unit, which is a being *(ens)* simply and complete.

19. *Why some forms cannot be naturally separated from matter.* Thirdly, the conclusion being drawn from this opinion of ours was that every form can naturally be without matter, and matter without form, because, if these parts have proper partial existences, each and every one, by its own existence, could exist without some part or without the whole. An answer is made by denying the sequence, and, as to

the proof, the assumption is also denied. For, by the fact that existence is not complete but partial, it can depend on an extrinsic formal cause or a material cause, if such an existence be also material. But when one objects, because it is the nature of existence to be sufficient for constituting a thing outside it own causes, a ready answer is that it is its nature to be sufficient in its own order, namely, in the order of formal act or intrinsic mode. It is not of its nature to be independent of every other efficient or formal or material cause. There is a clear example in an accident's existence which formally makes it exist, but not independently of a subject, as was also touched upon in the above sections. [60] But what is added in the same place, [61] because if matter and form cannot naturally exist except in a composite whose existence can be terminated, it would be superfluous to give it partial existence; this (I say) is already settled from what was said. [62] For, though these parts cannot exist except in the whole, still there is no existence of the whole unless it is made up of the existences of the parts; nor can the parts exist by the existence of the whole except [63] to the extent that it includes partial existences adapted to the single parts. So, the partial existences are not superfluous, but entirely necessary, for the parts to have an actuality sufficient for composing the whole, as well as to have the integral existence of the whole composite made up of them.

20.   Finally, in regard to that objection, [64] that if matter and form had proper partial existences, one would exist naturally prior to the other and, consequently, could exist naturally without the other, the answer must be that prime matter, by reason of the fact that it comes forth and is conserved by creation, does exist naturally prior to form. Yet, it must be said that it cannot be concluded from this that it exists naturally without form, because it can require that as a necessary condition and quality, or as a formal act without which there is no need for it to be. In this way it frequently occurs that what is naturally prior in one order cannot be without what is posterior. A lengthy statement about this was made in the above sections in the treatment about the causes, [65] especially in Discussion 18 [66] and in volume one of the third part about question two [67] and seventeen [68] I have touched upon many things about this matter. But, then, a material form which is educed from the potency of matter does not exist naturally prior to its union with matter, because the action by which it comes to be depends essentially on matter. And in this rests the difference between the rational soul and the other forms, that the former exists naturally prior to its union because it comes to be by creation, which is an act independent of a subject; and so, by that creation it receives being, in which it subsists naturally prior to its union to a body; and due to that creation it can naturally retain it,

though it be separated from the body. But the other forms, even though they receive a proper partial existence, are still not suited to subsisting naturally in themselves but are suited to being dependent on matter as the source of their support, and so, neither in themselves are the other forms naturally prior to being in matter nor can they be conserved in separation from matter.

21. *The existence of matter for comparison with the existence of form.* Fourthly, the conclusion was drawn that one partial existence is compared to another as potency to act, and this seemed to be repugnant to an existential actuality. But an answer was already made to this in the above sections, [69] and it was explained how some existence, although it constitutes a thing in act, that is, outside nothing and outside objective potency, could nonetheless be compared to another existence, as receptive potency to act, speaking of existence physically and really, as was set forth above. [70]

How existence is termed the ultimate actuality is explained.

22. Also, incidentally, an inference is drawn from this as to how the statement of many that existence is an ultimate act or the ultimate actuality of a thing is to be understood. For St. Thomas speaks this way in the single question *On the Soul,* a. 6, reply to the second, [71] and Cajetan, part 1, quest. 3, art. 4 on the second argument of St. Thomas. [72] But other Thomists [73] also say that existence is rather the first actuality of a thing, since being is the first act of whatever thing rather than the ultimate. This diversity, given the teaching we proposed, can consist in merely the meaning of the words. For actual existence is said to be an essential act or actuality, not physically or really, but metaphysically and according to reason; and in this way, for different reasons, it can be called a first act or an ultimate act. For in regard to the essential predicates, insofar as one is compared to the other as act to metaphysical potency, existence is called an ultimate act, because it constitutes in act the whole essence that includes all the essential predicates; and that is what, in our way of understanding, ultimately happens to an essence, in constituting the intrinsic and actual entity of a thing. But, then, in regard to those things which follow upon an essence, be they properties or operations or other accidents, the existence of a creature has the character of a first act, rather than of an ultimate one, for, in the teaching of Aristotle, 2 *On the Soul,* text 2 [74] and 5, [75] *form is first act,* because it grants being, on which follows operation that is second act. Consequently, for the same reason, every being compared to an operation or property which flows from it has the character of a first act rather

than an ultimate one. For this reason, as being has been, so will its actuality be, and it will be able to have such a character of first act. For, if it be perfect being, it will be an act in the manner of an efficient principle with regard to the things that flow from it. If it be imperfect being, it will be able to be a first act after the manner of a receptive potency. Consequently, it is not of the character of being as such that it be a pure or ultimate actuality in such a way that it cannot be perfected by a further act; but that pertains to the highest and the most perfect being. Whether existence be comparable to essence in perfection will be discussed below. [76]

THE EXISTENCE OF ACCIDENTS.

23.   Fourthly, it can be asked logically whether accidental forms have a proper existence and confer it on a subject. Certain of the more recent Thomists [77] hold it as likely that accidents have no other existence than the existence of the subject in which they are. And it seems that they have their basis only in this, that the being of the subject is sufficient so that through it all the accidents exist which have been really joined to it; therefore, there is no reason why more beings be multiplied in the same subject. In addition there is this, that an accident is not so much a being *(ens)* as a being *(ens)* of a being *(entis)*, as Aristotle attests in 7 *Metaph.*, in the beginning. [78] So it is commonly said that the being of an accident is being-in, because, surely, neither is it a being *(ens)* nor does it have being, except insofar as it shares in the being of its subject. Finally, the existence of an accident is not the very inherence, since, with inherence changed, an accident can retain the same existence. Nor is the existence of an accident the essence alone, for the essence of an accident consists in aptitudinal inherence, not in actual existence. Consequently, the very existence will be that of the subject. For nothing else is found in an accident besides these.

24.   *The rejection.* This opinion is supported neither by sound argument nor by any authority. Indeed, all the authors [79] who hold that existence is not a thing other than actual essence, must grant that just as an accidental form has a proper essence, so it must have a proper existence. This is what Scotus teaches, in 4, dist. 12, quest. 1, [80] and others [81] commonly. On the other hand, the ones who think that existence is a thing distinct from essence, still teach that the essence of an accident has a proper existence proportionate to itself, distinct both from its own essence and from the essence and existence of the substance. Thus the Thomists commonly maintain this, Soncinas, 7 *Metaph.*, quest. 5, [82] Flandria, quest. 1, art. 5, [83] Cajetan, c. 7 *On Being and Essence* after quest. 16, [84] and part 1, quest. 28, art.

2,[85] and it is drawn from St. Thomas, 3 p., q. 17, art. 2,[86] and 4 *Against the Gentiles,* c. 14,[87] and in 1, d. 3, q. 2, art. 3,[88] and d. 20, q. 1, art. 5.[89]

25.   Consequently, it must be said that an accidental form has its own proper existential being, which it imparts to a subject when it informs it. This statement is quite certain, as I have said,[90] if existence be not distinct in reality from essence. Thus it can be proved by the same arguments by which we have confirmed that opinion,[91] that is, because an accidental form, as distinct from a subject, is an actual entity. Therefore, in itself it intrinsically includes an existence distinct from the subject, and also, because an accidental form can be produced in a substance by a new proper action. But that new action must of necessity be terminated at some new existential being. Further, the mystery of the Eucharist especially confirms this, wherein numerically the same accidents are conserved without a substance. They are not conserved without existence. This argument[92] also appears in the position which distinguishes existence from essence. For what certain ones[93] have dared to say, that after the consecration of the Eucharist, even though the essence of bread does not remain, the substantial existence of the bread still remains in order for quantity and the other accidents to exist by it; this (I say) is more than false and improbable in Theology, because according to sound teaching and the definitions of the Councils,[94] the accidents alone remain in the Eucharist after the consecration has taken place, as was treated at some length in volume 3, on the third part of St. Thomas.[95] Consequently, since the existence of an accident remains, while the existence of the substance does not remain, one must say that an accident has a proper existence distinct from the existence of a substance.

26.   Nevertheless, the response could be made (if existence and essence are distinct things) that, indeed, the existence of the bread does not remain, but another is created by which the accidents would be conserved. In the first place, this reply proposes a new and unheard-of miracle. In the second place, it proposes that numerically the same actual entity is conserved with a different existence, which, as we have shown above,[96] is impossible, because, if numerically the same actual entity remains, then that being by which a thing intrinsically has such an actuality remains. But this is existential being. Finally, in reference to that existence which is said to be created anew, I shall ask if it is substantial or accidental? The first cannot be said. For, according to the faith, it is as certain that there does not remain any reality of whatsoever substance in that sacrament besides the body of Christ, as it is certain that there does not remain anything of the substance of bread. If the second be said,

then it is an admission that the accidental existence is of an order inferior to every substantial existence. Consequently, such an existence can also be naturally possible, and connatural to the essence of an accident. So we can go on in our argumentation, because such is the existence of things as the essence is, for whether they be distinguished in reality or in reason, they must maintain a mutual proportion. But the essence of an accident is such that by its own nature it depends on the existence of a subject. Therefore, it must be distinct from the existence of a substance, because the same existence cannot be dependent and independent of a suject.

27.   Indeed, these arguments are effective, given the true concept of existence, namely, that it be that by which a being in act as such is formally and intrinsically constituted. But if it be imagined that existence is something else, for example, a certain necessary condition for essential actuality but distinct from it, no effective argument can prove that such a condition is required for the being of accidents besides the being of a substance; unless such a condition be said to be actual inherence itself which some [97] confuse with the existence of an accident in not acknowledging that it is necessary they be distinguished in reality itself, since, as I have touched on above, [98] the existence of an accident can be conserved without inherence. I will speak about this again in what follows. [99] Consequently, in an accident, in addition to actual inherence, one must understand an existence distinct from the existence of the substance and naturally dependent on the substance by means of actual inherence, even though it can be conserved by God without the existence of substance and without actual inherence. But it is of itself unbelievable that an accidental form posits another distinct entity in a subject, which is the existence of an accident, besides its own actual or essential entity and its inherence, because neither what such an entity is for, nor what it contributes to, a subject, or to the accident itself, is conceivable.

28.   Thus, therefore, in regard to an existence which would not be a thing distinct from the actual essence of an accident, it is a certain and evident fact to me that an accident has its own proper existence distinct from substantial existence. This very point strongly supports the opinion expressed about the identity of essence and existence. But that an accidental form would impart to a subject an existence really distinct from itself, [100] I neither understand nor do I see a basis why it is to be believed. For whiteness, precisely by the fact that it inheres in a subject, constitutes that white thing by its very entity. This is to give it its whiteness. Consequently, every other being-of-whiteness is superfluous and is devised without foundation. Therefore, the ones who really distinguish existence from essence can say

nothing consistently on the present point. On the one hand, their procedure will appear not inept when they ascribe only a single and simple existence to a substantial supposit, which would primarily terminate the dependence of a substantial essence, and secondarily terminate the dependence of all accidents, lest they be forced to multiply so many entities without reason. For, if one denies that matter has a proper existence because of its imperfection, I do not see why one cannot deny that an accidental form, which is a less perfect being *(ens)* than matter, imparts a proper and distinct existence. On the other hand, it is well enough established that this very way of speaking is also not quite consistent with that opinion, because it can give no reason why a substantial form imparts a distinct existence, with proportion maintained, and an accidental form does not. Nor is it more able to explain what such a distinct existence imparts to a substantial form already, with a natural priority, informing matter, than what a distinct accidental existence imparts to an accidental form already inherent in a subject. In addition, it cannot explain what it is to terminate the dependence of an accidental essence, if already, by a natural priority, that essence is supposed as actual, that is, already effected in reality and inherent in a subject. Finally the mystery of the Eucharist has given sufficient evidence that that opinion is absolutely improbable. Consequently, we have only these things to show how much in accord with the truth is the opinion denying a real distinction of existence from actual essence.

29.   *How the being of an accident is a being-in.* Therefore, as to the basis of the opposite opinion, it is denied that substantial being suffices for accidents to exist by it, because it is not proportionate to them, and also because, as I have often said, [101] no thing can be formally and intrinsically constituted as a being *(ens)* in act (which is existing) by a being or entity distinct from itself. The answer to the second is that an accident is called a being *(ens)* of a being *(entis),* not because in the order of being *(ens)* it is intrinsically constituted by the being of its subject, but because it has its whole being along with a certain transcendental relation to a subject. For it is solely for perfecting that subject, and, because its being is such, and so weak and imperfect, it can be supported only in another. In the same sense must that axiom, *the being of an accident is being-in,* be interpreted, for if it be understood of actual inherence, that inherence is not formally the being of an accident. However, it can be so labelled causally, because naturally speaking, being is not imparted to an accident except by means of inherence. If that axiom be understood of aptitudinal inherence, then being-in is said to be the being itself of the accident, because that being is such that an actual entity constituted by it is in proximate aptitude to inhering; and it naturally demands actual inherence

so it can be. And from this there is a ready answer to the third argument, that the existence of an accident is not actual inherence, nor a potential essence or one only objectively conceived, but that it is the accident's very essence, actual and produced in reality.

THE EXISTENCE OF THE MODES.

30.   *The true opinion.* The question can be asked if the mode of a thing, not really but in reality or modally distinguished from it, has a proper and particular existence, distinct from the thing whose mode it is. There are many who[102] support the negative side. Indeed, they think that the modal distinction, as different from the real one, consists in this, that, although a mode has a distinct formal and essential character, still in no way does it have a distinct existence. However, given the principles already proposed, it must of necessity be said that, in the way that each thing and every thing is something made or produced in reality, it includes a proper being by which it is constituted in that actuality; and this must be entirely the same in reality with its constitute, and distinct from everything else from which its constitute is distinguished, and in the same way; for all these necessarily accompany one another. Accordingly, if it be a substantial mode, as subsistence, for example, which (as we now suppose) is not really but only modally distinguished, then that has its own proper existential being modally distinct as well from the existence of the substantial nature. And this can be shown from arguments used above,[103] namely, because that mode which is subsistence, is distinguished in the thing itself from the nature as something actual and posited outside its own causes is really distinguished from another being *(ens),* also actual; consequently, it must include a proper being distinct in the same way from another being *(ens).* Likewise, because that mode can be destroyed while the nature with its existence is conserved, and then it loses some being; and similarly it can be produced in an already existent nature. Every coming to be is terminated to some existential being, as was proved above.[104] Consequently, it is necessary that such a mode, just as it is in act in reality, so it has proper being.

31.   One must philosophize in the same way about an accidental mode with respect to that thing whose mode it is. As, for example, about figure in regard to quantity and about action or motion in regard to its terminus and so about others, for the argument is the same in all of these matters. I have said, *in regard to the thing whose mode it is,* because in that regard, such an existence is only modally distinct. But in regard to other things, a real distinction would also be possible, as the mode itself is distinguished. This is the case with

figure, which is only modally distinguished from quantity, yet has the same real distinction from the other things really distinct from quantity; we have spoken at length about this matter above, in Discussion 7 [105] where we also showed that a modal distinction is not distinguished from a real one in this, that it does not include a distinct existence, but in this, that the existence of the one term is not of such an essence which could, by itself alone, establish an entity, but it is that of a mode which essentially and in itself depends immediately upon some other entity, as was explained there at quite some length. [106]

Corollaries from the above teaching.

32.   From these remarks one understands at once the meaning to be acknowledged from what we said above, [107] that existence is not a thing distinct from essence. For essence can be taken in two ways. In one way, in the proper and most customary signification; and in this way it signifies the nature of a thing. Thus we say that humanity is the essence of man, and the theologians say that there is one essence in the three divine persons. Essence is taken more broadly in another way for any essential characteristic, as when we say that whatever is, has its own essence in the way in which it is because nothing [108] can be without its own proper and intrinsic essential character; and in this way also subsistence has its own essence, and so too figure and the other modes, whether substantial or accidental. Therefore, when we compare essence with existence, we are speaking in this latter signification and generality. For, accordingly, we are now concerned with being *(ens)* and essence, created in common, and so essence also should be compared to a proportionate existence. Each and every essence has identity with that existence by which it is constituted in its proper and precise actuality. So humanity is the same as its existence, by which it is precisely constituted in the being of such an essence or actual nature. But if it be compared to the existence of the whole man, it is not entirely the same as it, because man not only includes the nature or essence of man, but also subsistence; and thus, the adequate existence of man also includes the existence of the whole subsistence, in terms of which it is distinguished from humanity, as container from contained. Hence, to make a correct comparison, it should be made precisely between each and every actual essence with that being by which each is constituted in such an actual fashion. In this way there is a universally true rule that each and every being *(ens)* in act is really the same as its adequate being, and that each and every actual essence is the same as its existence: substantial with substantial, total with total, partial with partial, accidental with accidental, and modal with modal.

33.   Nor is it the case that we exempt relations from this general rule as certain authors[109] think, who, though they teach that an accidental form imparts a proper existential being, and at the same time also teach that created relations are realities or modes really distinct from their foundation, nevertheless exempt them; nor do they think they impart a proper existence, but they exist by the existence of the foundation, because otherwise the very existence of a relation would express a relation to a term and, as a result, existence would be relative. Consequently, either the relation would be expressed twice in regard to its term, if existence is a thing other than essence; or if they are identical, the same relation would be expressed twice, once to a subject by reason of existence, again to a term by reason of essence. This opinion is usually ascribed to Cajetan, 1 p., q. 28, art. 2.[110] But in that place he teaches rather that relation imparts a proper being along with itself, really distinct from its essence, even though he claims that that being is not related to a term but only to a subject, following St. Thomas, in 1, d. 33, quest. 1, art. 1, reply to the first.[111] Hence, this exception is not true, but just as relation has an essence, real, actual and proper and distinct from the other essences of things, so it must have a proper existence, accordingly distinct from the existence of the foundation, just as the relation itself was distinct. Consequently, if relation is an accidental entity really distinct from a foundation, it must have an existence really distinct as well, especially in our opinion, because existence is the actual essence itself. Similarly, the ones who[112] think that a relation is only distinguished as a mode of the foundation, should ascribe the same distinction to its existence for the same reason, and because the general arguments made above[113] have, in the present case, the same strength, given the supposition mentioned.[114] But if relation is distinguished from a foundation only in reasoned reason, in the same way will it have a distinct and proper existence for the same proportional reason.

34.   This is why logically it must be admitted in our opinion that the existence of a relation is relative in the same way the relation itself is, if we speak ontologically, because they are entirely and thoroughly identified. It is also because a relation, as actual and posited in reality, essentially includes both references, namely, to a subject whose form it is acccording to its whole self, and to a term to which it relates the subject which it informs. To be sure, these are not two real relations but are so according to reason only. For in reality there is one complete reference or difference of relation by which it looks to a subject in such a way as to refer it to a term, and looks to a term in such a way as to refer a subject to it. Just as a habit, for example, at once both by the same intrinsic and complete relation looks to the power whose habit it is, and the object to which it inclines the potency.

But this whole reference befits a relation, not only essentially, but also existentially, because such is the actuality of relation that it includes both in its actual entity. Therefore, relation has a proper existence proportionate to it, nor does it follow therefrom that a relation is expressed or referred twice to a term, because it is not referred in act except insofar as it is such a form existing in act; and so it is referred by one relation, or rather it refers the subject by reason of its actual essence or existence. But that it twice be related or express a relation according to reason, to a subject and a term, is not at all unsuitable, it is even necessary, even though that relation which looks to a subject, precisely considered, is not proper to a relation as it is a relation, but is common to the rest of the accidents. However, here there used to occur a theological difficulty, because it follows that also divine relations have proper existences; but I have discussed this matter at length in volume 1 of the third part, discussion 11, section 2. [115]

35. *How one thing is said to have only one being.* Finally, from all that has been said, it is understood how it is true that one thing has only one existence or one being. For this is true of being adequate and proportionate to that thing whose being it is. So also the soul and humanity and man have one being respectively (so to speak), even though absolutely and in itself there is not one and the same being for all of them. For the soul is one being *(ens)* and humanity as well, and even man, but not in the same way nor are they entirely the same being *(ens)*. For the soul is one partial being *(ens)* as a physical form, but humanity is one being *(ens)* as a certain whole in regard to the soul and as one complete nature, but not as an altogether complete being *(ens)* or complete substance, because it is not a supposit but a metaphysical nature or form. But man, whether Peter or Paul, is one being *(ens)* as a certain complete whole in regard to humanity. And so, each and every one of these has one being proportionate to itself, but not in itself entirely the same. For the being of humanity includes more that the being of the soul, namely, the being of the body and the union of each; and similarly the being of man includes more than the being of humanity, namely, the being of subsistence. Consequently, the being of the soul is one as simple, but the being of humanity is one as composed of the being of form and matter; and the being of man is one as composed of the being of nature and subsistence. Therefore, in this way, in every one thing there is one complete and adequate being which, in the case of composite things, includes many partial beings, as Scotus has rightly observed, in 4, d. 11, q. 3, § *To the arguments,* [116] where he also says that he himself does not understand that fiction that being be something additional coming to an essence and is not composite, if an essence is composite. [117]

This is something that I, too, (to tell the truth) do not understand. Indeed, I think there has been adequate proof that it cannot be true.

Notes

[1] See Section IX above.

[2] See Section X above.

[3] See Section I, 7-9 above.

[4] See Fonseca, *In V Metaph.*, cap. 18, q. 5; col. 988-998.

[5] See *DM* 5, II; XXV, 148-161.

[6] I read the *dixit* of the 1597 Salamanca and 1605 Mainz editions instead of the *dicit* of the Vives text.

[7] Aristotle, *Metaphysics*, I, 1, 980a 16.

[8] Aristotle, *Metaphysics*, VII, 13, 1038b 15.

[9] See paragraphs 3-4, this section, above.

[10] See Suárez, *In Sum. Theol.*, III, 17; XVIII, 260-272. Also see *Salmanticenses, Cursus Theologicus* (Paris, 1879), Tract. XXI, disp. 8, V, 95; XIV, 73-74.

[11] Capreolus, *Def. Theol., In III Sent.*, d. 6, q. 1; V, 111-124 and *In I Sent.*, d. 8, q. 1; I, 312-313. Also see Suarez, *DM* 34, IV, 2-3; XXVI, 367.

[12] See *Salmanticenses, Cursus Theologicus*, Tract. XXI, disp. 8, dub. III, I, 2; XIV, 54.

[13] See Section V above.

[14] See *DM* 34, IV; XXVI, 367-379.

[15] *Ibid.*, 17-23; XXVI, 372-374. See Cajetan, *In Sum. Theol.*, III, 17, 2; T. 11, 223-229.

[16] See Fonseca, *In V Metaph.*, cap. 8, q. 6; col. 540-556.

[17] I read the *sit* of the 1597 Salamanca and 1605 Mainz editions which is deleted in the Vives text.

[18] *DM* 34, IV; XXVI, 367-379.

[19] See paragraphs 7-9, this section, below.

[20] See Section IV above.

[21] See *DM* 34, IV, XXVI, 367-379.

[22] See paragraph 33, this section, below.

[23] *Sum. Theol.*, III, q. 4, a. 2; T. 11, 74.

[24] *Ibid.*, a. 3; T. 11, 81.

[25] *Sum. Theol.*, III, q. 6, a. 4 ad 3; T. 11, 100.

[26] See Section X, 18-20, above.

[27] See *DM* 13, IV; XXV, 409-414.

[28] See Section VIII, 6, above. Also see *DM* 13, V; XXV, 414-420.

[29] Dionysius, *On The Divine Names*, trans. C.E. Rolt (London: Macmillan, 1920) c. 5, 131-143 esp. 1-4.

[30] See *DM* 13, IV, esp. 6; XXV, 409-414.

[31] *Ibid.*

[32] *DM* 15, IX; XXV, 532-536.

[33] See Section IX, 6-13, above.

[34] See *DM* 13, IV-V; XXV, 409-420; *DM* 15; VIII, 525-532.

35 *Ibid.*

36 *Ibid.*

37 *Sum. Theol.,* I, q. 76, a. 1 ad 4; T. 5, 210.

38 *De Ente et Essentia,* c. 5; 39.

39 Cajetan, *In Sum. Theol.,* I, q. 76, a. 1 ad 4; T. 5, 213a; *In De Ente...,* c. 5, 165-169.

40 Sylvester of Ferrara, *In Cont. Gent.,* II, 63; T. 23, 434.

41 Scotus, *Opus Oxon.,* IV, d. 43, q. 1; T. 20, 4-29.

42 Scotus, *Quaestiones Quodlibetales,* q. 9; T. 25, 379-392, esp. 389-392.

43 *De Ente et Essentia,* c. 5; 39. I read the *c. 5* of the 1597 Salamanca and 1605 Mainz editions instead of the *c. 9* of the Vives text.

44 *Ibid.*

45 *Quaest. Disp. De Anima,* q. 1, a. 1; 281-285.

46 *Sum. Cont. Gent.,* II, 81; T. 13, 504-506.

47 *Quodlibet* 10, a. 3; 198-199. This seems to be incorrect.

48 *Quodlibet* 10, a. 6; 201-202.

49 *In I Sent.,* d. 8, q. 5, a. 2 ad 2; ed. Mandonnet, I, 230. I read *q. 5* of the 1597 Salamanca and 1605 Mainz editions rather than *q. 6* of the Vives text.

50 *Ibid.*

51 This reference seems defective.

52 See *Quaest. Disp. De Anima,* q. 1, a. 14; 332-335.

53 I read the *hominis* of the 1597 Salamanca and 1605 Mainz editions which is deleted in the Vives text.

54 See *DM* 13, V; XXV, 414-420.

55 I read the *tamen* of the 1597 Salamanca and 1605 Mainz editions instead of the *autem* of the Vives text.

56 See Section I, 7-9, above.

57 See paragraph 10, this section, above.

58 See, at least, Sections II and III above as well as Section VIII, 4 and Section X, 13.

59 See *DM* 3, IV; XXV, 125-131.

60 *DM* 16, I; XXV, 566-574. Also see Section IX, 24, above.

61 See n. 56, this section, above.

62 See paragraph 8 and following, this section, above.

63 I read the *nisi* of the 1597 Salamanca and 1605 Mainz editions instead of the *sine* of the Vives text.

64 See n. 56, this section, above.

65 *DM* 15, III; XXV, 512-516; VIII, 17 et seq.; XXV, 530-532.

66 See *DM* 18, I-III; XXV, 592-624. The Vives reference to *Disp. 28* is incorrect. The 1597 Salamanca edition carries the correct one.

67 See Suárez, *In Sum. Theol.,* III, q. 2, disp. 8, sect. 1; XVII, 328-340.

68 See Suárez, *In Sum. Theol.,* III, q. 17, disp. 36, sect. 1; XVIII, 260-270.

69 See Section X, 13-14, above.

70 *Ibid.* Also see *DM* 13, IV-V; XXV, 409-420.

71 *Quaest. Disp. De Anima,* a. 6 ad 2; 302.

72 Cajetan, *In Sum. Theol.,* I, q. 3, a. 4; T. 4, 43.

73 See D. Bañez, *In Sum. Theol.,* I, q. 3, a. 4, dub. 4; 155-156.

[74] Aristotle, *De Anima,* II, 1, 412a 10. The Vives reference to Bk. I is incorrect.

[75] *Ibid.,* 412a 27.

[76] See Section XIII, 20-23, below.

[77] See D. Bañez, *In Sum. Theol.,* I, q. 3, a. 4, dub. 5; 158-160 and Suárez, *In Sum. Theol.,* III, q. 75, a. 2, disp. 49, IV, 8; XXI, 130.

[78] Aristotle, *Metaphysics,* VII, 1, 1028a 10-30.

[79] See Section I, 12, above.

[80] Scotus, *Opus Oxon.,* IV, d. 12, q. 1; T. 24, 136.

[81] See B. Mastrius, *Disputationes in XII Arist. Stag. Libros Metaphysicorum* (Venice, 1646), Disp. 8, q. 4; II, 143-151.

[82] Soncinas, *In 7 Metaph.,* q. 5; 132a-134a.

[83] Dominic of Flandria, *In Duodecim Libros Metaphysicae Aristotelis* (Coloniae, 1621), VII, q. 1, a. 5; 471-473.

[84] Cajetan, *In De Ente...,* c. 7, q. 17; 140, 227.

[85] Cajetan, *In Sum. Theol.,* I, q. 28, a. 2; T. 4, 322.

[86] *Sum. Theol.,* III, q. 17, a. 2; T. 11, 222-223.

[87] *Sum. Cont. Gent.,* IV, 14; T. 15, 55-58.

[88] *In I Sent.,* d. 3, q. 2, a. 3; I, 103-105.

[89] This reference is defective for there is no art. 5 there.

[90] See paragraph 24, this section, above.

[91] See Section II and following above.

[92] See Section I, 10, above.

[93] See Suárez, *In Sum. Theol.,* III, q. 75, a. 2, disp. IV, esp. 8; XXI, 127-132. F. A. Cunningham, S.J., "The 'Real Distinction' in Jean Quidort," *Journal of the History of Ideas* VIII (1970), 19 n. 116 refers to the original edition of Bañez's Commentary on the *Summa Theologiae* as maintaining that the *esse* of the bread continued in existence without its essence.

[94] *Ibid.,* disp. 49, III, 3; XXI, 124-125.

[95] *Ibid.,* disp. 49, I-III; XXI, 109-132.

[96] See Section III above.

[97] See *DM* 37, II, 2; XXVI, 493.

[98] See Section V, 2-4, above.

[99] See paragraph 29, this section, below as well as *DM* 37, II; XXVI, 493-498.

[100] See paragraph 24, this section, above.

[101] See Section I, 13 and following above.

[102] See Fonseca, *In V Metaph.,* cap. 8; col. 546-551. esp. 548-549.

[103] See Sections V-VI above.

[104] See Section IX, 11-15, above.

[105] See *DM* 7, I-II; XXV, 250-271.

[106] *Ibid.*

[107] See Section I, 12-13, above.

[108] I read the *quia nihil potest* of the 1597 Salamanca and 1605 Mainz editions instead of the *quia esse non potest* of the Vives text.

[109] See *DM* 47, II, 7-11; XXVI, 787-789.

[110] See Fonseca, *In V Metaph.,* cap. 15, q. 2; col. 808-821, esp. 812 and 817. See reference to Cajetan in n. 85, this section, above.

[111] *In I Sent.,* d. 33, q. 1, a. 1 ad 1; I, 702.

112 See Fonseca in n. 110, this section, above.
113 See paragraph 23 and following, this section, above.
114 See paragraph 27, this section, above.
115 See Suárez, *In Sum. Theol.,* III, q. 3, a. 1, disp. 11, II; XVII, 434-440.
116 Scotus, *Opus Oxon.,* IV, d. 11, q. 3; T. 24, 125-126.
117 *Ibid.*

Section XII

Whether a created essence is separable from its existence.

1. *The various ways in which essence is considered to be separated from existence.* This question has been settled for the most part from the principles set forth thus far, however, I propose it to answer more clearly and distinctly some difficulties and arguments touched on in Section 1. [1] Consequently, that a created essence is separated from existence can be understood in different ways. First, by destroying essence and preserving existence which some [2] have thought takes place in the sacrament of the altar, wherein the substance of bread as to essential entity is destroyed or transubstantiated and conserved as to existential entity. It is understandable in a second way, if essence is conserved when existence is destroyed; this in turn can be thought of in three ways. One is, if, with one connatural existence removed, another is gained, as many [3] think takes place naturally in prime matter which, as to essential entity, endures under the form of the generated and the corrupted, yet changes existence. Almost all deny that it can take place naturally in the case of a form or a composite of matter and form, because being follows immediately and essentially upon form. Consequently, it is not separable from it except insofar as it it separated from a subject on which it depends, as it is gathered from St. Thomas, part 1, quest. 50, art. 5 [4] and other places. [5] There has been no lack of those who [6] would say that an exchange in existence takes place in the intension of a form. This is unlikely, as we shall see below in Discussion 46. [7] Another way this separation can be thought of is that a created essence without a proper existence would remain subject to another higher and supernatural existence. This, it is agreed, cannot take place naturally; but many [8] think it can be done supernaturally, indeed, has happened in the humanity of Christ the Lord which is said to have a created essential entity without a proper existence, but is also said to exist by the uncreated existence of the Word. A third way it can be understood is that

essence and existence are separated by the destruction of the union and the conservation of both in reality. Finally, one can think that a created essence is separated from a proper existence in such a way that, without it and without another which would supply its function, it is conserved in reality. Also in this way (which is amazing) certain modern commentators say in part 1, quest. 3, art. 4 (although under the particle *perhaps*)[9] that God can conserve a created essence outside its causes, and outside nothing, without any existence. Finally, the essence of a creature can be said to be separated from actual existence in such a way that it does not remain in reality, but from an existent it becomes non-existent and a non-being *(ens)* in act.

THAT EXISTENCE CANNOT BE CONSERVED WITHOUT
A PROPER ESSENCE.

2.   Consequently, I say first that it is impossible for existence to be separated from essence in such a way that existence be conserved while essence is destroyed. I do not find one of the ancient theologians who taught the opposite of this contention, but only one or another of the moderns.[10] In the first place, given the true opinion on the identity of actual essence and existence, this assertion is evident, because the same thing cannot be separated from itself; and as often as in the thing itself one is separated while the other is conserved, there is a clear sign of some distinction in reality, as was shown above in the seventh discussion.[11] Further, also those Doctors[12] who grant some distinction in reality between essence and existence, yet not the real one but only a modal one, are logical in teaching this assertion. For, if existence and essence are modally distinguished, the essence is not a mode of existence but just the opposite, as is self-evident. For existence is, or is conceived of, as the act of an essence, and logically as its form or its mode. But a mode is not separable from the thing whose mode it is, because by itself it is essentially united to it, as was treated in the seventh discussion already referred to.[13] Consequently, if existence be only a mode of an essence, it is not separable from it in the way mentioned above.[14]
3.   But, then, the ones who think that existence is a thing altogether really distinct from created essence, even though they commonly teach that it is not separable in the way mentioned, or that it cannot be conserved without it,[15] are still hardly able to give a sufficient reason for this statement in regard to the absolute power of God. For naturally it could be said readily that an existential entity cannot be conserved without an essential entity, because it depends on it either as on a receiving subject or in another way. Nonetheless, it certainly

cannot be proved by a sufficient reason that God could not furnish
that dependence. For neither is it repugnant because of an identity
since a real distinction is supposed; nor because of a dependence,
since, even though that be said to belong to the genus of a material
or formal cause, in that genus it is still in some way extrinsic, that is,
not be an intrinsic composition of one entity from another in the way
a whole depends on the parts, but by the influence of one entity on
another. But God can furnish this type of dependence. Indeed, He
does that when he conserves an accident without a subject. Consequently, on this score, the separation noted would not be repugnant
in the present instance. Nor can any other suggestion of contradiction be thought of, given the principle of that opinion. The reason
why I point this out is to show how difficult it is to speak consistently
in all that follows upon that principle. Indeed, that the conclusion as
set forth is simply true, is shown in this way. If the essence in an
existing thing be destroyed and done away with and separated from
existence, then some being in it, actual and outside causes, which it
had beforehand, is destroyed. Consequently, some existential being
is destroyed; therefore, the existential being of such a thing does not
remain; hence, it is impossible that existence be separated from
essence in the above-mentioned way. The first consequence is evident, because first it was shown above[16] that every coming-to-be is
terminated at some being outside its causes. Therefore, for the same
reason, a destruction must necessarily be terminated at some non-
actual being, and outside causes or (which is the same) some actual
being outside its causes has to be destroyed by it. Furthermore, the
first consequence is evident because, when an essence is destroyed or
not conserved, it does not lose being in objective potency. For it
always remains in[17] that, at least in view of divine power. Therefore, it loses the actual being which it had outside its causes. But the
second consequence is based on that principle, demonstrated
above,[18] that every being, actual and outside its causes, is existential
being. While the third consequence is also evident from another
principle proved above,[19] that in a single thing there is only one existential being, and in fact, that in addition to that actual being, by
which an essence first and intrinsically becomes a being (*ens*) in act
outside its causes, no other existence is found in it. So it is finally
concluded that it is an obvious contradiction for an actual essence to
be destroyed while existence is conserved; otherwise the same being
would be destroyed and would remain.

4. You will say that, when the essence is destroyed, the being is not
necessarily destroyed but is separated from the essence, which is
destroyed by that very fact, if another being be not imparted to it;
just as matter could be annihilated by the mere separation of the

form, without the annihilation or destruction of the form, whose place would not be taken by another form. The answer is that it is impossible for an essence to be destroyed without some being *(ens)* intrinsically in act, that is, in terms of a proper actual entity, ceasing to be in reality. So it is not sufficient that the union of two entities be destroyed, because from this there merely follows the immediate destruction of the composite. In the present instance the composite of essence and existence is not only said to be destroyed, but also the actual essence itself is entirely destroyed and does not remain outside its causes, nor is it a being *(ens)* in act as it was before. Consequently, it not only loses a union to another entity but also loses a proper entity and actuality; and this is to lose its own intrinsic actual being. The argument offered proceeds in this way. Nor is it true that this kind of separation of being from essence has occurred in the mystery of the Eucharist; because, as I have said above, [20] just as the essence of bread in that mystery does not remain after consecration, so neither does existence. Just as the essence of the accidents is conserved, so too existence.

IT IS QUITE REPUGNANT FOR AN ESSENCE TO BE CONSERVED WITHOUT ANY EXISTENCE.

5.   I say secondly that it is impossible, even with regard to absolute power, for a created essence to be conserved in reality and outside its causes without any existence. This contention is also common to every opinion, even though a convincing reason for it cannot be given equally by all, as I shall explain at once. Accordingly, there is an evident reason, because if an essence in itself and in its entity be conserved outside its causes, it therefore exists. For what else is it to exist than to be outside causes? But if it exists, it certainly has existence, just as, if it is white, it has whiteness. For these are related as form and intrinsic formal effect. Consequently, it is absurd and quite unintelligible, what certain authors [21] say, that an essence conserved in reality without existence is certainly a being *(ens)* and outside nothing, yet it is not formally in the order of existents. However, these men speak consistently to some extent, for since they suppose that such an essence is deprived of existence, they logically say that it is outside the number of things formally existing, and accordingly they ought also to say that it does not exist, because to exist and to be among the number of existing things are the same. Yet [22] the astonishing thing is that they would not see in this a patent contradiction, in saying that a thing is in reality, outside causes and outside nothing, and does not exist. For these words are clearly equipollent. For what can be conceived of as being added to a thing when

it is said to exist, if that was already produced by its causes in reality? Or, were we to imagine that a real essence is thus conserved by the omnipotence of God without a superadded existence, what does it lack for it to be said to exist? For, both to come to be and to have come to be and to be a real being *(ens)* in act outside its causes belong to it; and consequently it will also belong to it to be a cause in every order appropriate to it. Consequently, nothing else can be wanting on behalf of existing.

6.   Perhaps they will say that the act or term which they call existence is lacking to that thing. Unless they give a further explanation of the necessity, or the formal effect of such a term, the reply is of no importance; but from this it is concluded rather that a term of this sort is nothing, since it has no effect or use. This is why, even on this score, the authors who hold that existence is a thing entirely distinct from actual essence seem to me to be quite puzzled. For from this do they rightly blush to admit that an actual essence can be conserved in reality without any existence, because it is impossible for an essence to be conserved without existence and existing; and it is no less impossible to understand an essence in act outside causes and as non-existent. But from another angle, since they say that essence and existence are mutually distinct things, they are unable to give[23] any reason why God cannot conserve that bare essential entity and without that formal effect which it receives from existence. For, if they are distinct entities, the dependence of one on the other cannot be so intrinsic that one is constitutive of the other. Consequently, there is no reason why God cannot conserve the essential entity without the existential entity. To say vaguely that they have a mutual essential relationship and dependence which God cannot supply, is to beg the question or to claim the same thing in other words, but not to explain in what this dependence consists, because it is not by way of a relative reference, as is self-evident. Therefore, it should be reduced to some causality, which[24] is not wholly intrinsic, as I have explained,[25] and thus, there is no reason why God cannot furnish that. Hence, the reason is to be derived from this, that, by the fact that an entity is actual and outside its causes, it is intrinsically and most formally existing; nor can existence as such add some new formal effect to it, and so there is[26] a patent implication of contradiction because the essence would be conserved with actuality and without existence. But just as this argument agrees that an actual essence cannot remain without existence, so it proves that in reality it cannot be distinguished from it.

ESSENCE AND EXISTENCE CANNOT BE CONSERVED SEPARATELY.

7. I say thirdly, that created existence and essence cannot be separated in such a way that both are preserved in reality, after only their mutual union has been destroyed. We are speaking of the absolute power, for in terms of the natures of things, the matter is quite clear. There is a basis, because there is no union between actual essence and existence, but an identity which cannot be separated or dissolved. Also, because the arguments which prove that existence cannot be conserved with essence destroyed, on the contrary, do not logically prove that they cannot be conserved in separation and without a union between them. One reason is that, if once they were understood to be disjoined and yet conserved in reality, since they are not mutually related as relation and term, no reason can be given why one cannot remain upon the destruction of the other. Another reason is, because, with the union dissolved, all formal or material causality of one upon the other would cease. Consequently, if they could be conserved without a union, one could also be conserved without the conservation of the other, for there is nothing against it. Also from this the *a priori* reason, already often insisted upon, is made clear, because an actual essence cannot be conserved without the intrinsic effect of formal existence. But this effect would be necessarily destroyed if, by way of the impossible, the mutual union between essence and existence were to be destroyed. Consequently, such a union cannot be dissolved with both terms conserved.

8. This argument certainly seems to be effective even in the opinion affirming that existence and essence are distinct things, and indeed, it is absolute and effective. But if its strength be carefully pondered, it cannot be effective without destroying that opinion and proving that there is no union, but an identity, between essence and existence, and proving that existing is called the formal effect of existence in such a way that it cannot be a quasi-physical effect deriving from or imparted by a distinct thing, but a quasi-metaphysical effect deriving from an intrinsic mode, not in reality nor modally, but distinct in reason. This (in addition to the arguments offered) can thus be clarified and corroborated because, if essence and existence are distinct things, then they are mutually joined with some sort of a union coming between them, for all distinct things are so[27] united. Why, therefore, could not God dissolve such a type of union while conserving the terms? Surely no sufficient reason can be given, as the reasonings offered in the previous assertions readily prove; and they can be applied here equally. Besides, one could ask what existence that union has, for there is also something essential in that,

which is able to be and not to be. Consequently, since it is not formally existence itself, it will have to have an existence distinct from itself; and this is quite absurd. For in this way one could keep going almost unto infinity.

A THING CANNOT EXIST BY AN ALIEN EXISTENCE WITHOUT A PROPER EXISTENCE.

9.   I say fourthly that a created existent essence cannot be conserved by the absolute power of God through an alien existence without a proper existence. So do all the theologians think,[28] who maintain that there is created and proper existence in the humanity of Christ, and that that humanity does not formally exist by the existence of the Word. For these authors were not able to depend upon another foundation, except because they judged it to be impossible to take place in another way. Otherwise, why would they deny this, since the greatest possible substantial union is to be ascribed to the humanity of Christ as long as the truth of both natures, divine and human, remain intact? But the proper basis for this conclusion should be what we have set down about the identity of existence and actual essence. For if actual existence were either a thing or a mode distinct in reality from an actual essence, no sufficient reason (as I have often said)[29] can be given why God could not conserve an actual essence without a proper existence and provide for its dependence in another way, just as He conserves a substantial nature without a proper subsistence and an accidental form without a proper inherence, even though subsistence as well as inherence is only a certain mode distinct in reality from a nature. If, therefore, God prevents this mode and provides for it in another fashion, why could He not do the same in the case of existence, if that were a thing or mode distinct in reality from actual essence?

10.   I perceive that it can be said that existence is a more intrinsic mode because first and formally it constitutes a thing outside its causes. However, this reply either proves what we intend, that is, that existence is not separable due to an identity; or it cannot make clear what that more intrinsic being consists in, or how existence formally constitutes a thing outside its causes, if it already supposes in the natural order an actual essential entity produced by causes and not formally constituted in that actuality by existence. For, in regard to such an entity, existence will be just as extrinsic as subsistence or inherence, or it will certainly not be more intrinsic. Indeed, in the estimation of many Thomists,[30] subsistence influences an actual essence naturally prior to existence. Consequently, in this case it seems to be in some way more intrinsic to it. But others[31] think

that the existence of a substance is the same as subsistence. Consequently, if once there be supposed a real or modal distinction between existence and actual essence, no effective reason can be given for the claim set forth. So I have said in the above sections [32] that the authors who deny that the humanity of Christ could be assumed without a created existence, must logically assert that existence is not a thing or mode distinct in reality from actual essence.

11.   This, then, is the complete basis for the present assertion and when it is set down the inference is clear. This is clarified and explained further from the above considerations. For an actual essence cannot be conserved in reality without a proper and intrinsic existence; the arguments given prove this. For it is not distinguished in reality from its proper existence; consequently, just as it cannot be conserved without itself, so also it cannot be conserved without a proper existence. Also, because the very conservation of a created essence is a certain effecting of it; but every effection is a communication of some being and it receives this effect in itself and has it outside its cause, and, as a result, there is the communication of some existential being, intrinsic and proper to the produced essence. Also, because an actual essence must of necessity be constituted in that actuality by some real being indistinct from it, as was proved above. [33] Consequently, it cannot possibly be conserved in its actuality unless such being be conserved in it. But it was shown above [34] that such being is true existence, because it is temporal being. Therefore, an actual essence cannot be conserved without such an entirely intrinsic and proper existence.

12.   There is a further conclusion from this, that God cannot conserve any existent essence by an existence (so to speak) extraneous and foreign to it. First, of course, because an essence cannot exist by a foreign existence unless it be deprived of a proper existence; but it cannot be deprived of a proper existence, as was shown. [35] Therefore. Secondly, because the reasons given prove that that formal effect, which we can conceive of as imparted by existence, cannot be from a thing or mode distinct in reality from the existent essence itself. However, it is unintelligible that a thing be made existent by an extraneous thing unless that be distinct in reality from the essence, to which it is said to be joined to make it existing. Thirdly, because God cannot bring it about that some created essence be an actual essence or a being *(ens)* in act outside nothing by an actuality extraneous to and distinct from itself. But precisely from the fact that a created essence is a being *(ens)* in act outside nothing, it is existing. Consequently, it cannot be made existing by an extraneous and foreign actuality. The consequence is clear. However, the major and minor have been frequently proved in the above sections. [36]

13.   *An objection: Solution.* No natural argument of any significance can be raised against this assertion. For, that certain authors [37] argue that existence is not a perfection essential to a created nature and so can be separated from it and can be supplied by a foreign existence, is of no significance. First, because it is not a formal consequence, for the attributes of being *(ens)* are not essential predicates and yet cannot be separated nor supplied from without. Consequently, an identity without any distinction in reality is sufficient for a separation to be out of place, even though the perfection not be considered essential. Indeed, there are those who think [38] that there are some properties neither essential nor involving an identity, but rather a distinction in reality from essence, which cannot be separated nor supplied from without. Just how probable this may be will be taken up elsewhere. [39] But the best objection is, because, as in the common teaching, which the ones who argue in this way do not deny, the individuating principle as such, or haecceity, is simply not an essential perfection of an individual (Peter, for example); and nonetheless it cannot be separated from Peter nor supplied from without in order that Peter endure in this fashion. But if they should perhaps say that that individual difference, even though it is not absolutely of the essence, still it is of the essence of Peter as Peter is, we too shall say that actual and exercised existence is not of the essence absolutely, but is of the essence of an actual essence as it is a being *(ens)* in act outside nothing. So, even though an essence can be understood absolutely in potential or objective being, without actual existence, it is still not able to be understood that an essence be produced as a being *(ens)* in act and outside nothing without an intrinsic and proper existence.

14.   *Some theological objections.* However, there is another argument usually drawn from supernatural principles, namely, because a proper subsistence can be separated and supplied by another; and similarly inherence can be separated either absolutely or in a way that is opposite to being *(essendi)* substantially; therefore, it is the case with existence too. This was also settled from what was said, [40] because subsistence and inherence are modes distinct in reality from actual essence because they do not constitute it in the order of a being *(ens)* in act; nor do they first and formally distinguish it from a being *(ens)* in potency. So, even though they be separated from it, it is understandable that the actual essence remains the same, though subject to another mode of being *(essendi)*. But it is otherwise with existence, because it is the first formal constitutive of an actual entity and is not distinguished in reality from it.

15.   *Whether the humanity of Christ exists by the existence of the Word.* But some [41] insist upon a theological argument, because, from this meta-

physical principle laid down by us, it follows that the divine Word assumed the humanity with its created existence. This not only appears to be contrary to the teaching of St. Thomas[42] but also to that of other ancient Fathers, especially Leo,[43] Sophronius,[44] Fulgentius,[45] and Damascene.[46] Also it seems to be too little in agreement with other truths which the Catholic faith teaches about that mystery, as that the blessed Virgin not only conceived humanity but a true man; and that not only is Christ one but also one being *(ens)* simply; and that the humanity of Christ does not exist in itself but in the Word; and finally that the humanity of Christ could not operate, but the Word would operate through it.

16.   This problem could be passed over here both because it is theological and also because we discussed it to the best of our powers in the first volume of the third part, discussion 36[47] where we show that what was concluded in the objection presented is true; yet, because some modern writers[48] give a bitter reception to the doctrine put forth by us in that place and have tried to fight against it, I will not feel it burdensome to answer them again, even though they do not offer any new proofs or new arguments, but only new and unusual exaggerations. But what is the reason why they are astonished by a teaching that is not new but accepted by many and eminent theologians, both ancient and modern, such as Altisiodorus,[49] Albert,[50] Scotus,[51] Durandus,[52] Gabriel,[53] Bonaventure,[54] Almainus,[55] Harvey,[56] Paludanus,[57] and by St. Thomas himself, in question one *On the Incarnate Word,* art. 4?[58] And about[59] this, it is not quite certain that he ever changed his position, as I have explained at length in the reference cited.[60] There also, I showed that Sophronius, Leo and Fulgentius have taught nothing opposed to this teaching; and I had also touched upon this at length in the same volume, discussion 8, section 1.[61] But in the case of Damascene, I have shown that he is not only opposed to this teaching of ours but is even very much in favor of it. Consequently, I am very much surprised at how a certain eminent author,[62] who undoubtedly had read what we had written, had dared to write afterwards, and even commit to print, that Damascene, book 3 *On Faith,* c. 22, explicitly teaches that opinion which denies that there is a created existence in the humanity of Christ, even though in that chapter Damascene does not write a word about this matter, but only attacks the error of those who claim that Christ had advanced in grace and knowledge. This he refutes with these words; "But those who say that He made progress equally in wisdom and grace as if He were receiving an increase in them, do not claim that a union was made at that first birth of the body nor do they maintain a personal union."[63] And below: "For if the body was united to the Word from the first moment of birth, nay rather existed

in it and had a personal identity with it, then what, finally, can be alleged besides its very abounding in all the riches of wisdom and grace?"[64] What, I ask, is there found in these words which would support that opinion? Or what reference was there to a teaching of Damascene that there is no created existence in the humanity of Christ as long as it was united to the Word from the beginning? But no Catholic denies this nor is it repugnant to the created existence of the nature itself, because it was always able to exist in the Word, as Damascene says in the same place. In which case, he rather favors us, because he does not say that it existed by the Word or through the Word but in the Word.

17.   But they say that that teaching is hardly in keeping with the principles of faith. Then other eminent authors[65] think that it is almost evident that this opinion follows from the principles of faith. For Faith teaches that Christ assumed a true and real humanity, not having only objective being or being in potency in its cause, but having some real and actual being created outside its causes. This is existential being. Therefore, He assumed humanity with some created being. The consequence is evident and formal. The major is certain according to faith, which teaches that the humanity of Christ is a created thing and distinct from the divine Word and assumed in unity of the person; and faith teaches that from that nature Christ has a human being which is a created being, and consequently an actual being[66] and not merely potential. The minor was demonstrated in the above sections[67] and appears to us to be practically evident from the terms themselves if they be rightly understood, because to be actual and outside causes is nothing else than to exist, as was explained at length in the above sections.[68]

18.   For this reason, these absurdities seem to follow from the opposite opinion. First, that humanity is not a created being *(ens);* this is clearly false. The sequence is proved, because a being *(ens)* is named from being and is constituted a being *(ens)* in act by being. Consequently, if humanity is constituted a being *(ens)* in act by uncreated being, it is not a created being *(ens)* but uncreated; just as, because Christ is not constituted in personal being by a created personality but by an uncreated one, He is not a created person but an uncreated one. Also, either humanity is called a created being *(ens)* as it is existing in act, or only as it is in act in terms of essential being. In that opinion the first cannot be said because humanity is posited as existing in act by an uncreated existence; hence this existent, as such, must be either uncreated, if we were to speak formally and properly, or surely not completely created but made up of the created and the uncreated. If the second be said, I ask whether that essential being is only in potency, and if so, it is not created but crea-

table and in itself it is truly nothing, but in its cause it is the creative essence itself; or it is actual being in itself and outside its causes; and this must needs be existential being, because to exist is nothing else than to be in act outside causes, and because creation is formally terminated at existing, as was proved above. [69] Consequently, a being *(ens)* in act completely created without some created existential being cannot be understood.

19.   Secondly, one can conclude that the Incarnation was not a true and real union and assumption, because a true union can occur only between real actual beings *(entia)*, of which one does not intrinsically have its entity from another, even though one can depend on another; all these things were explained at length in the above sections. [70]But then if the humanity of Christ were existing only by the existence of the Word, it would be intrinsically constituted in the being of an actual entity by the existence of the Word.

20.   Thirdly, one can conclude that the Word was united to humanity as understood in essential being only which it had from eternity, because, besides that being, the humanity does not have another except existential being. Therefore, if this existential being in the humanity of Christ was nothing else than the being of the Word, then that being was immediately united to the humanity which in itself was eternal. Consequently, to be incarnated was nothing else than to draw an eternal essence to the uncreated being of the Word. But this is not an incarnation but a fiction, because that eternal essence was nothing. Nor is it assumable in terms of that which it has precisely from itself and from eternity. Consequently, some other being must be first ascribed to it by a natural priority or at least by a priority of reason, which is sufficient for that being to be distinct from the divine subsistence which is imparted by the union.

21.   Fourthly, one can conclude from that opinion that the humanity does not have a proximate capacity to be united to the Word from God through His efficiency; this is also very absurd in the teaching of faith. The sequence is clear, first, because that capacity is not present in the humanity in terms of some existential being, but only in terms of an eternal essential being, inasmuch as the essence of humanity is not from God as efficient cause. Then, too, because, if that capacity is present in the humanity by God's actual efficient causation, then it exists in virtue of that efficient causation. Consequently, it has some produced and created existence. Hence, this is the existence of the humanity itself. This argument also proves that humanity had that existence naturally prior to being united to the Word. This could have been only created existence, as is evident in itself. This sequence is clear, because that humanity was capable of union naturally prior to being actually united in act. But a proxi-

mate capacity is only in an entity already effected and existing outside its causes.

22.   *How the Most Blessed Virgin was associated with the existence of
Christ.* But let us see what the other truths of faith are with which
that teaching is thought to be scarcely harmonious. The first was,
because the blessed Virgin not only conceived the humanity but the
God-man; the opposite of this seems to follow if the humanity of
Christ had a created existence. The sequence is clear, because then
the humanity would have had that existence from the mother; and,
in consequence, the whole efficiency or causality of the mother, be
that it may, would have been terminated at that created existence
and would have stopped there. Therefore, since that existence be of
the humanity alone and not of Christ, the Virgin would have conceived the humanity alone, and not Christ, nor God. But this difficulty (whatever its worth be) is far more pressing if there is no
created existential being in the humanity of Christ, but only essential being. For it then follows that the whole action or causality of the
mother had been terminated at the essential being of the humanity
and had not advanced beyond. Consequently, much more does it
follow that she conceived the humanity alone in essential being, and
not the existing humanity, much less Christ Himself or God. The
antecedent is clear, because (as we suppose) the blessed Virgin did
not immediately cooperate in the union of that humanity with the
Word. Therefore, she did not cooperate in the action by which that
humanity was made existing, because that action was the act of uniting, according to that opinion. Therefore, the whole causality of the
Virgin was concerned with the essential being of the humanity and
rested in that. And the second consequence is clear from this, both
ad hominem, because it has the same form as that which they bring
against us; and *a fortiori,* because the humanity, in terms of essential
being alone, differs more from Christ than does the humanity
already existing. And no one can deny that that humanity had at
least essential being in the natural order, at least in some genus of
cause, namely, material, naturally prior to having been assumed or
united to the Word.

23.   Hence we conclude from this argument that one principle must
needs be granted by all Catholics, that is, that the Virgin is not said
to be the Mother of God nor to have conceived God for the reason
that she immediately effected the union of the humanity with God,
for it is agreed that she did not do that, either as a principal cause or
as an instrument. Therefore, she is said to have conceived God,
because to her causality, by which she cooperates toward the union
of the body and soul of Christ and for the formation of the humanity,
there was a simultaneous conjunction of the Holy Spirit's action, by

which that humanity, in the same instant in which it was formed, was united to God; by this it has happened that the entire conception, which involves both those actions, was terminated, not to the humanity alone, but to the God-man. All should philosophize in this way, whether they would say that the action of the Virgin concerned the humanity in terms of essential being alone, or also in terms of existential being. Indeed, those who affirm only that first one, ascribe much less concurrence to the Virgin in that conception, as was shown. [71] They can hardly explain how it is a true conception or generation wherein no existential being is imparted; and from this angle that teaching is also less in agreement with this truth of faith.
24.   Therefore, we reply to that easy difficulty by denying the sequence, because that conception has been terminated absolutely at God in the same instant and simultaneously in terms of real duration. Nor does it matter that the action of the Virgin and its terminus preceded in the order of nature, because that was only in the genus of material cause, and with some connection and dependence on another action, by which that humanity in that instant was united to the Word. Add that it is more probable that the soul and body were united to the Word naturally prior to being joined together themselves; and so, according to the communication of idioms, the Blessed Virgin is most properly said to have conceived God, for she concurred in joining the soul and body of God together, and which were already subsisting by the subsistence of God. So, of necessity, she has borne God, because generation is terminated at the supposit, and it was impossible then for such a generation to be terminated at another supposit. All of these things were explained at some length in the references given from the first volume of the third part [72] and in the second volume, discussion 1, section 1. [73]
25.   Another principle of faith said to be weakened by this metaphysical principle which we proposed, is, because Christ is simply one and one being *(ens),* the opposite of this seems to follow if there is in Him a created existential being of the humanity. But an answer is given to this by denying the sequence. For Christ is said to be simply one because of the unity of person. He is one person, even though He has two real and actual natures, which is to have them with their proper existences. Christ is called one being *(ens)* because of one being, complete and substantially one. However, Christ as Christ is not one simple being *(ens)* but composite (for He is a composite person), and so He does not have to have one simple being, but composite, according to the teaching established above. [74] Therefore, Christ has one being composed of the being of the humanity and the being of the Word or Its personality. Consequently, the twofold being of the nature or of the terms is not an obstacle to the unity of a

being *(ens),* if there be a true and real union between them, particularly substantial, and one which would suffice for composing a being *(ens)* substantially one. So the present metaphysical teaching detracts nothing; indeed, it is especially in keeping with the cited truth of faith and corroborates another which teaches that the unity of Christ is not simple but by way of composition; and the other teaching, which ascribes to Christ one absolutely simple being, is less in keeping with this truth.

26.   *How the humanity of Christ is said to exist in the Word.* The third principle of faith is that the humanity does not exist in itself but in the Word. For Sophronius so speaks in the sixth synod, eleventh action,[75] and Damascene as cited above.[76] The matter is most certain; but what (I ask) is that consequence: Humanity exists by a proper existence; therefore, it exists in itself and not in the Word? For this is similar to the form: An accident exists by a proper existence distinct from the existence of a subject; therefore, it exists in itself and not in a subject. Yet this is not valid, for the antecedent is true and the consequent is false. However, they prove that consequence, because, to exist in something is nothing else than to exist by its existence and in dependence upon it. But of these two, the first is false. The second is inadequately stated and not given enough explanation. The first part is proved from the example cited about an accident. For it exists in a subject, and not by the existence of a subject; and a form, especially a material one, exists in matter. All speak this way, and yet no one ever said that a form exists by the existence of matter; the reason will be established from what is to be said.[77] The second part is explained, because, in the first place, in order to say that something exists in another, it is not enough to exist dependently upon it. For matter exists dependently upon form and yet does not exist in form. Any creature exists dependently upon God and yet does not exist in God, in that way in which we are now speaking. Consequently, that some thing exists in another, in the present case expresses a relationship to a term or supposit by which that thing, said to exist in another, is supported in its existence; just as for an accident to exist in a subject designates a relationship to and dependence upon that in its existence in the genus of something supportive, although in a more imperfect way, and with material causality. Consequently, then, to exist in something is not to exist by its existence, but it is to have one's existence supported by another and dependent on it in that way. Hence, it rather supposes or includes the proper existence of that thing, but adds a union or conjunction to another thing by which it is supported either as by a supposit terminating the dependence without any proper causality, or as by a subject, as there is in inhering forms. But the first way belongs to the humanity of Christ

by reason of the hypostatic union. So its proper existence is not said to be of itself actual existence, because it is not terminated by a proper subsistence, but it is called inexistence because it depends upon the Word of God. It does not have this denomination from itself, but from the mode of union by means of which it has that it be in the Word.

27.   Consequently, if that existence of the humanity be considered precisely in terms of that which it has of itself, it does not constitute a thing existing in act in itself, or in another, but only existing substantially in such a nature. For those modes of existing designated by those words *in itself* or *in another* are not essential to such an existence. They are added to it to constitute or complete a supposit, though not in the same way. For the first mode of existing *in itself* is connatural and completes a supposit, without union to another, as a proper term or the subsistence of such a nature, as we will see below.[78] The second mode of existing *in another* is supernatural in relation to the complete substantial nature and it does not formally constitute a person but joins a nature to the person so that one composite person results therefrom. Consequently, because the humanity of Christ, though it had a proper existence, still did not have it with a proper way of existing in itself or by itself, but with a supernatural mode of union to the supposit of the Word of God, it thus cannot be said to exist or ever to have existed in itself, but always in the Word.

28.   *How the humanity of Christ in no moment (in nullo signo) has been able to operate but the Word acts through it.* There remains the necessity of speaking about the fourth proposition very much in keeping with the teaching of faith, namely, that the humanity of Christ has never been able to operate, neither in an instant of time nor in a moment of nature *(in signo naturae),* before the Word would operate through it; the opposite of this seems to follow from our opinion, for if it had a proper existence, it existed naturally prior to being united to the Word. Then it was also able to operate naturally prior, for action follows upon being. However, the answer is made by denying the sequence, even though there was no dearth of theologians[79] and learned men who have asserted that consequent, as I have discussed at length in the cited volume one of the third part, discussion ten, sections one and two.[80] But they have been mistaken in this as I have shown there. Therefore, the consequence referred to is denied. In the first place, some think that, even though the humanity has a proper existence, it does not follow therefrom that it existed naturally prior to having been joined to the Word, because it was able to receive that existence by an action dependent on the Word, as upon a supposital term; just as an accident has a proper existence, and yet does not exist naturally prior to being joined to a subject, because it

receives existence by an action dependent on a subject, as on a material cause. This manner of speaking is not altogether unacceptable, but it does not appear true to us, as we have discussed at length in the cited volume one, discussion eight, section one.[82] Consequently, I grant that that humanity existed naturally prior to its having been assumed. Nonetheless, I deny that it operated or was able to operate naturally prior to its having been assumed, because the existing nature is incapable of action until it is terminated by some subsistence which I have shown at length in the volume referred to, discussion ten, section two and three.[83] There is no need to repeat it here.

29.   I add only that the same argument can be turned against the other opinion and must needs be solved by the opponents in proportionally the same way. For they cannot deny that the humanity of Christ received actual essential being[84] naturally prior to having been assumed by the Word, as was proved above,[85] and which they teach in a number of places. Consequently, I shall conclude in like manner, that the humanity was able to operate in that prior state by that actual essential being, for that is proper being, from which operation follows from a formal principle; and it will be a sufficient condition because it would be in act outside its causes. This is especially so, since (in their opinion) also according to that being a nature is capable of a proper subsistence naturally prior to existing. Hence, they will answer by denying the sequence, because actual essential being is not sufficient for operating until it be terminated by existence. Why, therefore, will they not grant our answer when we deny a similar consequence, because existence does not issue into operation until it be terminated by subsistence? Especially, since they can give no sufficient reason why an essence demands such an existence for acting if, with that prescinded, it already has in act its whole essential perfection in itself and outside its causes, and especially if it also has that terminated by a proper subsistence, because, now one does not understand what existence can add which would be required for acting. But we offer a reason, because subsistence is a substantial and intrinsic terminus of a nature, pertaining in its own way to the substantial complement of a thing. So, it is altogether intrinsic and immediately springing from the nature or at least first effected with it: but action is more extrinsic and accidental, and so, according to the order of nature, supposes subsistence; and in Christ it supposes the assumption, because a proper and created subsistence is impeded.

30.   In the last place I shall not fail to mention that the author[86] noted at length above did not favor our opinion enough, when, after all those attacks and verbal exaggerations, he adds that, though in fact the humanity of Christ did not have a proper existence, it still

could have been assumed with a proper existence to the hypostatic union by the absolute power. In this he has certainly spoken cleverly, because in the teaching which he follows along with others[87] he will scarcely be able to give a reason why that is impossible, since it certainly involves no repugnance or contradiction, as we have proved enough and more in the above sections.[88] For they teach that existence and subsistence in a created nature are distinct things, and that the Word in the humanity of Christ the Lord has impeded and supplied both. Consequently, why was it not possible to impede subsistence alone, and not existence as well, at the same time? This is especially so, since in the teaching of these same men subsistence is naturally prior to existence, and so, speaking logically, the union of the nature for subsisting would be naturally prior to the union of the nature for existing; and accordingly, since the prior could be separated from the posterior (as has been generally accepted by philosophers), provided a special repugnance does not arise from some other place, then the union will be able to rest in the subsistence alone and proceed no further, by granting a proper existence to the nature.

31.　So we readily grant this statement, yet we are amazed that they did not realize that thereby (willy-nilly) the whole opinion is overturned, and all the basic reasons why it is denied that the humanity of Christ has in fact a proper existence. First, of course, because if a proper existence is not repugnant with a true hypostatic union and with the unity of person in a twofold nature, from what source or on what foundation can it be said that there is no such existence in the humanity of Christ, proper, that is, and created? For faith teaches nothing else but such a hypostatic union by which one person would subsist in a twofold real nature. Indeed, it further teaches that by such a union the Word assumed whatever it had deposited in human nature, which, of course, would not be repugnant to such a union. Hence, if the existence of the nature, as the author mentioned above[89] is not afraid to grant, is not repugnant to the union but could be conserved in the nature united personally, on what basis can it be said that it had been removed? An additional point is that, according to that opinion, two unions of the humanity to the Word are to be posited, one to the subsistence, the other to the existence, of the Word. For, even though there is no distinction in reality, on the part of the Word, between subsistence and existence, still, on the part of the humanity a distinction must necessarily be posited since, in the thing itself, one is said to be separable from the other; this is a clear sign of some distinction, at least modal. Consequently, there are two distinct unions, which is unheard of till now. The Thomists[90] themselves strongly criticize, and justly so, a similar teaching in Durandus.[91]

32.   I insist further upon this in the following fashion, for these unions are distinct in reality; therefore, just as it is said that God can conserve the union to subsistence without the union to existence, so it will have to be said that He can conserve the union to existence without the union to subsistence. For the reason is equal, since the distinction is the same, and one does not depend more essentially on the other, than the other way around. Consequently, there would then be a created person with a nature existing by uncreated existence alone. Also there would then be a substantial union between an uncreated [92] nature and God without a hypostatic union. But these are unheard of and scarcely in keeping with the teaching of the Holy Fathers and the Councils. However, we conclude further from this, that that union to existence is neither hypostatic nor intrinsically included in the hypostatic union; and so it was gratuitously invented in the union which took place. For, according to faith, only a hypostatic substantial union was produced between the humanity and the Word.

33.   Finally, if that is possible, let us agree that it took place; would Christ not be truly one and a being (*ens*) essentially and simply one? In truth, He would be, because He would be one substantially composite person, by reason of which not only would man truly and properly be God but God-man. For the same reason, as long as that man were conceived of a mother, God also would be conceived; and His humanity, even though it would exist by a proper existence, it would not exist in itself, but in the Word, nor could it operate properly but the Word through it. Therefore, this case clearly shows that the arguments brought against us above [93] are not effective. Let this suffice for this digression, which seemed necessary here in order to establish that those metaphysical principles are conveyed by us which may be of service to true theology; for this is what we especially strive for and desire. Now let us return to the unfinished discussion.

THAT AN ACTUAL ESSENCE WITH ITS EXISTENCE CAN BE ALTOGETHER DESTROYED.

34.   I say finally that actual existence is separable from the essence of a creature so that, with existence, essence itself perishes or is destroyed at the same time. This assertion is certain and evident. First, because a creature does not have existence from itself but from another, at least from God, on whom it always depends in its being. But just as God freely gives being to a creature, so He also freely conserves it in being. Consequently, He is able not to conserve. Hence, a creature can be deprived of being. But if it be deprived of

existential being, its essence must be destroyed and must perish at the same time, because, when existential being has been taken away, an essence is nothing, as was explained in the second section.[94] Accordingly, the proposed assertion is corroborated, because everything generable (witness Aristotle)[95] is corruptible and, for the same reason, everything which begins to be, can cease to be; and the cessation is proportionate to the beginning, that is, that very thing can be lost through the ceasing-to-be which was acquired by the coming-to-be. But when a creature begins to be, its essence begins to be something which beforehand was nothing or did not as yet exist. Consequently, in a like manner, it can accordingly cease to be or be separated from being so that it loses its very own essential entity altogether.

35.   Someone will ask how being can be separated from essence in this way, if they, in reality, are altogether the same, since it is clearly repugnant for the same thing to be separated from itself. For, those who claim that essence should be distinguished at least modally from the essence of the creature put great weight in this, especially Giles, in the references given above[96] and particularly in his little work *On Being and Essence*[97] when he claims that a creature can neither be produced nor destroyed unless its essence is something distinct from its being on which being can both be stamped and from which it can be separated. Before Giles, Alexander of Alexandria[98] referred to this manner of speaking in 7 *Metaph.,* text 22[99] and neatly refuted it. Because the being of a creature, before it comes to be, is purely objective if we are to speak absolutely of the entire creature, "And so (he says) there is no need to imagine that that is produced from this, or that it is impressed on something, the essence itself, for instance. For, if this were the case, since that on which a thing is impressed precedes and would not come to be by that production, the whole thing would not come to be."[100] Also we shall be able to make the same argument about ceasing-to-be simply, by which a thing is transformed into nothing. Keeping the proportion, the same argument can be applied to corruption, as we shall explain at once.

36.   Consequently, the same Alexander replies to the problem proposed, that a thing's coming-to-be must not be imagined as if being itself were impressed upon or joined to an essence, as an act to a potency, but only that the whole reality of essence, which previously was subject to a possible nature, would come to be[101] afterwards the whole in act:"And certain ones (he says) call that nature as it precedes, essence. But, as it is the term of divine action, they call it being."[102] Accordingly, in like manner, it must not be imagined that a thing ceases to be for the reason that being would be separated from essence, as an act from a receptive potency, either as one thing is

separated from another thing or a mode of a thing from the thing itself, but that it ceases to be only because the whole thing which was a being *(ens)* in act, loses its entity through God's action and ceases to be a being *(ens)* in act. Consequently, when it is said that a thing cannot be separated from itself, if there is no distinction in reality, that is true in regard to a proper separation by which that which is separated does not remain, and that from which it is separated does remain, either in the same duration or in the same place according to the type of separation. But then, as we have said, [103] being is not separated from essence in this way. However, if the same thing were said to be separated from itself because the whole ceases to be and goes from one state into another, that is, from a state of being *(essendi)* to a state of non-being *(essendi)*, or from an actual state to a potential one, then it is no more repugnant for the same thing to be separated from itself than it would be repugnant for the same thing now to be, and thereafter not to be, or for the same thing now in act to terminate the action of its cause, but thereafter to remain only in potency, or objectively in a cause. Hence, in this way and in terms of this last separation, the essence of a creature is said to be separable from being, because the same essence which is actual as long as it is, can lose that whole actuality and return to mere objective or potential being.

37.   Here it must be noted that that, even though it is true of every created essence, is separable from being in this way, or rather can be deprived of actual being, it still does not befit all to the same extent or in the same way. For there are certain ones which, after they once receive being, do not have an intrinsic potency to be without it or be separated from it, but only by the extrinsic potency of an agent, as they are incorruptible beings *(entia)*, as was touched upon above in discussion 18. [104] But there are other beings *(entia)* which can be deprived of being by an intrinsic potency, as they are corruptible beings *(entia)* which consist of matter capable of another being, whence follows the corruption or ceasing-to-be of an existing thing. Moreover, a difference is to be noted between a thing's ceasing-to-be by corruption and by annihilation. For, though in both cases an essence loses being or is separated from it, nevertheless it does so in a different way. For in annihilation, an essence in its whole self and all its parts is entirely destroyed, since it is wholly deprived of being. For this is the nature of annihilation, that it leaves no being, neither integral nor partial. So also it leaves nothing of essence. Indeed, it is also necessary that no being succeed such ceasing-to-be in virtue of such action, or change according to the more probable teaching of the theologians which I have discussed at length in the third volume of the third part. [105] But, then, in corruption, although the essence

which is corrupted, just as it loses being, so also is it destroyed so
that the whole no longer remains, nevertheless it is not so destroyed
that some part of the essence cannot remain; for the subject or matter always remains, and sometimes even the form, as in the case of
man. As much remains of essential being as there remains of existential being, because they are not separable in such a way, as we
have amply shown above. [106] The result is that, by corruption alone,
essence is not separable from being in its whole self and its every
part, unless annihilation be added to corruption. However, this is to
be understood of a proper corruption of the whole composite, for
were we to speak of an accident or of a material substantial form
alone, its essence is separated entirely from being or destroyed when
the whole is corrupted; but that is not properly deprived of being, or
corrupted, but is corrupted along with the ceasing-to-be of the
whole. So it is easily established how existing actually is separable
from any and every essence, whether integral or partial; and how,
with being removed, an essence at the same time and respectively
also perishes. This is also a strong indication that those two are not
distinct in reality.

THE OBJECTION DEALING WITH PROPOSITIONS OF
ETERNAL TRUTH IS TREATED.

38.   Immediately, though, the well-worn problem touched on
above in section one, in the first argument of the first opinion, [107]
presents itself, because if, with the removal of existence, the essence
perishes, then those propositions, wherein essential predicates are
attributed of a thing, are not necessary nor possessed of eternal
truth; but the consequent is false and contrary to the opinion of all
philosophers. Because otherwise all the truths dealing with creatures
would be contingent, hence there could be no science of creatures,
because this concerns only necessary truths. The sequence is proved,
because if, with the removal of existence, essence is nothing, therefore neither is it a substance, nor an accident and, consequently,
neither a body nor a soul nor other things of this kind. Therefore, no
essential attribute can be rightly predicated of it.

39.   *The opinion of some.* In the face of this difficulty, some contemporary theologians [108] grant that these propositions about creatures are
not possessed of perpetual truth, but begin to be true at the time
when the things come to be, and they lose truth when things perish,
because (as Aristotle said), "from the fact that a thing is or is not, a
proposition is true or false." [109] However, this opinion is opposed not
only to modern philosophers but also to the ancient ones, and, indeed, to the Fathers of the Church. For Augustine says, Bk. 2 *On*

Free Choice, ch. 8: "three and four are seven is eternally true, even if there be nothing to be numbered."[110] In the same sense he says, Bk. 4 *Literal Commentary on Genesis,* c. 7: "Six is the perfect number, not because God perfected all things in six days but rather the converse; and so God perfected all things in six days because that number is perfect, and it would be perfect even if those things were not."[111] Similiarly, Anselm, in the dialogue *On Truth,* c. 14,[112] expressly claims that the truth of these propositions is eternal, and not destroyed even if the things themselves be destroyed.

40.   Nor is it enough, were someone to answer with St. Thomas, part 1, quest. 10, art. 3, to the third;[113] q. 16, art. 7, to the first[114] and quest. 1 *On Truth,* art. 5, to the eleventh[115] and art. 6, to the second and third,[116] that, with the destruction of the existence of creatures, these enunciations are true, not in themselves, but in the divine intellect. For, in this way, not only enunciations, of the type wherein essential properties are predicated, have eternal truth in the divine intellect, but also all accidental or contingent ones, which are true. But were you to say that, there is a difference because, even though all are eternally in the divine intellect, still not with the same necessity are they there. For those truths, in which an essential predicate is attributed to a subject, are in the divine intellect in such a way that it was impossible for them not to be in it. Therefore, they are simply necessary and without any supposition. But then the other contingent truths, though they have always been in the divine intellect, are still not present there with absolute necessity, but only on the supposition that they would be at some time; if this be said (I say), then the difficulty against the preceding opinion[117] gains greater strength and increases, because those propositions, wherein essential predicates are affirmed of subjects, are not for that reason true, because it will be so in some species of time. First, because even if God had ordained that nothing would come to be in time, He would still know them to be true. Then also, because they are not only eternally true to the extent that, with regard to the future, they can be enunciated in relation to time, but they are true absolutely and in abstraction from every species of time; in both cases they greatly differ from contingent truths, which have truth only in relation to existence for some species of time. Again, those enunciations are not true because they are known by God, but rather they are thus known because they are true; otherwise no reason could be given why God would necessarily know them to be true. For if their truth came forth from God Himself, that would take place by means of God's will; hence it would not come forth of necessity, but voluntarily. Also, because in regard to these enunciations, the divine intellect is related as purely speculative, not as operative. But the

speculative intellect supposes the truth of its object, it does not produce it. Therefore, enunciations like this, which are said to be in the first, and even in the second, type of essential predication, have eternal truth, not only as they are in the divine intellect but also in themselves and prescinding from it.

41. *The common opinion.* Therefore, it is a very common and accepted opinion that these propositions have eternal truth. Albert the Great teaches this along with the ancient Arabs in the *Commentary on the Book of Causes,* proposition 8 [118] and in the *Postpredicaments,* c. 9. [119] And St. Thomas seems to follow this, in the references given, though he refers this whole eternity to the divine intellect. Capreolus defends the same opinion in 1, dist. 8, q. 1, conclus. 1, following St. Thomas and Albert; [120] and Soncinas, 9 *Metaphys.,* q. 5 [121] where he mentions Henry, *Quodlib.* 10, q. 2 and 3; [122] and Harvey, *Quodlib.* 3, q. 1; [123] Scotus [124] and other authors [125] in 3, dist. 21. Cajetan also holds it, 1 *Poster.,* c.9 [126] and Ferrara, 2 *Against the Gentiles,* c. 52. [127] It appears to be Aristotle's opinion in Bk. 9 *Metaphys.,* c. 6, [128] 7 [129] and 9. [130] However, many of the authors [131] cited explain this opinion in such a way as to say that in fact the essences of creatable things are not eternal, absolutely speaking, as we proved above in section two, [132] but the connections of the essential predicates with the essences themselves are eternal. In addition, they say that, when things are created, the essences of things are created and come to be, yet the above-mentioned connection does not come to be; for it is one thing for an essence to come to be, but it is another coming to be that such an essence belong to such a thing, for instance, that it be the essence of man, horse, etc. The first is true, for a created essence, speaking absolutely, has an efficient cause, because not only do the existences of things come to be, but the essences as well. But that an essence belong to such a thing does not have an efficient cause, nor does it come to be, because of itself it is necessary and eternal. This is to say, that man, for example, or animal have an efficient cause; but that Peter be a man or man an animal, does not have an efficient cause, because that connection of itself is absolutely necessary. Hence, they also say with consistency that, even though the essence of a creature has a cause, still the truth of an essence does not have a cause, because the truth of a thing consists in that necessary connection which of itself is eternal and has no cause, and in this way there is science of necessary and eternal truths.

42. *A judgement is rendered in regard to the opinion proposed.* But it seems that this opinion too, without further explanation, cannot be defended. First, because if that connection of such a predicate with a subject is eternal, I ask what it is outside God? For, it is either something or nothing. If something, how is it eternal without an efficient

cause? If nothing, it is indeed not surprising that it does not have an efficient cause; but it is surprising that it could be eternal or that there would be a real connection, if it is nothing. Also, a connection is nothing else than a union; but a union must be a thing or the mode of a thing. Consequently, if nothing is eternal, then there can be no eternal union of things, because the mode of a thing cannot be without the thing. Furthermore, how can an essence have an efficient cause and not have from it that it be the essence of such a thing? For if an essence comes to be, it comes to be in some thing or entity; hence, by the same effecting it has that it is the essence of such a thing. And there is corroboration, for, just as the essence of Peter did not exist before it came to be, so Peter did not have an essence before he was created or generated. Consequently, there was neither man nor animal etc. Therefore, he receives this whole thing from its efficient cause through generation, thus, not only do essences come to be but also the essential connections as well. There is a second corroboration. For, when a form (a soul, for instance) is impressed on matter, it formally begins to bestow upon the whole composite not only that it be, but also that it lives, senses, etc.; hence, the efficient cause which joined such a form to matter, not only produced that whole, but also made it to be living, animal, etc.; therefore, it brought it about that such an essence would come together with such a thing. Finally, either *being* in these statements is taken in the same signification or in a different signification. If taken in a different signification, there is patent equivocation and there is[133] no consistent teaching. If taken in the same signification, it must have the same efficient cause. This I explain accordingly, for when it is said that an essence absolutely has an efficient cause, it must be said to have it in relation to being, because nothing comes to be if not to exist. Consequently, either this is understood of being in act, and then it is true; or of being in potency, and then it is false, if the statement be strictly about an efficient cause in act, even though it is true of a cause able to effect. But it is entirely the same case, when an essence is said to belong to such a thing. For, if the statement concerns actual being, a created essence cannot belong to some thing in act except by an efficient cause; because what is not in act cannot belong to something in act. And the arguments already made also prove this, because, just as Peter does not exist unless he comes to be, so man is not in act unless a man comes to be, but man is only in potency. Consequently, if the statement is only about this being, then it is true that it does not have an efficient cause in act; nevertheless, it requires it at least able to effect. Hence, what is there that is affirmed of one and denied of the other?

43.   From this, the fact that it is said that an essence has an efficient cause, but the truth of an essence does not, also seems to be false. For the truth of an essence is really nothing else than the essence itself, or at most, it is thought to be a property intriniscally joined with essence. Consequently, it is impossible that it not have the same cause, either with equal primacy or concomitantly. For how can it be understood that some cause effects gold and does not effect true gold? But if in effecting gold it effects the essence of gold, how is it that, in effecting true gold, it does not effect the truth of the essence of gold? Therefore, we can use the same dilemma. It is either a statement about truth in potency or in act. Whichever of these be said, the character of an essence and of truth in potency or in act is the same, as will be readily clear, by applying the argument already made. [134] Finally, either it is a statement about complex truth, which is properly in an intellect composing and dividing and this, thus, has an efficient cause, just as the composition itself and the division of our intellect, for it inheres in that and begins with it in the way in which it is, as St. Thomas said, part. 1, q. 16, art. 7, to the fourth. [135] It is the same, keeping the proportion, about the truth which obtains in the composition of a word as in a sign. Else it is a statement about the truth of a thing, which gives foundation to the truth of intellect, and this does not differ from being itself. Hence, there is that text of Aristotle:"From the fact that a thing is or is not, a proposition is true or false." [136] Therefore, it has the same cause as being itself and it is subject to the same change. Consequently, St. Thomas himself, q. 1 *On Truth,* art. 6, to the fourth [137] says that the truth of these pronouncements, even in regard to the essentials of the things themselves, is not entirely immutable, unless the things abide.

44.   This entire controversy (as it seems to me, at least) consists in the different signification of that copula, *is,* by which the terms in these enunciations are connected, for it can be taken in two ways. First, to indicate a connection, actual and real, of the terms existing in the thing itself, so that, when it is said, *man is an animal,* it is an indication that it is really so. Secondly, it only indicates that the predicate is of the nature of the subject, whether the terms exist or not. In the first sense, the truth of the propositions undoubtedly depends on the existence of the terms, because, in terms of that signification, the word *is,* is not divorced from time. Or (which is the same thing) it indicates a real and actual duration, which is nothing, after the existence of the terms has been removed. And so, such a proposition is false, for it is affirmative of a subject not supposing. In this same sense, the arguments just made prove very well that the truth of these enunciations depend on an efficient cause, on which the existence of the terms depend. Likewise, it is proved that not only a

created essence, taken absolutely, has an efficient cause, but also the application of an essence (so to speak) to this thing has an efficient cause; that is, not only man or animal has an efficient cause, but also that man is really an animal has an efficient cause. For, even though there is not twofold action or efficient causation, one by which man comes to be, another by which man comes to be an animal, still both truly come to be when man is generated. There is a difference only because by these words, *man is an animal,* it is signified in the complex way we conceive of it. But in the thing itself, it comes to be by the simple action by which man and animal come to be in reality, insofar as they are the same in such a thing. So taught Harvey at length in *Quodlib.* 1, quest. 10[138] and Javellus, 5 *Metaphys.,* quest. 12[139] has defended him against Soncinas, in the same book 5, quest. 10,[140] who clearly struggles in an equivocation, as was said.[141] Finally, our assertion that existence is not separated from essence except by the destruction or cessation of the same essence goes along in this same signification. Nor does the objection made[142] make any progress against it. For it is denied that the propositions, in which essential predicates are predicated of subjects, are true in that sense, when actual existence is removed. For, thus, that text from the chapter on substance in Aristotle's *Predicaments* is true, namely, "with first substances removed, it is impossible for something to remain."[143] And Averroes has spoken in the same way, 1 *Physics,* com. 63:"When a thing ceases to be, it loses its name and definition."[144]

45.   But then propositions are true in another sense, even though the terms do not exist; and in the same sense they have necessary and eternal truth, because, since the copula *is,* in the stated sense, does not indicate existence, it does not ascribe actual reality to the terms in themselves. So, for its own truth, it does not require existence or actual reality. Likewise, this is explained from the authors cited above,[145] because propositions in this sense are reduced to a hypothetical or conditional sense. For, when we say man is animal, while abstracting from time, we say nothing else than that this is the nature of man, that it is impossible for man to come to be without being an animal. Consequently, just as this conditional proposition is eternal: *If it is man, it is animal,* or, *If it runs, it moves,* so, too, this is eternal: *man is an animal* or, *running is motion.* From this it also follows that these connections, in this sense, do not have an efficient cause, because every effecting is terminated at actual existence from which the stated propositions in this sense abstract. The other[146] arguments which Soncinas brings together, in the references cited,[147] prove only this. Indeed, in this same sense these connections not only do not require an efficient cause in act, but also they do not seem to demand one in potency, if we take our stand formally and

precisely on their truth. This can be clarified by the argument made about a conditional proposition, whose truth does not depend upon an efficient cause or one able to effect; and so is it found as well in impossible things as in possible ones. For this conditional: *If a stone is an animal, it is able to sense,* is true as well as that: *If man is an animal, he is able to sense.* Consequently, also this proposition: *Every animal is able to sense,* does not of itself depend on a cause which can effect an animal. Thus, if, by way of the impossible, there were no such cause, that enunciation would still be true, just as this is true: *A chimera is a chimera,* or the like. Yet, on this point, we should assign a difference between necessary connections, conceived and enunciated between possible things or real essences, and between imaginary things or beings *(entia)* of reason, that in the former the connection is so necessary in terms of an intrinsic relationship of terms abstracting from actual existence, that it is still possible in relation to actual existence. This whole can be indicated by the copula *is,* even as it abstracts from time, so that when it is said: *Man is a rational animal,* it is indicated that man has a real essence so definable, or (which is the same thing) that man is such a being *(ens),* which is not a fiction but real, at least possible. In this respect, the truth of such enunciations depends on a cause able to effect the existence of the terms. But then in the case of fictional beings *(entia),* the necessary connections only come to be without a relationship, even with regard to the possible, to existing, but merely with a relation to the imagination or fiction of the mind. Finally, in terms of this sense, also the objection [148] raised against our assertion is stilled, because, although these connections are necessary independently of existence, the essences signified by them are still not true and actual beings *(entia),* if they are deprived of existence.

46.   Two objections still remain. The first one is because it has still not been explained what that necessary connection of nonexisting terms is. For, since it posits nothing in reality, it is difficult to understand how it can afford a basis for necessary truth. For, neither is it satisfactory if we were to say that, with the existence of things removed, this connection remains only in the divine exemplar and such a necessity arises from that. This (I say) is not satisfactory, for, although the truth of these connections, as real and actual truth, remains only in the divine intellect (in the sense St. Thomas spoke of in the references cited, [149] especially part 1, quest. 16, art. 7; [150] and it is also taken from Anselm, *Dialogue on Truth,* c. 7 [151] and 8 [152]), nevertheless the necessity of this truth and the primary source and origin of such a connection, does not seem to be able to be referred to the divine exemplar. For the divine exemplar itself had this necessity of representing man as rational animal; nor was it possible to represent

that of another essence; this proceeds from no other source, except because man cannot be of another essence, for, by the very fact that a thing be of another essence, it is no longer man. Consequently, this necessity arises from the object itself and not from the divine exemplar. Therefore, the difficulty touched upon always remains, namely, how, if that object in itself is nothing, it could have of itself such a connection of predicates to furnish in some way a foundation for the necessity of such a science, and such a truth, and such an exemplar. To this it seems we have to say that this connection is nothing else than the identity of the terms which are in essential and affirmative propositions (the same thing is to be said proportionally about the difference of the terms in negative propositions). For every truth of an affirmative proposition is founded on some identity or unity of the terms which, though conceived of by us in a complex way, and by way of the joining of a predicate with a subject, is still in reality nothing but the very entity of the thing. But identity, since it is a property of being *(ens)* (for the same and the different are reduced to unity, as we said above), it is found proportionally in every being *(ens)* or in every state of being *(ens)*. Consequently, just as an existing man and animal are the same in reality, so a possible man, or anything that can be an object to the science or exemplar of man, has identity with animal taken proportionally. Hence, this identity is sufficient for founding that necessity, and it can be found in a being *(ens)* in potency, though it is nothing in act, because it adds nothing to a being *(ens)* in potency except a relationship of reason in regard to our concepts.

47. *A minor problem is solved.* But then a second difficulty arises. For it follows that this connection is also necessary: *man is* or *exists* or *is existing,* and consequently is true, even though it does not exist in act. But this is clearly false and contrary to every sense and meaning of the words. But the sequence is clear, because man and existing also have an identity, either objective and possible, or actual, if they be taken proportionally. Also, because, if that proposition be reduced to a conditional proposition, it will be found to be true and necessary, because man cannot come to be without being existent, just as he cannot come to be without being an animal. However, the whole necessity of this proposition, *Man is an animal,* was said to be, because man cannot be without animal, the necessity which some [153] call composite or suppositional. Therefore, the necessity is the same in, *Man is existing,* because man cannot be without existing. The answer is that, in reality, of course, there is hardly any difference, if existence be taken with the same proportion, either in act or in potency, as the argument proves, and as is sufficiently established from what was treated above. [154] But nevertheless there is a diffe-

rence in the manner of speaking. So the consequence must be denied absolutely, because the word, *existing,* used simply, does not signify potency, but the exercise of existing. Consequently, that statement, *Man exists,* used simply, does not render a composite sense, that is, if[155] man is, he is existing, but a simple and absolute sense. So, if it were necessary, it would indicate the absolute necessity of existing, which cannot belong to a man.

Notes

[1] See Section I, 4 and 10, above, esp. n. 47 there.

[2] See Section XI, 25, above, esp. n. 93 there. Also see the comment of L.A. Kennedy, C.S.B., in regard to Pedro of Ledesma on this issue in "Peter of Ledesma and the Distinction between Essence and Existence." *The Modern Schoolman* XLVI (1968), 35-36.

[3] See *DM* 15, VIII; XXV, 525-532.

[4] *Sum. Theol.,* I, q. 50, a. 5; T. 5, 11-12.

[5] *Sum. Cont. Gent.,* II, 55; T. 13, 393-395.

[6] See *DM* 46, I, esp. 5 and following; XXVI, 753-766.

[7] *Ibid.*

[8] See Suarez, *In Sum. Theol.,* III, q. 17, a. 2, disp. 36, I; XVIII, 260. Also see n. 47 in Section I, 10, above.

[9] See Franciscus Zumel, *In Primam D. Thomae partem commentaria* (Venetiis, 1597-1601), I, q. 3, a. 4; 95a:"Dico secundo quod forte Deus potest conservare essentiam sine existentia formali reali superaddita essentiae, per manutenentiam Dei." Peter of Ledesma thinks that it is probable that essence can exist without existence. See L.A. Kennedy, C.S.B. in article cited in n. 2, this section, above. Bañez espoused this position initially but later repudiated it according to L.A. Kennedy, C.S.B., "Thomism at the University of Salamanca in the Sixteenth Century: The Doctrine of Existence," *Tommaso d'Aquino nella storia del pensiero, Atti del Congresso Internazionale,* 1974; II, 256-257 where in n. 5 he refers to "A new commentary of Domingo Bañez," *Archivo Teológico Granadino* 36(1973), 153.

[10] See n. 2, this section, above.

[11] *DM* 7, II; XXV, 261-271.

[12] See B. Mastrius, *Disputationes...,* disp. 8, q. 2; II, 94a for a listing of some proponents of the modal distinction.

[13] *DM* 7, I, 16-30; XXV, 255-261.

[14] See the beginning of this paragraph.

[15] See D. Bañez, *In Sum. Theol.,* I, q. 3, a. 4, dub. 2 ad 1; 147 and Capreolus, *Def. Theol., In I Sent.,* d. 8, q. 1 ad 9 Godf.; I, 327.

[16] See Section IX above.

[17] I read the *in* of the 1597 Salamanca and 1605 Mainz editions which is deleted in the Vives text.

[18] See Sections III-IV above.

[19] See Section VI above.

[20] See Section XI, 25, above.

[21] See F. Zumel, *In Sum. Theol.,* I, q. 3, a. 4; 95a.

[22] I read the *tamen* of the 1597 Salamanca and 1605 Mainz editions instead of the *autem* of the Vives text.

[23] I read the *reddere* of the 1597 Salamanca and 1605 Mainz editions instead of the *addere* of the Vives text.

[24] I read the *quae* of the 1597 Salamanca and 1605 Mainz editions instead of the *quia* of the Vives text.

[25] See Sections III-IV above.

[26] I read the *est* of the 1597 Salamanca and 1605 Mainz editions instead of the *esse* of the Vives text.

[27] I read the *ita* of the 1597 Salamanca and 1605 Mainz editions which is deleted in the Vives text.

[28] See Suárez, *In Sum. Theol.*, III, q. 17, a. 2, disp. 36, I, 2; XVIII, 261. Also see Section XI, n. 10, above.

[29] See paragraphs 3 and 6, this section, above as well as Sections V-VI above. Also see *DM* 7, passim.

[30] See *DM* 34, IV, 17-22; XXVI, 372-374.

[31] *Ibid.*, 1-16; XXVI, 367-372.

[32] See paragraph 9, this section, above. Also see Section VI, 19, above.

[33] See Sections III and VI above.

[34] See Section IV above.

[35] See paragraph 2 and following, this section, above.

[36] See Sections III-VI above.

[37] See F. Zumel, *In Sum. Theol.*, I, q. 3, a. 4; 94b-95a.

[38] See Fonseca, *In VIII Metaph.*, cap. 1, q. 1; col. 442-445, esp. 444.

[39] See *DM* 32, I; XXVI, 312-319.

[40] See Sections V and XI, 23, above.

[41] See n. 8, this section, above as well as *Salmanticenses, Cursus Theologicus,* Tract. XXI, disp. 8, dub. 3, I-IV; T. XIV, 54-73.

[42] *Ibid.*

[43] *Ibid.* Also see Suárez, *In Sum. Theol.*, III, q. 17, a. 2, disp. 36, I, 19-21; XVIII, 267-268.

[44] *Ibid.*

[45] *Ibid.*

[46] *Ibid.*

[47] *Ibid.*

[48] The 1597 Salamanca edition has a marginal note here:"Joan. Vinc. lib. de gratia Christi q. 7, dub. de hac re, conclus. 2" and it is also carried by the Vives text. This would be John Vincent, a Dominican contemporary of Suárez at Salamanca. The work in question has been unavailable to me but his position on essence and existence is well analyzed in L.A. Kennedy, C.S.B., "La doctrina de la existencia en la Universidad de Salamanca durante el siglo XVI," *Archivo Teológico Granadino* 35 (1972), 50-70.

[49] See Suárez, *In Sum. Theol.*, III, q. 17, a. 2, disp. 36, I, 2; XVIII, 261.

[50] *Ibid.*

[51] *Ibid.*

[52] *Ibid.*

[53] *Ibid.*

[54] *Ibid.*

[55] *Ibid.*

[56] *Ibid.*

⁵⁷ *Ibid.*

⁵⁸ *Ibid.,* II, 5-8; 271-272.

⁵⁹ I read the *De* of the 1597 Salamanca and 1605 Mainz editions which is deleted in the Vives text.

⁶⁰ *In Sum. Theol.,* III, q. 17, a. 2, disp. 36, I, 2; XVIII, 261.

⁶¹ See Suárez, *In Sum. Theol.,* III, q. 2, a. 8, I; XVII, 328-340.

⁶² See G. Vasquez, *In Sum. Theol.,* III, q. 17, a. 2, disp. 71, cap. II; 476-477. See an allusion to Vasquez on this point in *Salmanticenses, Cursus Theologicus,* Tract XXI, disp. 8 dub. 3, V; T. XIV, 74b.

⁶³ See John Damascene, *De Fide Orthodoxa,* cap. 66, edit. E.M. Buytaert (St. Bonaventure, N.Y.: Franciscan Institute, 1955), 263-264. However, Suárez is using the Billius edition of 1577 as reference in n. 61, this section, above indicates.

⁶⁴ *Ibid.* See Suárez, *In Sum. Theol.,* III, q. 17, a. 2, disp. 36, I, 20; XVIII, 267-268.

⁶⁵ See nn. 49-53, this section, above.

⁶⁶ I read the *esse* of the 1597 Salamanca and 1605 Mainz editions instead of the *est* of the Vives text.

⁶⁷ See Section II, 5 and Sections III-IV above.

⁶⁸ *Ibid.*

⁶⁹ See Section IX above.

⁷⁰ See Sections II-VI above.

⁷¹ See paragraph 22, this section, above.

⁷² See Suárez, *In Sum. Theol.,* III, q. 17, a. 2, disp. 36, I, 25; XVIII, 269-270.

⁷³ *Ibid.,* III, disp. 1, I; XIX, 3-7.

⁷⁴ See Section XI above.

⁷⁵ See Suárez, *In Sum. Theol.,* III, q. 17, a. 2, disp. 36, I, 19-25; XVIII, 267-270.

⁷⁶ See nn. 63-64, this section above. Also see *Salmanticenses, Cursus Theologicus,* Tract. XXI, disp. 8, dub. 3, I; T. XIV, 54-59.

⁷⁷ See the rest of paragraphs 26 and 27, this section, below.

⁷⁸ See paragraphs 28-33, this section, below.

⁷⁹ See Suárez, *In Sum. Theol.,* III, q. 2, a. 12, disp. 10, I-II; XVII, 386-400.

⁸⁰ *Ibid.*

⁸¹ See Suárez, *In Sum. Theol.,* III, q. 2, a. 7, disp. 8, I, 13-26; XVII, 334-340.

⁸² *Ibid.*

⁸³ See Suárez, *In Sum Theol.,* III, q. 2, a. 12, disp. 10, II-III; XVII, 390-406.

⁸⁴ I read the *essentiae* of the 1597 Salamanca and 1605 Mainz editions instead of the *essentiale* of the Vives text.

⁸⁵ See paragraphs 17-20, this section, above.

⁸⁶ See n. 48, this section, above. Also see *Salmanticenses, Cursus Theologicus,* Tract. XXI, disp. 8, dub. 3, V, 101; T. XIV, 79. *Asturicensis* referred to there would seem to be John Vincent who hails from *Asturia.*

⁸⁷ *Ibid.*

⁸⁸ See paragraphs 9 and following, this section, above.

⁸⁹ See n. 86, this section, above.

⁹⁰ See Suárez, *In Sum. Theol.,* III, q. 2, a. 8, disp. 8, III, 6-39; XVII, 346-349. Also see *Salmanticenses, Cursus Theologicus,* Tract. XXI, disp. 8, dub. 2, III, 45-47; T. XIV, 34-36. See also dub. 3, V, 102; T. 24, 80.

⁹¹ *Ibid.*

⁹² I read the *increatum* of the 1597 Salamanca and 1605 Mainz editions instead of the *creatum* of the Vives text.

⁹³ See paragraphs 22 and following, this section above.

⁹⁴ See Section II above.

⁹⁵ Aristotle, *On Generation and Corruption,* I, 3; 318a 29-33.

⁹⁶ See Section I, 3, esp. nn. 24-25 above.

⁹⁷ Giles of Rome, *Theorema de Esse et Essentia,* edit. E. Hocedez (Louvain, 1930), Theorema 12, 67-68. Also see Hocedez in Introduction, (63).

⁹⁸ See Section I, n. 59, above.

⁹⁹ Alexander of Alexandria, *In 7 Metaph.,* text. 22; 207rb-207vb.

¹⁰⁰ *Ibid.,* 207va.

¹⁰¹ I read the *fit* of the 1597 Salamanca and 1605 Mainz editions instead of the *sit* of the Vives text.

¹⁰² Alexander of Alexandria, *In 7 Metaph.,* text. 22; 207rb-207vb.

¹⁰³ See paragraphs 2-9, this section, above.

¹⁰⁴ See *DM* 18, XI; XXV, 684-687. The Vives reference to Disp. 28 is incorrect.

¹⁰⁵ See Suárez, *In Sum. Theol.,* III, q. 75, a. 8, disp. 50, VII; XXI, 171-175.

¹⁰⁶ See paragraphs 2-9, this section, above.

¹⁰⁷ See Section I, 4 above.

¹⁰⁸ See F. Zumel, *In Sum. Theol.,* I, q. 10, a. 5, concl. 21; 157b and Michael de Palacios, *In Primum Librum Magistri Sententiarum Disputationes* (Salmanticae, 1574), *In I Sent.,* d. 8, disp. 2; 81v.

¹⁰⁹ Aristotle, *Metaphysics,* IV, 7, 1011b 26-28.

¹¹⁰ St. Augustine, *De Libero Arbitrio,* II, 8; *PL* 23, 1252-1253. See Capreolus, *Def. Theol., In I Sent.,* d. 8, q. 1; I, 303b.

¹¹¹ St. Augustine, *De Genesi ad litteram,* IV, 7; *PL* 34, 301. See Capreolus, *Def. Theol.,* I, 304.

¹¹² St. Anselm, *De Veritate, Opera Omnia,* c. 13, edit. F.S. Schmitt (Edinburgh: Nelson, 1946); I, 196-199.

¹¹³ *Sum. Theol.,* I, q. 10, a. 3 ad 3; T. 4, 98.

¹¹⁴ *Op. cit.,* I, q. 16, a. 7 ad 1; T. 4, 215.

¹¹⁵ *De Veritate,* ed. Spiazzi, q. 1, a. 5 ad 11; 12.

¹¹⁶ *Op. cit.,* a. 6 ad 2 and 3; 15.

¹¹⁷ That of the *moderni theologi* noted in paragraph 39, this section, above. See n. 108, this section, above.

¹¹⁸ St. Albert, *De Causis et Processu Universitatis,* I, 1, 8; X, 377.

¹¹⁹ St. Albert, *Liber de Praedicamentis,* tract. VII, c. 9, ed. A. Borgnet; I, 289-290.

¹²⁰ Capreolus, *Def. Theol.,* I, 301-306. Also see III, 73-75.

¹²¹ Soncinas, *In 9 Metaph.,* q. 5; 232b-234b.

¹²² *Ibid.* See Henry of Ghent, *Quodlibet* 10, q. 2 and 3; T. 2, 137-139. However, this reference seems incorrect.

¹²³ *Ibid.* See Harvey, *Quodlibet* 3, q. 1; 67vb-70ra.

¹²⁴ Scotus, *Opus Oxon.,* III, d. 21, q. 1; T. 24, 743-747.

¹²⁵ I have been unable to find these to date.

¹²⁶ Cajetan, *Commentaria in Posteriora Analytica Aristotelis* (Laval reprint of Lyons edit., 1597), I, cap. 6; 115.

¹²⁷ See Section I, n. 21, above.

¹²⁸ Aristotle, *Metaphysics,* IX, 6, 1048a 25-1048b 34.

[129] *Op. cit.,* IX, 7, 1048b 35-1049b 3.

[130] *Op. cit.,* IX, 9, 1051a 3-34.

[131] See Soncinas and Ferrara in references cited in n. 121 and n. 127, this section, above. See Bañez, *In Sum. Theol.,* I, q. 10, a. 3; I, 227. See also Bañez in the 1584, Salamanca edition of his Commentary on the *Summa Theologiae, In Sum. Theol.,* I, q. 44, a. 1 ad 3; col. 646:"...dico quod illa maxima, essentiae rerum sunt aeternae, est vera quoad connexionem, non quia illae essentiae existant ab aeterno...."

[132] See Section II above.

[133] I read the *est* of the 1597 Salamanca and 1605 Mainz editions which is deleted in the Vives text.

[134] See paragraph 42, this section, above.

[135] St. Thomas, *Sum. Theol.,* I, q. 16, a. 7 ad 4; T. 4, 215.

[136] See n. 109, this section, above.

[137] *De Veritate,* q. 1, a. 6 ad 4; 15.

[138] Harvey Nédellec, *Quodlibet,* I, q. 10; 22vb-24va.

[139] Javellus, *In V Metaph.,* q. 12; 751b-753a.

[140] Soncinas, *In 5 Metaph.,* q. 10; 64b-66a.

[141] See paragraph 42, this section, above.

[142] See paragraph 38, this section, above.

[143] Aristotle, *Categories,* c. 5, 2b 5.

[144] Averroes, *In I Physics,* c. 3; Vol. 4, fol. 37v.

[145] See the references to Harvey and Javellus in nn. 138-139, this section, above.

[146] I read the *aliae* of the 1597 Salamanca and 1605 Mainz editions instead of the *illae* of the Vives text.

[147] See nn. 121 and 140, this section, above.

[148] See paragraph 38, this section, above.

[149] See paragraph 40, this section, above.

[150] *Sum. Theol.,* I, q. 16, a. 7; T. 4, 214-215.

[151] St. Anselm, *De Veritate,* c. 7; I, 185-186.

[152] *Op. cit.,* c. 8; I, 186-188.

[153] See Fonseca, *In V Metaph.,* cap. 5, q. 1; col. 318 and Harvey, *Quodlibet* 1, q. 10; fol. 22vb-fol. 24va.

[154] See Section XI above.

[155] I read the *si est* of the 1597 Salamanca and 1605 Mainz editions which is deleted in the Vives text.

Section XIII

The type of composition there is from being and essence or the type of composition that is of the nature of created being (ens).

1.   This question is necessary, first, to explain some problems touched upon in the second [1] and third [2] arguments for the first opinion proposed in the first section, then it is necessary to consider or explain many things written by the authors about this composition, especially by Cajetan, *On Being and Essence,* chapt. 5, a little after question 9, [3] where he explains the composition of being and essence by a comparison with the composition of matter and form, which he says agree on two counts, but differ on ten.

A COMPARISON OF THE COMPOSITIONS OF BEING AND ESSENCE AND OF MATTER AND FORM.

2.   There is a first likeness, because both are compositions of act and potency. This is self-evident in regard to the first composition; he [4] proves it of the second, because any quiddity is posited in reality by reason of the fact that it obtains existence. But this proof is especially weak, if it is a statement, as it certainly is, of a receptive potency, because an essence is not said to obtain being because it was first in potency to the reception and afterward receives an act, because the whole was first in objective potency or in the active potency of its cause, and afterward comes to be a being *(ens)* in act. There is a second likeness because in both compositions act and potency are reduced to the same genus. This is true; for it also occurs between a real composition and one of reason or between a physical composition and a metaphysical one, as is clear in the composition of genus and difference. However, on this point some difference could be noted, for in a physical composition, both parts, namely, matter and form, are only reductively placed in a predicament; but in a metaphysical composition, only the difference is placed reductively in a

predicament. But even though the genus as a part could also be reduced or located alongside, still as it is a certain whole, it is directly placed. And the same thing, in its own way, is found in the composition of being and essence, which is also a metaphysical composition, as I will state below.[5] For the integral essence is directly located in a predicament, but existence, considered as a certain mode, is located only by reduction; we have said enough about this in the above sections.[6]

3. The differences can be read in the above-mentioned author.[7] For the first six all suppose a real distinction between essence and existence, and that existence is an act only of a complete essence and composed of matter and form; and so for us they are not necessary nor must we attack all over again many of the things said therein; as, for example, that in a composition of being and essence neither term is a substantial part. For this is true in the compositon of a complete being *(ens),* but not in every composition of being and essence. For this is also found in matter itself, and form and in the separated soul. Also, as is said in the second difference, that in a composition of matter and form, one term is pure potency but not in a composition of being and essence, this (I say), in the first place, is not general, since matter itself is made up of being and essence; and, furthermore, if an essence be prescinded from being, it is more potential being *(ens)* than matter prescinded from form, or as it is supposed to form with its own being, these potentialities are of a different sort. For, in an essence as such, it is objective, but in matter it is receptive. And rather similar things can be pointed out in the four remaining differences; I pass them over.

WHETHER A SUBSTANTIAL UNIT IS FORTHCOMING FROM BEING AND ESSENCE.

4. What Cajetan says in the seventh difference, that a substantial unit comes to be from matter and form, but not from being and essence, I judge to be false, even in the opinion that essence and existence are really distinguished. First, because they are compared as act and potency of the same genus which essentially and of their very nature are ordained for composing a unit, and an essence without existence does not have a complete actuality, indeed, it is not a being *(ens)* in act. Why, then, does not a being *(ens)* substantially one result from them? Secondly, I judge it as false because an accidental unit does not come to be from them. Hence, a substantial unit comes to be. The antecedent is admitted and proved by the same Cajetan,[8] because an accidental unit joins together things of different genera. But the consequence is proved, because something truly one comes

to be from being and essence. For there is a real union between them, indeed, (and this is astonishing) Cajetan himself says, in the same place, *that essence is substantially united to being.* [9] But it is impossible to conceive of a medium between a substantial unit and an accidental one. Thirdly, it is because otherwise no created being *(ens)* would be substantially one, insofar as it is a being *(ens)* in act. Fourthly, because Cajetan's argument [10] is especially weak, that is, because a being *(ens)* substantially one comes to be from substantial parts. But being is not a substantial part. For the assumption is false; indeed, a substantial unit also comes to be from a substance and a substantial act or term, otherwise a substantial unit would not come to be from nature and subsistence, nor would a substantial supposit, as such, be substantially one; this is clearly false. Therefore, we can attack that teaching theologically, because it follows from it that Christ is not a substantial unit, because He is composed of the humanity and the Word not in the manner of substantial parts, but as from nature and subsistence or from essence and being.

THAT THE COMPOSITION OF BEING AND ESSENCE IS A COMPOSITION "OF THESE" (EX HIS).

5. And, from this, in a similar fashion, it is established that the eighth difference which the same author [11] points out, is false, that is, that a composition of matter and form is a composition "of these" *(ex his),* and a third unit comes to be in that case; but the composition of being and essence is a composition "with these" *(cum his),* because in this [12] composition a thing composed of essence and existence is not given, properly speaking, as there is given a thing made up of matter and form, but essence composes with *(cum)* existence and vice versa. And so (he says) it was stated that they were substantially united, not, however, by composing a third thing. But this distinction of a twofold composition "of these" *(ex his)* and "with these" *(cum his)* is a figment (as I have shown elsewhere in a similar issue against Durandus [13]). For every true composition in terms of different relationships is a composition "from these" *(ex his)* and "with these" *(cum his)* or of this to this, as Durandus has more appropriately said. [14] For, in relation to the term which results from the composition, it is called a composition "of these" *(ex his),* because a composite does not compose with its components, but it is composed of them. However, in terms of the relationship of the components to each other, it is called a composition "with these" *(cum his)* or of this to this, because one with the other composes a third. But it is impossible for some true composition to be given unless there were to be given something composed by it which would have some unity proportionate to the composition.

Consequently, it is impossible for a true composition to be given unless there be a composition "from these" *(ex his)*. The consequence is evident from what was said[15] and from the very signification of the terms. For what else is it to be a composition "of these" *(ex his)* except to be the composition of one thing consisting of many? But the antecedent is clear, because every true action, especially a transient one, has some adequate term. Consequently, composition also has an adequate term at which it would be terminated; and this can only be the composite, also, because every composition comes to be by a union of components. But a unit results from a union, not simple but composite. So, therefore, if the composition of being and essence is a true and real composition, as they say, it cannot be denied that it is a composition "from these" *(ex his)*. Also, it cannot be denied that one composite thing results from it. For if this is not[16] given, what, I ask, is that which is composed of being and essence? Moreover, Cajetan gives no reason, nor can he give one, why one thing is not composed of being and essence. And so, he would otherwise say, with equal reasoning, that something one does not come to be from nature and subsistence, which is clearly false, because a substantial supposit is one. The sequence is clear in the argument noted above,[17] because also this composition is not of substantial parts but of an essence and an essential term or mode. Consequently, here also a theological argument has urgency, because it follows that the Incarnation is not a composition "of these" *(ex his)* because it is a composition of nature and supposit, or of being and essence. And so it also happens that Christ is not made up of a divine and human nature, which is contrary to the Councils'[18] manner of speaking, when they say that Christ subsists of two natures and in two natures.
6.   Hence, with the differences disregarded, according to the opinion asserting that being and essence are distinct things, it would be necessary to say that the composition of being and essence is univocally like the others, in the common feature of a true and real composition of a real potency and an act, pertaining, in some way, to the same genus or predicament; and so it is also alike in the feature of composition by which a substantial unit comes to be from many. But it would be necessary to say that it differs because the act of this composition is not properly a form, neither substantial nor accidental, but a certain simple essential term or mode, intrinsic and proportionate to it. And, consequently, that it also differs from the side of the other term, namely, essence, because it is not a proper matter, but a potency receptive of another feature, and proportionate to such an act.

THE COMPOSITION OF BEING AND ESSENCE IS
DESIGNATED A COMPOSITION ANALOGICALLY.

7. But then, according to our opinion, it must be stated that the composition of being and essence is only analogically called a composition, because it is not a real composition, but one of reason. For there is no real composition except of terms distinct in the thing itself; but here the terms are not distinct in the thing, as we have shown. [19] Consequently, a composition of them cannot be real. However, just as a being *(ens)* of reason is not a being *(ens)* save analogically and almost by name alone, so this composition does not have a univocal likeness with the real composition of matter and form, for instance, but only an analogous proportion. And this is the primary and generic difference between this composition and that which is of matter and form. But with this there is associated another difference which pertains to the present case, namely, that the composition of matter and form is found only in bodies and sensible things, but this composition of being and essence is common to all created beings which are beings *(entia)* in act. And so, the former is a physical composition, because it does not abstract from matter in terms of being. But the latter is metaphysical, because it does abstract, and is common to immaterial beings *(entia)*. Hence, it also happens that that first physical composition is the basis for physical change; but the latter not at all. But, of itself, it abstracts from corruption or physical change, except insofar as it is joined to things in which the first composition is found. But it differs from other metaphysical compositions, generally speaking, because it is ordered to a different term and [20] quasi-formal effect. But, in particular, it differs from a composition of nature and subsistence, because this is real, the former is of reason. But it differs from the other compositions of reason, as that of genus and difference, etc., because they of themselves abstract from actual existence and are considered also in being in potency. But this one is considered only in a thing existing in act.

HOW THE COMPOSITION OF BEING AND ESSENCE
IS ONE OF REASON ONLY.

8. But some objections go counter to this explanation; in answering them this matter will be better explained. The first is, because if this is only a composition of reason, it cannot be said to be of the nature of a creature, because either it is not common to all creatures, or not proper to them, for a composition of reason is devised by reason. Hence, it comes to creatures from without. Therefore, it is not of their nature nor can it be called common to all. But if it be

called common, not to the extent that it is thought of in act, but inasmuch as it can be thought of in regard to all creatures, it will not in this way be proper [21] to created being *(ens)* but it will be possible to be thought of and imagined to be in God as well. For a composition of reason is not repugnant to perfect real simplicity. And so, it is not repugnant to God. For thus do the theologians [22] say, that the divine persons are constituted by relations or personal subsistences; and this constitution is clearly a certain composition of reason. For the relations are distinguished in reason from the essence, and the persons are constituted by the relations and the essence itself; and they are understood, as it were, to be composed. So also do some theologians [23] ascribe a composition of genus and difference to God. Nor have there been lacking also those who thought that being is distinguished in reason from essence, even in God.

9.   The answer is that this composition of being and essence is of reason in such a way that it has not been concocted by the intellect, merely gratuitously, but it has some basis in reality. Consequently, this composition is said to be of the nature of created being *(ens)*, not insofar as it is completed or thought of by the intellect, but in terms of the basis which it has in the created being *(ens)* itself. But this basis is nothing other than that a creature does not have of itself existing in act, for it is only a potential being *(ens)* which can partake of being from another. From this it comes about that we conceive the creature's essence as something potential, yet its being as a mode or act by which such an essence is constituted a being *(ens)* in act. And in this sense it is best understood how this composition be of the essence of created being *(ens)*, for it is of its essence not to have being of itself, but only to be able to partake of that from another. However, I say that it is of its essence, if created being *(ens)* be taken as being *(ens)* in act, for if it be taken in potency, it will not be possible that it be of its essence to be composed in act in this way, for there is a repugnance involved in this. But it will be of its essence to be apt for existing with such a composition and not otherwise. And in this the proper character of created being *(ens)* in act or in potency is completed, which is what we have especially aimed to make clear in this whole discussion.

10.   *How the composition of being and essence is proper to creatures.* Further, from what was said, it is readily understood how this composition is proper to created being *(ens)* and cannot be ascribed to God. For its basis includes imperfection, repugnant to a God who is a being *(ens)* in act by essence. And He is not, nor can He be conceived of, as a potential being *(ens)*, because the very potentiality of an essence is repugnant to God, as He is God. Therefore, whatever be of the composition of reason in common, or insofar as it is such, would be repugnant to divine perfection. For perhaps some compo-

sition is not repugnant, unless it be a question of the name, and to avoid the prejudice of the word, it would be called constitution, and not composition, even of reason; nevertheless, that composition of reason, which in reality has a basis involving imperfection, is clearly repugnant to God. For this reason, those of the theologians [24] who are better thinkers, deny a composition of genus and difference in God, even though it be one of reason, because it demands in reality some foundation involving imperfection, namely, a limitation of perfection which could be defined by a genus and a difference, as was touched on in the preceding discussion. [25] Thus, for a much greater reason, is the composition of being and essence repugnant to God. But those [26] who ascribe such a composition to Him or make a distinction of reason between being and essence in Him, either do not have a concept of what God is, or do not sufficiently understand in what the character of this composition consists, or do not speak of the distinction of reason with which we are now concerned but one which can be thought of between being and essence in common as it abstracts from God and creatures.

11.   *An objection.* A second objection is possible, because, according to our opinion, a composition of reason of being and essence cannot be derived from thought. For essentially a composition of some thing should be of real terms, even though it is of reason. Indeed, it is not said to be of reason because the terms themselves would be concocted by reason, but because, though they are something real, they are still not two in reality, but one. But, then, essence and being are not two real terms in reality nor can they even be conceived of as two real terms, because, when there are two terms, in the way in which they are two, one is not included in the other. But essence is not conceived of as a real term, except as containing being, as we said above. [27] Consequently, this actuality which essence is understood to have from being cannot be conceived of in the manner of a composition. And this difficulty has greater urgency in created existence itself, for that is a created being *(ens),* and hence, also in that, this composition must have place; for that is potential and can sometimes be, and sometimes not be, and yet in it a composition of essence and being cannot be understood, otherwise there would be a procession to infinity.

12.   *The solution.* The response is that, for a composition of reason, the terms need not be or be conceived of as real actual beings *(entia)* especially taken precisely, insofar as one is not included in the concept of the other; but it is enough that the terms be some real natures apt for existing in some way. This is clearly evident in a composition of reason made up of a specific nature and an individuating difference. For a specific nature, as conceptually prescinded from all

individuating differences, is not a being *(ens)* in act, but only a certain real nature apt to be in act in individuals (but we are speaking about that composition as it is predicated of real things, or as it has a real term). Consequently, that the terms be real beings *(entia)* in act is, of course, essentially necessary for a real composition, but scarcely for a composition of reason. Therefore, one can distinguish a threefold composition of reason. One, which would be of terms as they are beings *(entia)* in act in the thing itself, even though they are not actually distinct. Another, which would be between terms, real, indeed, aptitudinally or by a real objective formality, but abstracting from existential actuality. Another, finally, which would be a quasi-middle, such that its one term would be only a nature or real essence precisely conceived, but the other would be actual existence. This is the best answer and consistent enough with the manner of conceiving.
13.   But, secondly, it could be said that not every composition of reason is of terms which are mutually exclusive or of which neither is included in the concept of the other; but it is enough that one can be prescinded from the other, even though, conversely, the other cannot. For, thus, a substance is in some way composed according to reason, because it can be broken down into two concepts of a being *(ens)* and of a substantial mode, even though being be necessarily included in the concept of a mode. Hence, it will be stated accordingly in the present case. In both ways a corroboration can be furnished about existence itself; for, first, it can be said probably enough that actual existence, by the very fact that it is abstracted from the exercise of actually existing, is confused with the essence itself. And thus existence, as exercised is not conceived of as composite, but as a simple mode composing created being *(ens)* in act. For this reason, when this composition is said to be of the nature of created being, it is understood either of that which is conceived of as that which is, and not as the precise character of being *(essendi),* or it is understood proportionally, namely, that this composition is of the nature of created being *(ens)* as composed by it or as composing. Or it can be stated, in the second place, that this composition can be conceived of in the existence itself without a procession to infinity, because existence itself, as long as it is the reason for the being *(essendi)* of the essence, it is also the reason for being *(essendi)* to itself, as was discussed rather amply in the above sections. [28]

How the being of a creature is received being.

14.   There was a third objection which was touched upon in the second argument cited for the first opinion, [29] because, from what was said, it follows that the being of a creature is not received in some receptive potency, but is subsistent being. Consequently, it was a

further conclusion that it is most perfect and infinite because it does not have a source of limitation. The first sequence is proved because, if a composition in reality does not come to be from being and essence, as from act and potency, then, in reality, being itself is not an act received in a potency; therefore, it is unreceived and in itself subsistent. In the first place, this difficulty does not arise concerning the being of accidents; for this is received in a subject. Secondly, it does not arise concerning the being of a substantial material form; for this too is received in matter by which it can be limited. And for almost the same reason it does not arise concerning the being of the rational soul, because, [30] though it be not received in matter as dependent upon it, still it is adapted to it and by relationship to it can be limited. Consequently, it further follows that the argument arises much less in the being of matter itself, which is much more imperfect than the being of form, and can be more limited by relationship to form than the being of form itself by relationship to matter. Consequently, the ones who really distinguish them say almost this very thing of essence and being; for they say that being is limited by the essence whose act it is, and that essence is limited by being, because it is a potency receptive of it. In addition, because of this, that difficulty in the being of the entire composite substance is easily put to rest, for it will be limited from its component parts, since that cannot be unlimited which is made up of limited parts.

15.   Therefore, only the being of angels remains, about which it must be acknowledged that it is not properly received in a subject properly taken, neither in terms of a part, since it is indivisible, nor in terms of its whole self, because it is substantial and complete. Yet it can be said that it is received in a supposit distinct in reality from essential being itself, and that this is enough to be limited and finite. This can be explained as follows, for either we are speaking of the being of the angelic nature alone, or of its subsistential being, or of the complete being of the whole composite. The being of the nature is received in a supposit distinct in reality from it and it is limited from this angle, because it is drawn into composition and is limited and determined by such a mode of subsisting. But subsistential being itself is plainly limited from this, because it is only a certain mode of such a nature. Finally, the complete being of the whole supposit, since it is made up of limited terms, it too must be limited. So, then, there is no need for the being of a creature to be unlimited, even though it be unreceived in a subject.

16.   But the inference that it will be subsistent can be understood in different ways. First, that essentially and adequately and by itself it would be subsisting being, secondly, that it would be subsisting denominatively, as it were, by some mode or term intrinsic to it.

Taken in this second way, in none of the opinions can it be denied that created being, if it be substantial and complete, would be subsistent by its nature, because it is not inhering nor supported by something else, but terminated by a proper subsistence. And because this subsistence is distinguished in reality from such being and it has from it that it subsists, this is why I call that subsisting denominatively and not essentially. And this mode of subsisting being denotes no infinity or lack of limitation in such being, since it is an imperfect mode of subsisting and with some composition. But we acknowledge that, in the first way, only the being of God is so subsisting in act by Himself, essentially and substantially, and He has this in virtue of His infinity. Nor does it follow, from the fact that the composition of being and essence in a creature be not real, that its being be subsisting in that way. For if it be a statement about the being of a substantial nature, this subsists only by a superadded mode. But if it be a statement about subsistential being itself, that is not properly subsisting, but the reason for subsisting. Finally, if it be a statement about the whole supposit, that, of course, is subsisting, but still not in a primary essential fashion and adequately, but by some other term or mode of its own. And so complete satisfaction is given to the difficulty set forth, even if we should grant some principles which have not yet been proved adequately, such as that subsistent being is proper to divine being, or that it require infinite perfection.

17.   But, in another way, it would be possible for the reply to be that being unreceived is understood in two ways. In one way, that it be unreceived both in something and by something; and in this fashion, it does not follow, from our opinion, that the being of a creature be unreceived, as is self-evident. And it is rightly said about such being that it is infinite because it is independent being and not participated, but rather the source of the whole participated being. Such being can be justly called, in a unique way, subsistent being itself, because, since it be not participated, it is and subsists of itself with every perfection of being *(essendi);* and, in this sense, it is rightly said to be proper to God that He be subsistent being itself. But to be unreceived in something can be said in another way, even though it be received by another; and, in this way, it is conceded that created being can be unreceived. Yet, I deny that it follows from this that it be unlimited and infinite. First, because, although it be unreceived in a subject, it is only subsistent by some composition with subsistence itself. From this, infinity cannot be inferred, as was explained in the first reply. Then, too, I deny the contention because it would not be pure act, but by participation. But, they say if being is participated, then it is participated by something; hence it is participated

by the essence, whose being it is. Consequently, it must be distinct from that and make a real composition with it. The answer is from Alexander of Alexandria cited above [31] that, when created being is called being by participation, *it must not be imagined that there be one thing which participates, as essence, and another which is particpated, as being; but that one and the same thing is a reality in a participated manner, and by virtue of another, as by virtue of an agent; for this reality of itself is only subject to a possible mode; but that it would be and could be called act, this it has by virtue of an agent.* This very thing is clarified in the essence itself or the created substance; for it is an essence and a substance by participation, not because it be participated subjectively (so to speak) by some other thing or substance, but only because it is effectively from the divine substance, in which there is a certain participation.

18.   But it was objected, because being is not received in something, it does not have that whereby it is limited, because it is limited neither by a receptive potency nor by some contracting difference. There could be an adequate reply to this in one word, that by itself and in virtue of its own entity it is limited and finite; that it does not need something limiting or contracting, distinct in reality from itself, but that intrinsically, its own nature is of so much perfection by its own formal entity; and that extrinsically it is limited by God, either effectively, because it receives from Him so much perfection of being *(essendi)* and no more, or as from an exemplar cause, because it is commensurate to such a divine idea representing so much perfection and no more. But to make this more clear we can distinguish a twofold contraction or limitation, one metaphysical, the other physical. A metaphysical contraction does not require an actual distinction in reality between the contracted and the contracting, but a distinction of concepts with some foundation in reality suffices for this. In this way, (if we wish to speak as many do), we can grant that an essence is rendered finite and limited because it is the act of such an essence. For this circle is not repugnant under distinct aspects and in a different genus of causes, just as we distinguish in the essence itself a genus, and the difference by which a species is constituted and limited to a certain quality and quantity of perfection. The difference itself, as it is a difference, can be said to be limited in relation to such a genus whose act it is, and conversely. But, then, speaking physically, if an essence be simple, substantial and complete, as an angelic substance is, it truly does not need some formally and intrinsically limiting thing besides itself; but just as a composite substance is limited by its intrinsic components or principles, (and it is not distinguished in reality from these taken together and united), which is nothing else that to be intrinsically limited by its very own entity, so a simple created substance is physically and really limited by itself.

It has this limitation either in potency, before it comes to be, or in act, when it does come to be. Consequently, since existence is nothing else than an essence constituted in act, just as an actual essence is formally limited by itself or by its intrinsic principles, so, too, created existence has limitation from its very essence, not as it is a potency in which it is received, but because, in reality, it is nothing else than the very actual essence itself.

THAT AN ESSENTIAL DIFFERENCE OBTAINS AMONG EXISTENCES.

19.   It is understood from these remarks that, just as the essences of created things differ specifically, so, too, existence which even those who think that essence and existence are distinct things do not deny. For they claim rather that the differences of essences, especially in immaterial substances, are obtained through the relation to different being, as is taken from Cajetan, *On Being and Essence,* c. 6.[32] This could not be true unless there were diversity in the existences themselves. Further, because they say that existence is compared to essence, either as to an intrinsic principle from which it flows, or as to a proper and connatural receiver. Consequently, under both aspects, existence must be proportionate to essence and, consequently, that the distinction between existences would be as great as it is between essences. But this is much more of a necessity according to our opinion because, if existence in reality is nothing else than an actual essence, just as actual essences are distinguished specifically, so must existence be distinguished. You will say, therefore, that just as genera and species are distinguished in essences, so they can be distinguished in existences. For, just as all created essences agree in the common and transcendental character of essence, so all existences agree in the common character of existence. And just as certain essences agree more with each other than with others, and then differed among themselves, and from this the different genera and differences of essences are obtained, so the existences of Angels, for instance, agree more among themselves, than with the existences of men; and again they differ essentially from each other. Consequently, it will be possible for the concept of genus and difference to be abstracted from them. The response is, indeed, that, in reality, it is true that a greater agreement or similarity is discovered between certain existences than among others; indeed, that in this, almost the same proportion is maintained between existences and among essences, for the reasons set forth. Consequently, even Cajetan, *On Being and Essence,* chapt. 4, a little before question 6[33] says, that actual existence is constituted by the proper principles of the being *(ens)* itself, and so it is not of a nature extraneous to the being *(ens)*

itself. It necessarily follows that it has the same proportion of similarity and difference to the existence of other things as there is between the natures and essences themselves. And Scotus in 2, dist. 3, quest. 3,[34] says that existential being, in the way it is distinguished from essential being, is not of itself distinct nor determined but is determined according to the determination of the essence. From this it also follows that being[35] is such as is essence and that one being maintains such a proportion to others as one essence has to others.

20.   But, still, (as Scotus says in the same place[36]), there is no need to distinguish the differences of existences from the differences of essences, nor to distinguish the predicamental coordinations, because these are only properly distinguished in that which is, or which has the character of a complete being *(ens)* in each and every predicament, or which is conceived of as a complete being *(ens)*. But we do not conceive of existence as that which is, but as some simple mode by which an essence is constituted in the order of actual being *(ens)*. Just as also among the differences themselves some greater agreement of some among themselves than with others can be understood, and yet in them we do not distinguish a concept of genus and difference, but only simple modes by which each and every difference is determined to a proper and a sort of specific character. Thus, it must be understood about existences, inasmuch as we conceive of them metaphysically, as modes of essences, for they can be conceived of under an aspect or concept more or less common and proper. Yet, in particular, those concepts do not have the character of a genus and species, properly taken, but are either reduced to them or are related rather as a transcendental concept and its mode. And so it can be understood also metaphysically that each and every created existence is limited by a proper and particular mode by which it is determined to such an existence. Nor is this abstraction and determination of concepts repugnant to the actuality of existence because, even though existence in relation to essence is compared as an act to an objective potency, nevertheless in the actual existence itself a similarity and a diversity with another existence can still be conceived of; this is enough to provide a basis for above-mentioned concepts with a distinction of reason alone.

WHICH ONE IS MORE PERFECT, THE ESSENCE OR EXISTENCE?

21.   And from this, at last it is understood what the thinking must be in that comparison between essence and existence, which is disputed by many,[37] as to which of them is more perfect. This comparison is properly pertinent only in the opinion which grants a distinction in reality between actual essence and existence, and there is a

difference of opinions even between the authors who follow this opinion. For certain ones[38] think that, in every thing, existence is more perfect than essence because its actuality is such that without it an essence would have no perfection. And for this reason St. Thomas said, part 1, q. 4, a. 1, to the third: *that being itself is the most perfect of all; for it is related to all things as an act, for nothing has actuality except insofar as it is.* [39] And Dionysius is drawn into the same opinion, chapt. 5 *On the Divine Names,* [40] when he says that being itself is the greatest of all the perfections we receive from God. And Aristotle, 8 *Ethics,* c. 11,[41] calls being itself the greatest gift of God.

22. But others[42] contend that the essential entity is more perfect, because it is in each and every thing as its substance. Indeed, existence is only a certain mode or term of it. Truly it is in itself unbelievable that there is in man some entity connatural to him more perfect in regard to its essence than the rational soul, in terms of which he is in the image of God, by which he has the formal and principal power to perform his most perfect activities. Moreover, were we to wish to argue theologically, the Word (according to their opinion) assumed the essence of man and not existence. Consequently, if existence is that which is most perfect in man, it follows that the Word has assumed that which is less perfect in man, but left what is most perfect unassumed; this is quite absurd. Finally, (according to that opinion) it needs to be said that an actual essence has a proper entity by which[43] it is formally and intrinsically outside nothing, and not by existence itself, as was shown in the above sections,[44] because, otherwise, a proper entity cannot be conceived of in an essence in terms of which it would be distinguished from existence. But by positing this, the basic reason why essence could be considered of less perfection than existence is utterly overturned, that is, because from it it has every actuality in the order of being *(ens).* For this is a false and illogical statement in that opinion, because some actuality must necessarily be posited in the essence according to itself. Consequently, in that, it could surpass existence. Nor is it a difficulty that existence is posited as an essential term or mode, because from that source alone a relative excess can be inferred, just as subsistence also is an essential mode and term and yet is absolutely less perfect, even though it surpasses it relatively, inasmuch as it actuates it, as we will see below.[45]

23. But although this is an *ad hominem* argument or is being forced from acknowledged principles, still, absolutely speaking, the contrary opinion contains another inconsistency, that is, that an actual essence, as such, would formally and intrinsically include actuality in the order of being *(ens),* and be outside nothing, and that it would not include existence in the same way, since the proper concept of

actual existence can neither be understood nor explained except by the first actuality by which being *(ens)* in act is distinguished from being *(ens)* in potency, as was proved at length in the above sections. [46] Consequently, a clear repugnance is involved when it is said that an essence, with existence prescinded, [47] includes actual perfection in which it can surpass existence. For this reason, even though this comparison properly comes to be in the thing itself, given a distinction in reality, nevertheless nothing sound and sure can be said on this matter in the above-mentioned opinion. But then, in supposing that existence in reality is not distinguished from essence, it is established that the above-mentioned comparison, in terms of the thing itself, and speaking of the actual essence, has no place, because, since they are the same, one cannot be more perfect or less perfect than the other. But if those two be compared in terms of reason or a mental precision, existence is placed before essence, because, when existence is prescinded, an essence is not understood to remain in act but in potency only; and because nothing is actually perfected unless it is in act, being itself is therefore called the perfection of all perfections and the greatest of all perfections. And St. Thomas interprets Dionysius in this way, quest. 20 *On Truth,* art. 2, to the third, [48] where he says that being is characterized as more noble than living or understanding, if the comparison be made with being separated intellectually from living. For this reason, if a comparison be made between existence precisely conceived of as a mode, and an essence as existing in act, then essence is conceived of as something more perfect, because it is conceived of as that which is or as including the whole perfection of essence and existence.

WHAT COMPOSITION IS OF THE NATURE OF CREATED BEING (ENS)?

24.   There was a fourth objection set forth in the third argument on behalf of the second opinion in section one. [49] In this it was asked whether some composition is of the nature of created being *(ens)* and what it is. On this matter it must be briefly observed that it can be a discussion either about a composition according to reason or about a real composition, which results from things really or modally distinct. Again we can speak of created being *(ens)* either as it exists in reality itself, or as it is mentally prescinded in terms of some aspect. This precision can sometimes be based on some distinction which would be in the thing itself, as when we prescind a nature from a supposit or a substance from an accident. But sometimes it can be based on some agreement, property or distinctiveness of a thing without an actual distinction, as when we prescind genus from difference, and the like.

25.   Consequently, it must be said that a composition of reason, or rather its foundation, is of the nature of created being *(ens)* existing in the thing itself. For in this way a composition of being and essence is of the nature of created being *(ens)* as was explained above.[50] Again, it must be said that there is no created being *(ens)* which, as it really exists, would not include some real composition, modally speaking. But it must be said that this composition is not of being and essence but of other things or real modes. It is explained by induction. For a created substance, as it exists naturally in reality, includes a composition of nature and supposit; this is to be discussed below.[51] But an accident, since it naturally exists in a subject, includes a composition with it, and in itself includes a composition with actual inherence itself, as with a mode of its entity (for we are talking of a proper accident, really distinct from substance). And for this reason, even though we consider a substantial nature existing in a supernatural way, as humanity is in the Word, we shall find a real composition also in that, not only of its parts, but also with the Word, and with the mode of union which it has with the Word. And, similarly, in an accidental form existing in a supernatural way, as is the quantity of the Eucharist, we shall find (according to the probable opinion) a composition of the entity[52] of an accident with a mode of existing substantially, incompatible with actual inherence.

26.   Again, actual dependence on a first cause is necessary in[53] every created being *(ens),* and this dependence is distinct in reality from the being *(ens)* which comes to be or is conserved by it. Therefore, it makes a real composition with it, which is inseparable from every created being *(ens)* existing in act, because neither can such a being *(ens)* be without some dependence nor can the dependence itself be without some term. Finally, it is probable that no created being *(ens)* is possible which would not have in the thing itself some composition of subject and accident. For if such a being *(ens)* would be a true accident, or a real accidental mode, it necessarily requires a subject with which it would make composition, as is self-evident. But if it be a substance, since it is necessarily finite, it must of necessity have a definite place or location or local presence in terms of which it can undergo change. And so it must be distinct from it and make composition with it. For the same reason it can have a composition with really distinct accidents. But whether this is necessary in every created or creatable substance, is not sufficiently established, nor does it seem able to be demonstrated from the mere character of created being *(ens)* as such, even though the opinion which asserts this is more probable. We have made some comments about this above in discussion 18,[54] when we were treating of the powers which are the proximate principles by which creatures act. And below[55] we

shall add something while discussing quantity and quality. From these, therefore, it is well enough established that, in every created being *(ens)* as it exists in the thing itself, a real composition is found which is not based on the distinction of being from essence, but it is based on other distinctions of the existing thing from some mode of its own or from some accident. This distinction, indeed, arises from the limitation of created being *(ens)*, but we come to know it from the separation or change which can take place between a thing and such a mode. But this distinction has no place between being and actual essence, as was shown. [56] And so the argument is not the same about this and the other compositions of nature and supposit, and the like.

27.   And we draw a further conclusion from this, if we be talking about created being *(ens)* which exists in the thing itself, yet not in terms of all the things which it has in the thing itself, but according to some mental precision, that then it is not necessary that every created being *(ens)* include some real composition. This is also demonstrated by induction. For were we to regard a substantial immaterial nature as prescinded from accidents and from a proper actual subsistence or from a union with a foreign one, so no real composition is found in it. But in natures composed of matter and form, even though an integral nature cannot be prescinded from such a composition, still in the parts themselves precisely conceived of there is no such composition. And, in this way, matter precisely conceived of is a simple substantial entity and, in a like manner, form; simple (I say) in relation to essential composition. For, a composition of integral parts cannot be excluded, due to the imperfection of matter. And, for this reason, an accidental form precisively conceived of is simple, unless it be material; thence it would have a composition of integral parts, unless it could be increased or decreased, and thus would have latitude and composition in degrees, which are imperfections or compositions arising from the characters peculiar to some beings *(entia)*, but not from the character itself of created being *(ens)* as such. Hence, it is not repugnant to created being *(ens)* as such, that, under some precisely conceived of aspect, it be simple, without real composition.

28.   Nor can those authors who really distinguish created essence and existence repudiate this, because they are forced of necessity to acknowledge that existence itself precisely conceived of is a simple entity, especially if it be a spiritual or angelic existence. The reason is that in it no parts or terms distinct in reality can be thought of from which it would be composed. And in a similar way, some created essence precisely conceived of will be simple without real composition. For as such, it does not include a composition of being and essence, since it is supposed to be prescinded from its being,

which (according to that opinion) can happen not only mentally, but also in the thing itself, Just as, for instance, were we to posit that an angelic nature is assumed by the Word, such a nature, as quite distinct from the Word, would include no real and substantial composition, because, as such, it would consist neither of being and essence, nor of nature and subsistence. Consequently, it is not of the nature of created being *(ens)* to be unable to be prescinded from a real composition, when it is not integrally and adequately conceived of as it is in reality, but in terms of some precise or essential aspect. Nor is any objection against this made in that third argument[57] which would introduce a new difficulty or which would have necessarily to be solved in every opinion, even by those who think that the composition of being and essence is real and made up of distinct things; for that composition can be analyzed into its components; and I shall ask whether the components themselves are simple or composite. This latter cannot be said for the reasons given, and because otherwise there would be an infinite procession. But if the first is said, we have what we intend, because the essence itself, which is said to compose with existence, is created, and an actual entity.

29. For this reason, it must be finally added that every created being *(ens)*, however precisely and incompletely conceived of, includes at least an aptitude for composition; that is, that it could compose one being *(ens)* with another being *(ens)* or mode of being *(ens)*. Indeed, it must be added that it also includes the necessity or need for some similar composition with another being *(ens)* or mode of being *(ens)* in order to be able to exist in reality. In this it necessarily falls short of the perfection of pure act and divine simplicity. This whole point is clear from what has been said, because a substance cannot exist except with some mode of subsisting, or something else which takes the place of it, with which it necessarily makes some composition. There is the same or stronger argument about an accident in relation to a subject or[58] with respect to actual inherence. And (what is more certain) every created being *(ens)* requires actual dependence, and to that extent composition with that. Consequently, this imperfection is enough to explain the character and imperfection of created being *(ens)* as such, nor for this reason is a real composition of being and essence necessary in creatures.

Notes

[1] See Section I, 5, above.
[2] See Section I, 6, above.
[3] *In De Ente...*, c. 5, q. 10; 90, 141-144.
[4] *Ibid.*, 142.

[5] See paragraph 7, this section, below.

[6] See Section VII above.

[7] See Cajetan, *In De Ente...*, 142-144.

[8] *Ibid.,*143.

[9] *Ibid.*

[10] *Ibid.*

[11] *Ibid.,* 143-144.

[12] I read the *ea* of the 1597 Salamanca and 1605 Mainz editions instead of the *eo* of the Vives text.

[13] See Suárez, *In Sum. Theol.,* III, q. 2, a. 6, disp. 7, IV, 12; XVII, 315-316.

[14] *Ibid.*

[15] See paragraph 3 and following, this section, above.

[16] I read the *non* of the 1597 Salamanca edition which is deleted in the Vives text.

[17] See paragraph 4, this section, above.

[18] See Suárez, *In Sum. Theol.,* III, q. 2, a. 6, disp. 6, IV, 4; XVII, 312-313.

[19] See Sections II-VI above.

[20] I read the *et* of the 1597 Salamanca and 1605 Mainz editions which is deleted in the Vives text.

[21] I read the *propria* of the 1597 Salamanca and 1605 Mainz editions instead of the *proprie* of the Vives text.

[22] See *DM* 30, IV, 28-29; XXVI, 83-84 as well as VI; XXVI, 89-95.

[23] See *DM* 30, IV, 28-29; XXVI, 83-84.

[24] See *DM* 30, IV, 30; XXVI, 84.

[25] See *DM* 30, IV, 34; XXVI, 85.

[26] See Suárez, *In Sum. Theol.,* I, cap. 2, 4; I, 6.

[27] See Sections II-V above.

[28] See Section XI and following.

[29] See Section I, 5, above.

[30] I read the *quia* of the 1597 Salamanca and 1605 Mainz editions instead of the *qui* of the Vives text.

[31] *In 7 Metaph.,* text. 22; 207vb.

[32] *In De Ente...,* c. 6, q. 15; 131, 209-214, esp. 213.

[33] *Ibid.,* 89.

[34] *Opus Oxon.,* II, d. 3, q. 2; T. 22, 590.

[35] I read the *esse* of the 1597 Salamanca and 1605 Mainz editions which is deleted in the Vives text.

[36] See n. 34, this section, above.

[37] See B. Mastrius, *Disputationes...,* disp. 8, q. 3, 151-155; II, 133-137 for a good historical dossier on this point.

[38] *Ibid.,* where Mastrius lists Bañez, Navarettus, Ledesma, Blasius a Conceptione and Manca. But in light of the following three references to Aquinas, Dionysius and Aristotle, Suárez would appear to have Bañez in mind. See *In Sum. Theol.,* I, q. 3, a. 4, dub. 3; 149a.

[39] *Sum. Theol.,* I, q. 4, a. 1 ad 3; T. 4, 50.

[40] *On Divine Names,* c. 5; 6, 137.

[41] *Nichomachean Ethics,* VIII, 11, 1161a 15-16.

[42] See B. Mastrius, *Disputationes...,* disp. 8, q. 3, 151; II, 133 where, in addition to some *Scotistae,* the *Thomistae,* Soncinas and Ferrara, are mentioned. On this see C. Fabro, "L'obscurcissement de l'*esse* dans l'ecole thomiste," *Revue Thomiste* LVIII (1958), 443-478. Also L.A. Kennedy, C.S.B., "La doctrina de la existencia...," *Archivo Teológico Granadino* 35 (1972), 69 notes that John Vincent follows Soncinas and Ferrara in this matter.

[43] I read the *qua* of the 1597 Salamanca and 1605 Mainz editions instead of the *quae* of the Vives text.

[44] See Sections III-VI above.

[45] See *DM* 34, IV, 39-40; XXVI, 379.

[46] See Sections II-IV above.

[47] I read the *praecisae existentiae* of the 1597 Salamanca and 1605 Mainz editions instead of the *praecisa existentia* of the Vives text.

[48] *De Veritate,* q. 20, a. 2 ad 3; 365-366.

[49] Suárez's location here seems defective. It should refer to the third argument of the first opinion in Section I, 6, above. Moreover, both the 1597 Salamanca and 1605 Mainz editions, in addition to referring to *secunda sententia,* also refer to "section 2".

[50] See paragraphs 8-9, this section, above.

[51] See *DM* 34, IV; XXVI, 367-379.

[52] I read the *ex entitate* of the 1597 Salamanca edition instead of the *ex identitate* of the Vives text.

[53] I read the *in* of the 1597 Salamanca and 1605 Mainz editions which is deleted in the Vives text.

[54] See *DM* 18, III, 15-24; XXV, 619-624.

[55] See *DM* 40, II; XXVI, 533-538 and *DM* 42, IV; XXVI, 615-621.

[56] See Section VI above.

[57] See Section I, 6, above.

[58] I read the *vel* of the 1597 Salamanca and 1605 Mainz editions instead of the *et* of the Vives text.

Section XIV

Whether actual dependence and subordination as well
as subjection to the first and uncreated being (ens) is of
the nature of created being (ens).

1.   Up to now we have explicated the nature of created being *(ens)*,
by an absolute consideration of its intrinsic composition and its entity by relation to a proper act of being *(essendi)* from which it formally
has that it be a being *(ens)*. Now this character of created being *(ens)*
is to be further explicated and made clear by the relation and comparison to the first and uncreated being *(ens)*. For since it is a being
(ens) analogically in comparison to that, its nature will be best explained by comparison to that.
2.   Consequently, at the beginning, it must be supposed (something which is certain for all) that created being *(ens)* insofar as it is
such, includes essentially a dependence on a first and uncreated being *(ens)*, because this is the first feature distinguishing a created being *(ens)* from an uncreated being *(ens)*, as was shown in the above
treatment of this division. [1] Also, because, at least in this way, it is of
the nature of created being *(ens)* to have being received from
another, which is to have dependent being; therefore, it is especially
dependent on a first being *(ens)* which has being of itself, not received
from another. Finally, every being *(ens)* of this type is a being *(ens)* by
participation. Consequently, it essentially depends on that from
which it shares the character of being *(ens)*. We have spoken at
length on this matter in discussion 20 [2] and 21 [3] where we have explained what this dependence is and how it would be said to be
essential to a creature, because it needs that in virtue of its essence,
not because the dependence itself would compose the creature's
essence intrinsically. But the relation or reference to a creator which
created being *(ens)* includes, either by reason of its essence or by
reason of its actual dependence, will be established from what is to
be said below, in discussion 47 [4] on transcendental and predicamental relation, and in discussion 48 [5] on the relations of every dependence or action.

3. Consequently, from this principle it first follows that every created being *(ens)* is subject to the dominion of God with respect to its being, that is, it is subject to God in such a way that it can be reduced from that to nothing and be deprived of its being by the mere suspension of the influence by which He conserves it. It is proved from what has been said,[6] because a created being *(ens)* depends essentially on an uncreated being *(ens)*, in the sense presented.[7] Consequently, the above-mentioned subjection necessarily follows from this dependence. For by the very fact that a creature requires divine influence to be, it is of itself subject to annihilation, if it be deprived of such an influence. But you will ask whether this very subjection, in relation to annihilation, be as essential to the creature as is the positive and radical dependence itself. The answer is that, in regard to that which it connotes or requires on God's part, it does not seem as essential, if we speak precisely and formally. There is an explanation, for the essential dependence of a created being *(ens)* on an uncreated being *(ens)* formally regards only the uncreated being *(ens)* itself[8] as an infinite principle and sea of being *(essendi)* and most efficacious so that it can of itself impart the participation. And this perfection precisely taken would be sufficient for understanding the nature of created being *(ens)* in a creature. But then the above-mentioned subjection of the same being *(ens)* in relation to annihilation connotes in God liberty in conserving a creature which He once produced; though this liberty be essential to God Himself and, on God's part, the use of such freedom be necessary in such a way that the creature receives being and is conserved in it, still, on the part of the creature itself, and in regard to the order of created being *(ens)* as such, this seems to be accident like. For if, by way of the impossible, we were to understand that God communicates Himself *ad extra* not freely but necessarily, we would still understand the true character of created being *(ens)* in a creature without subjection to God in relation to annihilation, because we would understand in God the power to effect and conserve a created being *(ens)*, which would be enough to understand the essential dependence on God on the part of created being *(ens)* itself. Yet on God's part, we would not understand a complete dominion over the being of the creature, because such dominion is not without liberty, and so a subjection in regard to annihilation would not be understood in a creature, because this subjection and dominion are correlative and, with one removed, the other must be removed.

4. For this reason I have said that this subjection, in regard to what it connotes on God's part, is not included in the order of created being *(ens)* taken precisely and formally. But in regard to what is introduced in created being *(ens)* itself by this subjection, and in regard to

what it requires on its part, this subjection is essential to it, and indicates absolutely the same origin or same grade of being *(ens)* as essential dependence. For nothing else is meant by this subjection than that a created being *(ens)* is of such a nature and essence to which it is not repugnant to be reduced to nothing, if, on the part of its cause, there be no lack of the freedom to suspend the influence by which it communicates being to that. And, in this sense, it can be said that this subjection is essential to created being *(ens)* as such, especially, because, even though we prescind conceptually one perfection from another, still it is absolutely of the essence of God to have complete dominion over all created beings either in act or potency, so that were He to wish to produce them, He could not constitute them outside His dominion. Therefore, conversely, or by the same proportion, it is of the essence of created being *(ens)* to be always subject to God and to His dominion so that it could be reduced by Him to nothing. Consequently, from this dominion, which seems more known to us, we confirm best the dependence which created being *(ens)* has on God, not only in coming to be but also in being conserved, because, if it did not so depend, God, at the nod of His will, could not reduce a being *(ens)* once created to nothing; so He would not have complete dominion over it, which is repugnant to divine perfection. This argument is treated more at length in discussion 21, [9] already cited.

5.   From this we can draw a further conclusion or add that there is also another subjection or dependence on God intrinsic to created being *(ens)* as such, that is, in acting or in causing. But this dependence or subjection can be explained in two ways. First, absolutely, and in this way it can be seen that it is not universal, because it is not of the nature or essence of created being *(ens)* to be able to do something. In another way, this subjection can be understood only conditionally or hypothetically, namely, that this is a condition of created being *(ens)*, that if it be able to effect anything, in the very effecting it necessarily depends on an actual concursus and support of a first cause and uncreated being *(ens)*. Indeed, if we were to speak about proper efficiency, this second explanation will have to be used. But if the discussion be about causality generically, this condition must be explained in the first way, because there is no created being *(ens)* which would not have some kind of causality, for if it is an accident, it is either a proximate principle for effecting something or it at least formally affects the subject. But if it is a substance, it is either matter, and that has material causality or it is form, and this has formal causality. And perhaps there is no form which would not be a principle for effecting something, just as also every spiritual and complete substance has some operation of which it is the efficient principle.

Consequently, in every created being *(ens)*, there will be found some type of causality and some mode of imparting its perfection, in which it depends essentially on the actual influence of God yet in a different manner, for the efficient causality of a created being *(ens)* depends on God certainly as on a first and principle efficient cause. But the other causalities, for instance, material and formal, are not dependent in the same genus but in the genus of efficient cause, for, that matter cause materially, God must cause that very thing efficiently. And all these things have been treated and explained at greater length above in discussion 22.[10]

6.   However, it can also be asked here whether this subordination in acting or causing pertains formally to the essential character of created being *(ens)* as such, or it exists rather as its property. For it seems that this latter must be asserted, because to cause or to effect, or even the power of effecting, do not pertain to the essence of created being *(ens)*, but to its properties. Hence, dependence in causing does not pertain to the nature of created being *(ens)*, but at most it will exist as a property following upon that. But in favor of the opposite view is that this dependence would not be based on some quality or property of created being *(ens)*, which would be outside of its essence, but is based upon its intrinsic limitation; therefore, in this way it belongs to the essence no less than dependence in being. And so it certainly must be said, that it is one thing to speak of the formal causality itself or dependence, another to speak about the condition of created being *(ens)*, by reason of which it can produce or cause nothing by itself alone without God's cooperation. As to the first, it is evident that it does not formally pertain to the essence of created being *(ens)* as the argument given proves, and because the integral essence of created being *(ens)* can be conserved without actual causality or the actual assistance of God for causing. But, then, as to the latter condition or root of this dependence, it must be said that, in reality, there is nothing else but the essence itself of created being *(ens)* as such, because, even when every other thing superadded to such an essence has been removed by the intellect, it will be found to have this limitation and imperfection in virtue of itself, so that by itself alone it is not adequate to doing or causing something. And so, by the absolute power of God, a created being *(ens)* cannot come to be which would not have such subordination to an uncreated being *(ens)*. Hence, it is a sign that it is based in the essential nature itself of created being *(ens)*. Therefore, even though dependence in being *(essendo)* could be grasped by a precision of reason and inadequate mental concepts as logically prior to dependence in causing, and so the first could also be conceived of as primarily constituting and modifying the common character of being *(ens)* to the character of

created being *(ens),* so the second can be conceived of as a property or attribute of created being *(ens),* still, in the thing itself, this is not an accidental attribute but a sort of transcendental one, since, in reality, it adds nothing to the essence of created being *(ens),* even though it be conceived of by relation to something extrinsic and, under this aspect, be considered as a metaphysical rather than a physical property, in that way in which the transcendental attributes of being *(ens)* are its properties.

7.   Finally, about the nature of created being *(ens)* it must be said that it be subject or subordinate to an uncreated being *(ens)* for obeying Him in receiving or in doing whatever would have involved no contradiction. This condition of created being *(ens)* looks more to the theologians than to natural philosophers. For this property differs from the preceding one in that the former consists only in the dependence of created being *(ens)* with respect to the natural power of effecting or causing effects proportionate to its nature. And so, such dependence can be readily known by the natural light. But this latter condition adds that created being *(ens)* in virtue of its entity is apt to be obedient to God in receiving or in performing any possible and non-repugnant effect, even if it surpass the natural power or capacity of such a being *(ens).* This cannot be known so readily by the natural light, because in some way it touches on or expresses a relation to supernatural effects, which a creature cannot reach, except as it is raised by divine power; this raising is more evident to us by things which have been revealed than by the natural light. Consequently, from those thing which have either been revealed by faith or are more in accord with what has been revealed, this property of created being *(ens)* is concluded with sufficient probability. For we believe that man receives supernatural perfections from God which his nature did not demand nor were due to him. Also, the humanity of Christ was raised to the hypostatic union, of which it was not naturally capable. Also, the same humanity and the sacraments and other such things are raised by God to do something beyond their natural power. But all these things suppose that creatures of this sort, of themselves, and before they be raised, as born to be obedient to God willing to work in such a way in them or through them. And, to this extent, it is the same argument in the case of these creatures and of all creatures. Therefore, it must be said that created being *(ens)* as such has this subordination to God, so that it is born to be obedient to Him in doing and receiving whatever would not have been repugnant.

8.   And from this was born the teaching of the theologians about the obediential potency of creatures with regard to God, which Augustine had first noted, Bk. 9 *Literal Commentary on Genesis,* c. 17,[11]

and then St. Thomas, part 1, q. 115, art. 2, [12] and 4, [13] and in 1, dist. 42, quest. 2, art. 2, to the fourth, [14] whom the rest of the theologians, especially his disciples, have followed; and they explain it more explicitly under passive potency. However, there is the same proportional argument about active obediential potency as I have treated at length in the first tome of the third part, discussion 31, section 6. [15] Finally, the reason for this subordination is to be taken *a priori* from the complete dominion which God has upon his creature, so that He could use it in every application which would not involve repugnance or contradiction. For a complete dominion of this sort pertains to the infinite omnipotence of God. Indeed, there is no dominion perfect in every part, unless it contain power for every possible use. But to this complete dominion of God there is a corresponding complete subjection in the creature, for these two are correlative. But such a condition on the part of the creature is necessary for this subjection, by reason of which it is apt for accomplishing whatever God may have willed, either by receiving or by doing. Consequently, just as God cannot effect a created being *(ens)* over which He would not have complete and perfect dominion, so a created being *(ens)* cannot come to be which does not have the previously mentioned condition, and subordination or subjection to God.

9.   You will say that this condition or subjection neither formally pertains to the essential nature of created being *(ens)* precisively conceived of, nor is it even a property following upon it naturally and necessarily; therefore, in no way does it belong essentially and necessarily to created being *(ens)*. The antecedent is clear as to the first part, because the essential nature of created being *(ens)* consists precisely, and is sufficiently saved, in this, that it be a being *(ens)* essentially dependent on God. But as to the second part, it is proved, because that subjection is in relation to supernatural actions or effects, and so it pertains not to the natural order but to the supernatural. Consequently, it cannot follow upon the nature of created being *(ens)* as such, because created being *(ens)* abstracts from natural and supernatural. The answer is that this sort of condition of created being *(ens)*, which we have explained by this ultimate subjection to God, does not add to the very being *(ens)*, to which it belongs, some thing or real mode distinct in reality from the being itself, but it only explains the intrinsic condition itself of created being *(ens)*, subject to a different relation to God and to His omnipotence and His supernatural actions. For this reason, nothing else in the thing itself is expressed by this condition than the essence of created being *(ens)*. But it is explained by way of a certain metaphysical attribute or property, similar to the attributes of being *(ens)*, as we were saying in the point immediately above. [16]

10.   Therefore, the answer to the argument is that, if we should speak of the thing itself, the essential character of created being *(ens)* is not fully and adequately explained by this alone, that it is a dependent being *(ens)*. For, although in this relation every other subjection to God be contained implicitly, still it is not explicitly made clear what we do, when we expose all the above-mentioned subjections to God. Among these, as we distinguish them in reason by inadequate concepts, we also understand a certain aspect of order and grasp one as the primary and essential aspect; but we grasp the others after the fashion of properties. Consequently, under this consideration we grant this to be a property of created being *(ens)*. But we deny that it essentially and intrinsically pertains to the supernatural order, because it does not constitute a mode or a determinate order of beings *(entia)*, but it is such as the entity is, in which it is found, as we said more at length in the place cited above. [17] But, rather, (and this must be heeded) not only is this last subordination in relation to divine omnipotence, as working above the law of nature, common to natural and supernatural beings, but also the first subordination, which is in relation to actions and causalities connatural to each thing. For from theology we suppose that certain beings *(entia)* are natural, others supernatural, especially those which are called supernatural as to substance, which are only certain accidents which can be connatural to no created substance. Hence, these supernatural beings *(entia)* have actions or causalities proportionate to their entities, in which also they are subordinate to God and dependent on Him, in which dependence they agree with the rest of natural beings *(entia)*, with the proportion maintained. Also, for this reason, the dependence of created being *(ens)* on God, in all of its own and proper causality, is common not only to natural beings *(entia)* but also to supernatural ones. However, these supernatural beings *(entia)* can be raised to doing or causing something beyond the causality connatural to themselves. For in this they are no less subjected to God than the rest of the beings *(entia)* of the natural order. Also, for this reason, all this subjection and dependence in regard to God abstracts from natural and supernatural being *(ens)* and is common to all created being *(ens)* as such.

11.   Through these considerations, then, the common aspect of created being *(ens)* seems adequately explained and, along the way, we have already explained its causes, effects and properties. For created being *(ens)* as such, taken precisely and abstractly, requires no other cause than uncreated being *(ens)* itself, in which it has an adequate efficient, exemplar cause. But it does not demand essentially and positively, from the mere common aspect of created being *(ens)*, a formal and material cause, but it admits them in some beings

(entia); we shall see about these later. [18] In like manner, although certain created beings *(entia)* require other efficient causes besides God, at least in order to come to be or exist in a connatural way, still, the aspect of created being *(ens)* as such does not require them. In a similar fashion we must philosophize about effects. For created being *(ens)* in virtue of this common aspect, even though it be capable of causality, still determines no definite type of causality for itself, but only this, that in its every causality, whatever it may be, it is subordinate to God and depends on Him, as has already been explained. From this, finally, the properties of created being *(ens)* as such are also sufficiently taught. For it has no others besides the common attributes of being *(ens)*, which it shares in a way suited to itself, and the other attributes which accompany its limitation and perfection, such as composition, dependence and subjection are, about which it was discussed. [19] But that primary condition of created being *(ens)*, that it would necessarily have to be finite and limited, could be explained more at length here, but I have decided to omit it, because limitation as to the essential perfection of created being *(ens)* has no difficulty, since it was demonstrated above [20] that a creature cannot adequately receive divine perfection, which, if it be inferior, must be infinitely different from that, because an absolutely infinite thing (as God is) cannot surpass another by a finite excess, otherwise they could arrive at equality by a finite increase. But if created being *(ens)*, of necessity, differs infinitely from divine perfection, it must be that it is of finite essential perfection. But what looks to the infinity of being *(ens)*, either in quantity of mass or intension of some quality, is no concern of the present discussion, since it does not pertain to created being *(ens)* as such, but to the determinate aspects of being *(ens)*. Philosophers properly discuss these in 3 *Phys.* [21] and they are touched upon by the theologians, part 1, q. 7 [22] and in 1, dist. 43. [23]

Notes

[1] See *DM* 28, I, 14; XXVI, 5.

[2] See *DM* 20, IV; XXV, 769-779.

[3] See *DM* 21, III; XXV, 794-801.

[4] See *DM* 47, VII, 6-7; XXVI, 812.

[5] See *DM* 48, I; XXVI, 868-873.

[6] See paragraph 2, this section, above.

[7] *Ibid.*

[8] I read the *ipsum* of the 1597 Salamanca and 1605 Mainz editions which is deleted in the Vives text.

[9] See *DM* 21, I; XXV, 785-790.

[10] See *DM* 22; XXV, 802-843.

[11] *De Genesi ad litteram,* IX, 17; *PL* 34, 406.

[12] *Sum. Theol.,* I, q. 115, a. 2; T. 5, 540-541.

[13] *Op. cit.,* I, q. 115, a. 4; T. 5, 544.

[14] *In I Sent.,* d. 42, q. 2, a. 2 ad 4; T. 1, 992-993.

[15] See Suárez, *In Sum. Theol.,* III, q. 13, a. 4, disp. 31, VI; XVIII, 107-152.

[16] See Section XIII, 12-14 and 20, above.

[17] See Suárez, *In Sum. Theol.,* III, q. 13, a. 4, disp. 31, VI, 61-83; XVIII, 131-140.

[18] See *DM* 36; XXVI, 477-491.

[19] See paragraph 2 and following, this section, above.

[20] See *DM* 30, I-II; XXVI, 60-72.

[21] See *Complutenses, In III Phys.,* disp. VIII, esp. q. V; 362-393.

[22] See Suárez, *In Sum. Theol.,* II, cap. 1, 7-8; I, 47-48.

[23] See Peter of Tarantasia, *In IV libros Sententiarum Commentaria* (Tolosae, 1652), *In I Sent.,* d. 43, q. 1; T. I, 355-358.

Index of Names

Index of Topics

Abstraction, precisive, 17, 19, 20, 36n., 37n., 52, 96, 102; negative/privative, 20, 36n., 37n., 102, 103; metaphysical, 109.

Accidents and their existence, 166-170, 193; existence as accident, 106; existence as accident in predicament When or Quantity, 106; existence said accidentally of creature, 110.

Act and potency, 46, 47, 48, 49, 61, 67-71, 78, 88, 114, 147, 162, 212, 226.

Annihilation, 180, 181, 198, 199, 233.

Being (*esse*), existential, 7, 14, 45, 57, 61, 64, 73, 74, 75, 80, 81, 84, 87, 89, 93, 98, 99, 100, 116, 120, 130, 133, 134, 136, 146, 147, 150, 151, 156, 163, 167, 180, 185, 189; essential, 7, 14, 45, 58, 60, 61, 63, 64, 73, 74, 75, 79, 97, 98, 99, 100, 116, 117, 120, 127, 129, 130, 136, 163, 188, 189, 190, 194, 199, 224; of being known in Scotus, 57; equivocation and essential being, 63-64; essential being attributed to creatures in two ways, 63-64; created being as received, 46, 219-223; being unreceived understood in two ways, 221; ultimate actuality, 49; extrinsic to essence, 50; a supreme perfection, 134; subsistential, 7, 45, 220, 221; of a true proposition, 7, 61, 62, 64; diminished, 57, 67; actual essential being is true existential being, 73-77, 146; separable from essence, 50, 197; possible, 64; objective or potential, 57, 62, 63, 64, 143, 145, 198; entitative and formal, 116.

Cause, efficient, 8, 9, 10, 11, 12, 13, 14, 18, 46, 79, 95, 96, 97, 98, 113, 118, 119, 121, 130, 146, 149, 150, 151, 164, 201, 202, 203, 204, 234, 235, 238; exemplary, 9, 34n., 61, 63, 97, 98, 222, 238; actual efficient, 11, 12, 13, 18, 19, 26, 202, 204; potential efficient, 12, 13, 23, 34n., 42, 202, 204; material, 78, 79, 113, 114, 115, 117, 120, 130, 144, 145, 147, 150, 151, 164, 180, 183, 194, 234, 238; formal, 78, 89, 90, 113, 115, 116, 117, 118, 119, 144, 145, 147, 148, 150, 164, 180, 183, 234, 235, 238; twofold relation of formal cause, 89-90; final, 113, 120, 143, 144; instrumental, 25, 136; second, 124, 125, 126, 128, 130, 131, 135, 136, 138, 149; proximate, 125, 126, 135, 136; principal, 125, 135, 136.

Chimera, 18, 22, 26, 37, 58, 64, 105.

Composition, 78, 212, 213, 215, 216; real, 46, 47, 92, 99, 215, 216, 219, 220, 222, 226-229; physical, 212, 216; metaphysical, 212, 213, 216; of matter and form, compared to composition of being and essence, 212-219; of being and essence, compared to composition of matter and form, 212-223; *ex his,* 214-215; *cum his,* 214; genus and difference, 47, 216, 217, 218; of reason, 212, 216, 217, 218, 219, 226; threefold composition of reason, 219; in God, 217, 218.

Conservation, 91, 179, 181, 182, 183, 184, 185, 196, 233.

Constitution, 78; of reason, 218; by identity, 99, 147.

Contraction, physical, 222; metaphysical, 222.

Matter and form, 47, 48, 49, 90, 147, 148, 163, 164, 165, 192; composition of, compared to composition of being and essence, 212-224.

Mode, 8, 9, 17, 30n., 50, 79, 80, 82, 83, 84, 89, 92, 93, 108, 109, 110, 130, 142, 143, 148, 156, 164, 170, 171, 172, 179, 183, 184, 186, 217, 221, 224, 225, 227, 228, 229, 238; modes and their own existence, 170-171; extrinsic and intrinsic, 30n.; existence metaphysically conceived of as a mode, 148.

Nature and subsistence, 81, 82, 83, 195, 216, 229.

Nature and supposit, 47, 80, 119, 155, 156, 157, 173, 184, 191, 193, 215, 226, 227, 228.

Necessity, composite or suppositional, 200, 206; absolute, 62, 96, 200, 201; hypothetical or conditional, 23, 24, 62, 204.

Nihil, 28; essential, 58, 59, 60, 139; existential, 58, 59, 60, 139.

Non Repugnantia, 15, 16, 24, 26, 27, 37n., 42n., 59; negation of impossibility, 15, 16, 38n.

Object terminating, 60, 61, 62; moving, 61; objective reality, 26, 43n.; objective presence, 26.

Omnipotence, 11, 12, 18, 22, 38n., 59, 69, 182, 237; absolute power, 89, 158, 179, 235; divine power, 50, 91, 126, 137, 146, 180, 236.

Participation, argument from, for real distinction between essence and existence, 46, 219-223; participated subjectively and effectively, 222; participated effectively, 232-239.

Possibility, 18, 19, 23, 38n., 39n., 59, 62, 69, 76, 131; intrinsic, 11, 23, 24, 25; pre-existential 24, 25, 41n.; post-existential, 23, 41n.; logical, 39n.

Possible, 18, 19, 33, 62, 63, 68, 69, 206.

Potency, 18, 33n., 88; active, 67, 68, 212; passive, 67, 68, 147; intrinsic, 12, 58; extrinsic, 18, 58; obediential, 236, 237; receptive, 60, 70, 85, 147, 149, 162, 213, 215, 217, 220; subjective, 68, 114; objective, 67, 68, 69, 70, 85, 88, 90, 91, 94, 147, 180, 212, 213; nature of objective, 67-69; Scotus and objective, 67-68; logical, 95.

Potentia, objectiva, 18, 19, 24, 25, 33n., 34n., 35n., 37n., 39n., 42n., *subjectiva,* 19, 21, 38n.; *logica,* 19, 21, 22, 23, 24, 25, 26, 37n., 38n., 39n., 41n., 42n.

Philosophy, Christian, 5; and theology, 5, 9, 28n.; and metaphysics, 5, 7, 9, 11, 21, 22, 24, 25, 26, 27, 28n., 31n., 38n.

Predicates, essential, 13, 60; bonds of essential, 11; connection of essential, 13, 97, 201, 202.

Propositions, truth and falsity of, 203, 204; being of truth in, 45, 61, 64; necessary and essential, 10, 13, 17, 50, 62, 199, 200, 204, 206; conditional, 204, 205, 206; contingent, 50, 200; eternal truth of, 62, 199-207; composite sense of 207; simple and absolute sense of 207; with second adjacent, 74.

Question, whether a thing is?, what is it?; 110-111.

MEDIAEVAL PHILOSOPHICAL TEXTS IN TRANSLATION

James H. Robb, Ph.D. is editor of the Mediaeval Philosophical Texts in Translation.

Copies of this translation and the others in the series are obtainable from:
Marquette University Press
Marquette University
Milwaukee, Wisconsin 53233, U.S.A.

Publishers of:
• Mediaeval Philosophical   • Père Marquette   • St. Thomas
  Texts in Translation   Theology Lectures   Aquinas Lectures